O America

Also by Luigi Barzini

Americans Are Alone in the World
The Italians
From Caesar to the Mafia

O America

When you and I were young

☙

Luigi Barzini

Harper & Row, Publishers
New York, Hagerstown, San Francisco, London

Grateful acknowledgment is made to the Oxford University Press for the quotation from Dante's *Inferno*, on pages 54–55, translation by John D. Sinclair, copyright 1939.

FIRST EDITION

Designed by Gloria Adelson

Library of Congress Cataloging in Publication Data

Barzini, Luigi Giorgio, 1908-
    O America, when you and I were young.
    1. Barzini, Luigi Giorgio, 1908- 2. Journalists—Italy—Biography. I. Title.
PN5246.B33A36   070'.92'4   [B]   76-5110
ISBN 0-06-010226-8

77 78 79 80 81 10 9 8 7 6 5 4 3 2 1

To Vivi,
my own private
Statue of Liberty

My needle is slow to settle, but it always settles between west and south-southwest. The future lies that way to me, and the earth seems more unexhausted and richer on that side. . . . Eastward I go only by force; but westward I go free.

—Henry David Thoreau

Prologue

MOST OF THIS BOOK was written in collaboration by two
authors who resemble each other and have the same name,
Luigi Barzini, but are vastly different. One is a young college student and cub reporter plunged into the turbulent
American life of the late twenties. Like all boys of his age
anywhere he is fascinated, hopeful, ambitious, bewildered,
frustrated, and frightened. He sometimes suspects he is
actually a fool, a hopeless fool. Once in a while he thinks
he is a sage. He knows little, to be sure, understands,
senses, or guesses a lot more, but is too young and inexperienced to distinguish, in the confusing life around him,
what is uniquely America, the new experiment, Europe
purified and corrected, anti-Europe, man's challenge to the
gods, from what is just life, the apparently meaningless and
heartbreaking game men have tried to beat in the Old
World as in the New, in the remote past as well as today.

He does not even suspect that the country he is trying to understand, scrutinizing it (he thinks) with the cold and cruel eye of the writer, exists, of course, but at the same time does not really exist. It is partly the invention of his immature yearnings. He has to believe in it; otherwise his agonizing efforts to destroy the European, Latin, Italian in him and adapt himself to the strange life around him would be ludicrously wasted. He does not suspect either that this is nothing new, because that is what America had been from the beginning: the sum of the imaginary landscapes of each individual American. Many of the things he senses and guesses he cannot formulate anyway, not even to himself, cannot define in crystal-clear, well-ordered sentences, as he does not possess the patience, the vocabulary, and the métier for the job.

The other Luigi Barzini is a gray-haired veteran in his sixties. He acquired the patience, the vocabulary, and the métier long ago. He is probably as much of a fool as, in a different way, his young namesake, but feels comforted by what the Italians call *il senno di poi,* hindsight, the fact that he can look back from the top of the ridge to the landscape he crossed. He knows how many things turned out in the end. He thinks he knows some of the answers. The reader may sometimes distinguish between the two authors' dissimilar styles.

⁂

I think I was lucky to be exposed to American life when both the United States and I were young and full of stupendous illusions. We have both changed. History, or the crash, the depression, tough, bloody, and expensive wars (some of them unwanted), a few glorious successes, and a few honorable but disastrous miscalculations, transformed the United States. The insidious and unpredictable convulsions of world events, the harrowing decisions, the discovery of how easy it was to make catastrophic and irreparable mistakes, and of how much duplicity and dishonesty were often inevitable in the conduct of public affairs (possibly as much as in the conduct of private affairs), the lost war in Vietnam (*"pire qu'un crime, une erreur"*), the fourth assassination of a President and that of his brother, the resignation of another President to avoid impeachment, the revolt of the young, the blacks, and the women, the questioning of all sacred principles, made many Americans suspect in the end that they, too, were ordinary human beings, Adam's sons, subject to the same laws. All this made them also bitterly acknowledge what a handful of them had secretly known all along, that it takes more than good men, good intentions, and high motives to avoid ruin. Since one of the fundamental presuppositions on which the Republic was placidly run for a long time was that with good men, good intentions, and high motives there was nothing to worry about because things would take care of themselves, this gradual discovery, above all, made Americans almost unrecognizable from what they were.

Nevertheless, I believe nobody can have an idea of what they really are today if one had not known them in the twenties. Those were the last years in which they appeared in their pure state, what they imagined they had been from the start, a new splendid breed of men, unafraid, spunky, ingenious, chivalrous, generous, strong, full of daring and hope, always on the side of God or with God on their side,

3

as confident as a people could be who had discovered the perfect formula to avert misfortune (or straighten things out in time when they went wrong). They were, as Emerson had said, "new-born, free, healthful, strong." Theirs was still "the land of the laborer, of the democrat, of the philanthropist, of the believer, of the saint," and, of course, of the self-made millionaire. They knew they were slowly building a better life not for themselves alone but for all men. They made mistakes, of course, stupid or terrifying mistakes at times, mainly because they were always in a hurry, but never irremediable mistakes. They never doubted the final outcome. The American eagle felt omnipotent, happy, and carefree. It did not know it was enclosed in an immense imperceptible aviary. It had never flown far enough to smash its head and break its wings against the wire netting and had not yet discovered the inflexible and mortal limitations of its freedom. Americans as I knew them in the twenties had not yet been really tested by spiteful and sardonic history.

In the following decades, whenever I returned to the United States, saw aging friends, or read the latest impressive books written by scholarly experts or clairvoyant poets on the American failure, the decadence, corruption, and imminent ruin of the country, I, too, was sometimes tempted to believe the people were no longer those I had known in my youth. They themselves talked about their past as if it were remote and almost irrelevant, with bitterness, irony, or nostalgia. Could the change be true? I did not begin to see the murky scene more clearly until the day I realized that what these contemporary disenchanted and realistic Americans secretly dreamed of, in the interminable winter of successive crises, was the untroubled and

4

thoughtless tranquillity as well as the placid faith in themselves of those years, the propitious years, the last warm and almost cloudless summer of American history, the twenties, the real twenties, that is, the years of the honorable, hard-working, trusting, and unsung average people—the people I knew well, and not those one sees in the movies today, the bootleggers and flappers, the drunken millionaires, the sex-mad women, people who were anyway only a picturesque, rebellious, adventurous, and noisy minority. Then, it was still possible for almost all Americans to believe virtue and industry were always—well, almost always—rewarded, fabulous hopes seemed soberly realistic, all Presidents (except perhaps Grant and Harding) were gentlemen, and everything would sooner or later turn out, placidly and automatically, more or less as the books said it would, because Time was a gentleman and a friend of the United States.

American events, decisions, and pronouncements are notoriously incomprehensible to foreigners. They startled and baffled the world long before and after the last war. They still startle and baffle it. Great thinkers asked themselves from the beginning what America was all about and where it was going. Nobody came up with a durable answer, with the exception of Alexis de Tocqueville, who was a seer. America-watchers (the majority of them American) developed a vast assortment of theories, the best of which managed to explain some new development for a while, until America got off on a new tack. In the last two centuries, the art of forecasting the consequences of American decisions and foreseeing American political and emotional weather, from an idle hobby for academic specialists has gradually become a vital and urgent matter. The fate of the whole world depends as never before on American moods. Wrong guesses about probable reactions of the United States brought Mussolini and Hitler to their ruin. De Gaulle, a perceptive and skeptical man with a vast knowledge of history, once contemptuously said to Giuseppe Saragat, who was the Italian Foreign Minister at the time: *"On ne peut pas se fier des Américains."* Saragat, who firmly believed the Americans were and would continue to be what they declared themselves to be that particular year, was shocked and protested violently. In the end, of course, de Gaulle's doubts were justified.

I admit that I, too, cannot always tell for sure what the United States is all about and what Americans will do next. This, however, I discovered: that inside each of them, inside older men, to be sure, but also inside their sons and grandsons, one can always see the man of the twenties in transparency, the man I know well. They may follow a zigzag course, but there is a secret, unconfessed, unmentioned single hope in them, a single belief animating them, a single goal they grope for. To save themselves (and the world) they try everything: they embrace newfangled utopian ideas and dream of a world peopled by law-abiding angels; they hope to establish peace on earth by the skillful use of rhetoric, noble proclamations, documents decorated with seals and ribbons and the signatures of important statesmen. In desperation, they sometimes allot immense sums of money to the solution of some urgent and agonizing problem in the hope of all rich people that, if enough dollars are spent, the problem will go away. They finance backward and sluggish economies in rickety countries; blindly trust foreign scoundrels who double-cross them;

occasionally try to apply Machiavelli's teachings against their very instincts, plot sinister intrigues, conduct secret conspiracies, then reveal everything to a stupefied world. At one time they put a finger in every pot, at another time they dream of isolating themselves from the rest of the world, becoming entirely self-sufficient behind walls of electronic apparatuses and diabolical weapons; sometimes lose patience and land Marines on distant beaches, fight insensate wars, and remorsefully dispatch half-naked natives. To be sure, all this meandering is not exclusively American (all nations meander), nor is it entirely new and unexpected. Americans' equally erratic decisions went unnoticed in the past because the United States was a distant and weak power, and what it did brought almost no serious consequences. One key, however, allows me to make some sense of present American twists and turns. I believe the United States does not want to dominate the world, exploit it, control its wealth, as the Communists think, nor does it want to cut itself away from it. It merely wants, by trying almost anything, like a mouse in a maze, to get back to the point in history when it was so rudely interrupted.

I, too, of course, have changed. I, too, have made grievous mistakes. I, too, have lost many illusions. With the years, all traces of the American student and cub reporter in the days of Calvin Coolidge and Herbert Hoover vanished. This was to be expected. I was born in Italy, the son of Italian parents, and lived an entirely Italian life. I served in the Army as a *bersagliere* with a plumed hat, the most Italian of all special corps, wrote for the only national newspaper, the *Corriere della Sera,* was jailed just before the war by the Fascist police for political reasons, and after the war

7

edited dailies and magazines, wrote a few books and plays. I fell in love mostly with Italian girls and married two of them. I went through the postwar political convulsions and was elected three times to Parliament (until I gave it up in 1972).

Above all, I look Italian. My clothes are Italian, but, more important, the expression on my face, the visible result of years of thinking Italian thoughts, is Italian. When my hair was black, I looked like an illustration in an anthropological textbook: "Typical Mediterranean Man." With drooping mustaches, a ring in my ear, a red kerchief, a monkey, and a barrel organ, I would have been inconspicuous in a New York East Side scene at the beginning of the century. I now look like the gray-haired father in *La Traviata,* or a variation of the De Sica type. Tourists who stop me in the streets speak to me in hesitant guidebook Italian, like the American tank commander, the night the Allies entered Rome, June 4, 1944, who asked me, *"Skewsee, dovay ay eel Tayvayray?"* and, when I answered in American English, "You want to know where the Tiber is? Just one block behind you, Captain," looked incredulous, surprised, and relieved. Americans, at the next table in European restaurants or in train compartments, always comment on my appearance in their native language, certain that, with my face and clothes, I cannot understand a word.

Nevertheless, there is an almost undetectable part of me which is indelibly American, pre-1929 American. I am not always aware of it. It has often complicated my life, forcing me to make uncomfortable non-Italian decisions which made me incomprehensible (and *antipatico*) to my friends and enemies, almost always to my own very Italian sons. The reason why I was jailed by the Fascists in 1940, I suspect, was my loyalty to Thomas Jefferson and the Bill of Rights. Obviously, I had been irremediably brainwashed in my youth. Similarly, I am now accused by Communist sympathizers of having been a CIA agent, or an agent's agent, and will surely end up in jail once again if the Communist Party ever reaches absolute power. This does not mean I am a professional Americanologist, one of those frightening European historians or literati who know everything about the United States, read every book, write well-documented disquisitions about American history and politics, and perceive the psyche of the American people in the prose of their best writers. I am something entirely different.

Once in Milan I lunched between William Faulkner and his Italian translator, Elio Vittorini, a famous novelist and a learned specialist in current American literature, so that I could interpret their conversation. English being for Vittorini purely a mute written language like some obscure form of an ancient Mesopotamian dialect, he could not recognize it when spoken, particularly, I suppose, with a Mississippi accent. At one point he said thoughtfully: "Tell Mr. Faulkner I think there is always something vaguely military about his prose . . . . Under it I feel the rolling of drums, the thunder of guns, and the blaring of bugles." I could not understand this at all. It sounded farfetched and vaguely preposterous, but who was I to disagree with the intuitions of one of Europe's notable authorities on American literature, on the American genius, and the translator of the greatest American authors, Faulkner and Hemingway among them? I carefully translated his words, without omitting or adding one. Faulkner looked at me with stupefaction, looked at Vittorini, shrugged his shoulders, and answered: "Tell him I wouldn't know. I am a farmer." I was consoled to see he could not understand either.

Obviously, I have not read all the books I should have read, have not developed an all-embracing theory that explains everything about the United States and could be labeled with my name, in the years to come, the "Barzini theory." I have not become a friend of celebrated Americans, the protagonists of American life, and the interpreters of the collective soul of the United States. My experience was that of an anonymous, befuddled, and almost penniless young man lost in the crowd, reading, studying, and occasionally working as an humble cub reporter, in contact with unknown people. My America, I am afraid, is that of an adolescent. Yet for some reason I often understand Americans better than the experts. I understand them even before they speak and can often extract the real meaning and motivation of an American official pronouncement at first glance. Moreover, Americans understand me to the point that they often forget I am not one of them.

Somehow, this invisible American in me ensured my entanglement with Americans all my life, whether I wanted it or not, as at the Faulkner luncheon. Once in China, in 1937, to mention one dramatic and memorable instance, during the Japanese invasion, I had reached Nanking from Shanghai, crossing the vast no-man's land between the two armies on a little flat-bottomed boat whose Chinese owner, a poor fisherman, knew his way through a maze of tiny canals, which looked like *couperose* on the maps. (Incidentally, when I got on board, I found I shared the boat with a couple of saintly white-haired missionaries from Scranton, Pennsylvania, husband and wife, who held hands most of the time. They were risking their lives, so to speak, in order to return to their mission and their waifs. Once again I realized I could not get away for long from Americans.) Nanking was still in Chinese hands but was being shelled by the advancing Japanese, each day a little more, and I was looking forward to writing a memorable description of its siege, inevitable fall, and the heroic holocaust of its people, for the *Corriere della Sera,* something that would be included in all anthologies for generations to come. I could not. The Italian Ambassador pleaded with me over the long-distance telephone from Shanghai to leave the city without delay. This was not to save my life, he said. The Italian authorities back in Rome, he was very emphatic, could not care less whether I lived or died killed by some loathsome Chinese disease. What they absolutely did not want was my death from a stray Japanese bullet. The Japanese were our political soulmates at the time. The Ambassador explained that such a death would also be inopportune and embarrassing for him personally. I could not do such a thing to him. Had he not always treated me courteously and once invited me to lunch?

I obeyed. Together with other prudent journalists I boarded the safest possible refuge, the U.S. gunboat *Panay* anchored on the Yangtze. It was an old and meek river boat, equipped only with two small machine guns. It really looked more like a pleasant Lake Como tourist steamer than a machine of war. But on its deckhouse roof an immense American flag had been beautifully painted as a warning to absent-minded or panicky Japanese and Chinese. She immediately steamed upriver and dropped anchor in a peaceful and silent spot far from both shores, where we would be out of all danger. She was sunk the next morning by Japanese naval planes flying over us in successive waves. I learned later that a group of fanatical officers had decided to create an irresistible *casus belli,* to force the hand of their own and the American Government. We did not realize it then, but we were seeing the first action of World War II, a rehearsal of Pearl Harbor. The American sailors in a rage tried to fire the two machine guns at the planes, but they were not made to shoot at a high enough angle. The cook from Chicago and my friend Sandro Sandri, another Italian journalist, were killed. Many, including the captain and his younger officers, were seriously wounded.

An American Army officer who was also on board then took charge of the party ashore, while a Chinese-speaking diplomat requisitioned a ricksha from a passing peasant and went to look for the nearest telephone. Without hesitation, the major appointed me as his adjutant. The fact that I was not American did not seem to bother him at all. It bothered nobody. I did what I could. The sailors obeyed me cheerfully as if I were one of them and called me "Chief." Later, the United States Navy awarded me an elegant decoration, called the U.S. Navy Expeditionary Medal with China ribbon. It must be rare because I could find no trace of it in the *Encyclopaedia Britannica.* It reached me a long time after the end of World War II. It had arrived in Rome four years after the sinking of the *Panay,* just before Mussolini declared war on the United States, and, as the Embassy officials had more urgent things to attend to, had been abandoned in a desk drawer. One day, in 1947, an American official rang me up and tentatively asked me: "Have you by any chance ever been in China?" When I said yes, of course, I had been in China, and had been on the *Panay* when she was sunk, he happily announced: "There is a medal here waiting for you. Come and get it." It was accompanied by an explanatory letter signed by a Secretary of the Navy who had been long dead. The medal was pinned on my civilian chest by the naval attaché in full uniform, in the Ambassador's office, by a standing American flag. It was a solemn moment. "Now you have to kiss me," I said. I knew that the request for this ritual, which incidentally is French and not Italian, would outrage him. I knew the United States Navy not only sternly disapproved of alcoholic beverages but, at that time anyway, of men kissing each other. He was horrified, corrugated his forehead, and hurriedly said: "No, I don't. It's against the rules." He shook my hand instead.

This intuitive feeling for American moods, inclinations, prejudices, and channels of reasoning was useful to me in many less dramatic, unimportant circumstances.

One hot summer night after the war (I was broke), an American motion picture company shooting a film in Rome offered to hire me as a temporary bilingual publicity man, to issue differently worded handouts in English and Italian, aimed at the two dissimilar mentalities, and to handle all kinds of visiting journalists. I was eager to get the job but had two reservations. One, I knew the food at the studio canteen was not only inedible but also indigestible (I had eaten there a couple of times). Two, I wanted to go on taking a leisurely siesta after lunch, as I had done almost all my life and as my ancestors had probably done for thousands of years. My body required it. After a leaden meal, without a tranquil snooze, I would be but an irritable wandering ghost with a burning stomach, swallowing magnesia pills or bicarbonate the rest of the afternoon, of no use whatever to anybody.

I knew, however, that both conditions could not even be suggested to an American. They were sacrilegious. The earnest and impatient producer from Hollywood, an elderly man brought up before 1914, would surely put up with no such nonsense from a native and would throw me out on my ass. In the eyes of Americans of his generation, the ones I knew best, to be fussy about food (to wish not to be poisoned by it) and to want to slip for an hour between cool sheets in the heat of a summer afternoon doubtless were decadent and contemptible forms of foreign laxity, not to be encouraged on any account, the principal reasons for the decline and fall of the ancient local empire. What, indeed, would the United States be today if the pioneers had paid too much attention to their cuisine and slept during working hours? The fact that the producer was an elderly Jew, an eminent Hollywood personage, who personally surely preferred good food to bad and after-luncheon siestas rather than milk of magnesia pills as much as I did, made the matter even worse. I knew from experience that successful American Jews could be more punctilious defenders of the Anglo-Saxon moral heritage, in public anyway, particularly when dealing with foreigners, than the Anglo-Saxons themselves. It was a difficult moment.

I was startled to hear myself improvising a complicated tale, the only one that would oblige an American of his generation to grant me my requests, and to do so not with acquiescence and resignation but with genuine enthusiasm. This fabrication of mine, which came out without premeditation, evidently spontaneously generated by my buried and half-forgotten American experience, not only surprised me but also vaguely disgusted me by the revelation of my deplorable Italian duplicity. I told him the job was what I had always desired, the duties were fascinating, the salary was adequate, but that there was one small difficulty. I had undertaken a previous engagement, which, however, with his help, would not prevent me from accepting his offer. I explained I had signed a contract: a job was waiting for me in Tokyo the following autumn, a well-paid, responsible job. The only condition was that I learn Japanese, a very difficult language. Therefore I had already paid in advance the best Japanese teacher in Rome, a university professor, for Japanese lessons, three hours a day, every day, between one and four, for the next few months. I would therefore have to leave the studio at lunchtime and come back four hours later. I pointed out that this would not seriously interfere with my duties as I could stay after hours when necessary. The best work was always done in the morning, anyway.

The American nodded with fatherly understanding as I spoke. He repeated the key words after me: "Signed a contract . . . a well-paid job . . . Japanese lessons . . . paid in advance . . ." He approved heartily. How could he stand in the way of an ambitious young man who wanted to get ahead in the world by hard work, had assumed firm commitments, and honorably wanted to keep them at all cost? A contract is, after all, sacred and inviolable. He gave me the job and patted me on the shoulder. "Don't worry," he said. The secret of my Japanese lessons lasted little more than a week. Some office gossip discovered what I really did in the middle of the day and spread the news. The producer, however, generously refused to change his word. In fact, he, the director, the cameraman, the star, Orson

Welles, and the lesser players openly envied me. When I left at the agreed time every day, the director waved a fist at me and cried derisively, in a thick Russian accent: "Japanese liessons, ha!" His name was Gregory Ratoff.

I am still haunted by those early years I spent in the United States, by the summer of 1929 in particular. Incongruous scenes from those days often break into my Italian grandfatherly dreams, like strips of old movies which get into the projector by mistake. In my sleep, I suddenly see bright girls laughing, roadsters careering in the tepid night, or gin bottles under the table. I feel moist kisses (the syrupy saliva of a girl who had been drinking, the minty taste of chewing gum), a warm marble breast in my cupped hand, or the irrepressible sprouting of young desire. I feel again (as elderly men often relive, in their dreams, the nightmare of a long-forgotten university examination) the tension that racked me at the time. Every young man, of course, has been at a loss even in his own familiar native country and in all historic periods when he discovers that tidy schoolbook rules are of limited use in the real world of grownups. Every man is haunted by the memory of his twentieth year or thereabouts, when every week bursts with the events, discoveries, and emotions of a decade. It is also impossible for him to forget his first job, his presumptuous dreams, and his first passionate love (the unquenchable desire for a young naked body whose every detail becomes as familiar as the eyes, nose, and mouth of a dear face, a body one could surely recognize by feel even if one were struck blind). But I was then a stranger in a strange country, a very strange, intimidating, incomprehensible, and sometimes pitiless country in which I had to play a game, the baffling local game of life whose rules I had to figure out somehow, appallingly aware all the time that my whole future, the interminable decades stretching ahead of me, could depend on one single casual move, hunch, word, decision, or encounter.

And the year was not any year. It was 1929 in the United States, the last of the decade, a year filled with fabulous promises and the shadows of unmentionable fears. It was, as we now know, a Turning Point in History, the End of an Era, A.D. 475 all over again, when solid beliefs crumbled, omnipotent gods were toppled, great wise men were shown to be asses, and no hope seemed to be left amidst the ruins. That happy and pleasant summer was the lull before the earthquake, the silent moment when the leaves are as still as in a photograph, the birds stop singing, and the horses in their stalls nervously paw the ground. It was, of course, the knowledge of what happened a few weeks later that added infinite nostalgia to our reminiscences. Each insignificant detail became worthy of being preserved, lovingly reconstructed, and relived. Adam and Eve surely spent the rest of their long lives recalling the short wonderful days before the Fall.

The year was a magic one perhaps because for the last time Americans were allowed to live happily unaware of the notorious and ancient contradictions of their nature. Few doubts troubled them. Most people then thought (if they ever thought about them) that the contradictions were not contradictions at all; they would be easily reconciled if they were, anyway, and in fact one beautifully complemented the other. Their country was, in my young man's eyes, a desperate, violent, and rebellious one, in which ugly and cruel things could happen, capable of brutal repressions at home and, at the slightest provocation, savage interventions abroad; but, at the same time, it was the world's best hope, an honorable model for all foreign nations and lesser breeds if they knew what was good for them, an experimental utopia which, like great European cathedrals, was always not very far from being completed. The country was (and still is, for that matter) filled with earnest people who abhorred violence, injustice, and war, dedicated their lives to erecting a New Society, and believed there was a saint in every man trying to get out. It was at the same time filled with realistic, rigorous, and cruelly intolerant people.

I looked at the American eagle (there was one on a calendar in the office where I worked in the summer of 1929) and thought that it properly held in its claws the two symbols of the double destiny of the nation. In one it clutched the lightning with which to incinerate whoever stood in the path of American progress, the enemies of private property, private initiative, law and order, or little dark men, Indians, Mexicans, Dominicans, Spaniards, Nicaraguans. In the other it held the olive branch of the eternal peace which would be established once all the world learned what was good for it and accepted the law. At that time history still clearly confirmed the people's faith. Had their might not won the last world war, the war that was to end all wars, and had the United States not generated a fabulous economic prosperity which grew and grew every year and probably would never end? This is why it seemed worthwhile at this point to reconstruct in my mind the last years in which Americans appeared to be what they imagined they had always been.

Chapter 1

THE FIRST DIRECT MESSAGE from the United States of America to me, written in white letters as high as a house, possibly loaded with awesome significance, was peremptory but sibylline. It reached me early one morning in August, 1925 (I was then a bookish sixteen-year-old). The Italian liner *Duilio,* on which my mother, brothers, sister, and I had crossed the ocean to join my father in New York, had arrived at the Narrows. The ship had stopped shivering and throbbing; the sea no longer rushed by its flanks with the roar of a waterfall. I peered through the porthole. In the gray-pink pearly light of a hot summer dawn I saw a low green cliff rising from the still brownish waters. On its flat top, at equal intervals, like teacups arranged on a tidy table, sat small wooden white houses. They were the dwellings of the Americans, as typical as the igloos of the Eskimos or the tents of the nomad Arabs. We had arrived in the New

World. This was the rising of the curtain, the turning point of my life, the moment I had been expecting for months, my first contact with the unknown, awe-inspiring country where I would finish my studies and possibly live forever, crowned by the laurel leaves of fame, fabulously rich or buried in abject and penurious obscurity. The immense white letters forming the cryptic message ran along the grass embankment, between the water and the houses. Were the words meant for me and what exactly was their meaning?

I dressed in a hurry and anxiously rushed above, streaking down passageways, breathlessly climbing companionways three steps at a time, running through the gloomy carved-wood reception rooms, to the promenade deck. I was astounded and frightened by what I saw on the way in the livid light of dawn. The ship was loaded with unconscious and prostrate bodies, dozens of them, lying everywhere, where they had fallen like dead and wounded after a battle, all dressed in rumpled evening clothes. I knew of course that before the bar had been sealed, in accordance with the Prohibition laws, late the night before, the moment we had entered American territorial waters, everybody had bought cases and cases of liquor, wine, and champagne, which had to be emptied or thrown away before the ship docked. Drunks sprawled open-mouthed, open-legged, and open-armed on the armchairs of the smoking room and the saloon; inert drunks were lying on sofas or had fallen on the carpeted steps of the companionways and along the passageways. Some looked waxy, pale, and unbreathing, like real corpses; some dribbled spittle, moaned, or mumbled incoherent invocations, mere animal sounds, as the wounded do before dying. Some smiled mysteriously to themselves as if they were enjoying some wonderful private show of their own behind their closed eyelids. There were middle-aged mothers and grandmothers with disheveled dyed hair, dressed in nursery colors, obscenely showing parts of their withered thighs above the strangling garters; pretty girls lay everywhere, abandoned in disarray like puppets after the show; and men of all sizes and ages, lean, fat, old, young. Here and there, clean and clear-eyed stewards just out of bed were patiently picking up empty bottles and wiping up the vomit. They did not look surprised. They had seen it all before. As I passed, I heard through some of the cabin doors the sound of tired, thick-tongued quarrels, weak and uncertain singing, or loud snoring. I was bewildered and terrified. I had never seen anything like it.

It looked as if the passengers of the *Duilio* had been struck down by a divine revenge, one of the lightning pestilences which Apollo hurled on the people who had displeased him. What god had they offended? What curse had been laid on them, which compelled them to turn themselves into demented brutes, to extinguish their consciousness, and desperately to seek refuge in the darkness of their minds? It was absurd to think they were doing it just because it was forbidden. Many things are forbidden that nobody feels obliged to do. What was it they wanted to forget? What consolation or respite did they seek? What was lacking in their lives? And, furthermore, what other cruel and mocking god had condemned so many venerable old ladies, like those on the *Duilio,* to masquerade as schoolgirls or blushing brides? (I was sixteen and women of forty looked decrepit to me.) Their disguise was so clumsy it was evidently meant to deceive nobody, but to rob the poor women of their dignity and make fools of them. Did the god blind them whenever they faced a mirror? Why did he not allow them to look like ordinary grandmothers, as they still did in Italy at the time, with kindly and serene and well-washed faces, gray or white hair, and dark dresses? Were these American women not happy to have reached at last the tranquillity of middle age?

There obviously were mysterious forces at work in the United States, which made many seemingly simple, straightforward, sane, and cheerful people try to obliterate themselves or turn themselves into something they were not, with the aid of alcohol or camouflage. Later I learned that many Americans also obliterated themselves in other ways, plunging into endless hard work until they died in harness, pursuing fanatical causes, amassing vast fortunes, or conquering immense power. I also learned in the following years that, as the world was more and more irrevocably transformed by the American example, more and more people everywhere tried to deface themselves one way or another, to the point that in the end even Italian grandmothers were condemned to disguise themselves to look like their granddaughters. This, of course, was one of the enigmas of American life, possibly the central enigma, whose solution would probably clarify every other.

I stepped gingerly over the spread-out corpses, avoiding a hand here and a nose there, until I reached the open air. The promenade deck was clean, tidy, and empty. The only people about were a few well-scrubbed children with their nannies, a couple or two of prim Americans with pince-nez glasses and sensible clothes, some Italian travelers, and a fat *Monsignore* with his finger in his breviary. The diabolical spell had somehow spared them. The ship was still, impatiently quivering a little, while it waited for the pilot, the immigration officials, and the journalists. My father, whom I had not seen for a couple of years, would surely arrive on the journalists' tug. Was he not the greatest journalist of them all? I read the cryptic white message once again, trying to squeeze from it an omen of sorts, just as one anxiously tries, in decisive moments of one's life, waiting for a woman's answer or the results of an examination, to read the future (as a haruspex read it in animals' entrails) in the number of a passing taxicab, a shop sign, or words heard at random.

I reached no conclusions then. It took me years, five to be exact, to formulate a possible explanation. The message said: "Do not anchor. Cable crossing." After the stock market crash, after my graduation from Columbia, after I had decided to give up my at best dubious chances of glory and wealth in the United States, the country I had come to know, commiserate with, and love, and after I had returned to Italy, I suspected the words "Do not anchor" had imperiously tried to warn me in time not to sink roots in the New World, not to let myself be deluded like so many others by its stupendous but often treacherous promises. The reason given ("Cable crossing") was more difficult to decipher. It looked like a mere pretext, one of those technical justifications experts glibly offer to the inexpert, but maybe it was more than that. It could have been a warning not to meddle with the serious business of Americans, with their efficient and ruthless technological pursuits. I surely was not made for a regimented industrial life. I was the type to foul up the best-laid cables.

The first hours in my new country were filled with indelible first impressions and other obscure omens. The Statue of Liberty we passed, coming up the bay, looked like the Statue of Liberty, still *"l'élégant presse-papier de M. Bartholdi,"* as Alphonse Allais wrote in 1894, *"qui garnit l'entrée du port de New York sans la meubler suffisamment."* The cluster of uneven skyscrapers at the end of Manhattan, with the sun still behind them, looked from a distance like a cluster of unlit candles at the foot of an absent saint. When Father took us in his car (the first we had ever owned) to a little wooden white house in Long Island (the first we had ever owned), I was impressed by the heat, the noise, the frantic bustle, the many automobiles, and the confusion of the immense city, but above all by the overwhelming, and overbearing, and unnecessary weight, size, sturdiness, and costliness of everything, bridges, buildings, newspapers, elevated railroads, fire escapes, policemen, trucks, and trees. As the car traveled into the countryside, the road, which in the Italy I had just left would have been covered with fine white dust and pitted with holes, was luxuriously paved with smooth asphalt like a city street, as if the city had infiltrated thin, mile-long tentacles into the green wilderness, just as some vines push their voracious roots all around them and slowly kill everything else.

In the brand-new house everything also looked heavy, expensive, shining, efficient, and belonging to the future. The plumbing, the bathrooms, the kitchen, the door locks, the gadgets, the appliances astonished me by their solidity, perfection, and ruthless disregard of habitual forms. The tubs were neatly walled in and not isolated on lions' claws as our single bath had been in Milan. The faucets did not drip (the sound like that of distant drums spelling unknown messages had comforted me during sleepless hours in the old country). The electric wires vanished inside the walls (in Italy at that time elegant braids, covered with silk in the color of the wallpaper, ran openly, gracefully suspended like festoons from little porcelain cups). This, I felt, was a confident modern country, slightly frightening, which did not want to be reminded of past shapes and habits, a country where money was no longer a problem and parsimony was evidently considered treason.

But the madeleine of that first day (possibly as important and pregnant with significance as the white words of warning on the green slope), the sensation which still reminds me of the United States of that August afternoon in 1925 every time I experience it again, and from which, in the ensuing years, I drew an endless chain of deductions about the nature of American life, was my first dish of American ice cream. In a way, as I will show, it assumed the importance of a national symbol. In the soda parlor where Father had taken us, not far from our house, the pert and impatient waitress, her red-brown hair permanently curled like Astrakhan fur, presented us with what I learned later was one of the dilemmas hovering persistently over American life: "Chocolate or vanilla?" We chose vanilla. The aroma was very agreeable but had no resemblance whatever to vanilla. In fact, it did not even try to imitate vanilla. We all knew the real taste well, of course. Vanilla was a small dark dry pod, imported from the Orient, which Mother usually kept in a jar with the powdered sugar. Like any product made by nature, it is always slightly unpredictable. Just as the bouquet of wine and the taste of country honey change from year to year and from spot to spot, one specimen of real vanilla is always perceptibly more pungent or fainter, smelling more like a gardenia, a carnation, or whatever, than other specimens, and the unexpected variation is somehow part of the pleasure.

What the waitress called vanilla without hesitation evidently was a slipshod attempt, which had clearly missed its mark, to approach the natural taste chemically. It was (as I learned in the next few days, when I tried cakes, biscuits, apple pie, and more ice cream) as implacably unvarying as the smell of commercial brands of soap. Maybe (I reflected later) American chemists were wizards, one generation or two ahead of their European competitors, but unfortunately had wooden palates; maybe they, like all Americans, were too impatient, too eager to proclaim their success; maybe they were too easily satisfied, and, like the American inventors of "invisible" wigs, improbable hair dyes, and preposterous dentures, had stopped work too soon; or maybe that was, at that stage in the ineluctable march of human progress, the best that could be done. I also wondered (having read Upton Sinclair) whether that particular flavor might not have been forced, for some sordid reason, on the guileless American public by a faceless conspiracy of greedy monopolists.

Presumably, I speculated later, the acceptance of their own improbable vanilla had taken time. In the beginning, years before, I imagined, most Americans surely could still distinguish the real from the sham, but, as time passed, the chemical flavor gradually became the real thing, the one and only vanilla. After all, what is vanilla, or anything else for that matter, but what people think it is? Perhaps a few obstinate snobs, proud of their epicurean European habits, a few maniacal Nature lovers, and stubborn immigrants clung to the taste of the Oriental bean, which in the end could probably be bought only in fewer and fewer exotic and esoteric little out-of-the-way shops. Surely the sons of the immigrants were ashamed of the natural flavor and brutally forced their primitive parents to abandon the old and adopt the new progressive American vanilla and like it. Americans traveling abroad, when suddenly faced with the genuine spice, were probably startled and vaguely disgusted. "What is this bizarre flavor?" they would diffidently and sternly ask the foreign waiter. "Vanilla, you say? Preposterous. Who do you take us for? We are not fools. We know vanilla when we taste it!"

But all this was not the point. I had to admit that everyone everywhere relished strange flavors and pined for them on their travels. The Milanese love their yellow *risotto* with saffron, which definitely reeks of iodine; the Irish love carrageen, a trembling pale green *bavaroise*-like jelly made of seaweed; people from the Near East far from home miss the all-pervasive smell of rancid mutton fat. What was strange about Americans liking their own vanilla, which was far from unpleasant anyway? The real point was that they called it "vanilla" *tout court,* and not one of those fancy mouth-watering names their experts invented all the time. The real point, and a puzzling one, was that the Americans seemed to believe it was vanilla, the true and only vanilla, and that anything else was but an imperfect and unreliable approach to their own, the perfect Platonic idea, the eternally unvarying vanilla. Maybe the Americans at times preferred to surround themselves with a picture of the world, a conception of man and history, of their own making, as reliable and constant as their vanilla, and to reject the unpredictable and treacherous reality. They liked to inhabit a mental Disneyland which would reassure but could also deceive them and occasionally lead them to disaster.

That first evening after dinner two old American friends dropped in, a well-known journalist and his wife. He had met Father in Tokyo during the Russo-Japanese War twenty years before, had seen him again in Mexico at the time of the troubles in 1914, but had only become a dear friend of his in Paris in 1919 during the peace conference, when they discovered they had the same passion for billiards. We had seen him intermittently in Milan during the last few years. The Italian situation was always good for a few picturesque and blood-curdling reportages, and Father's ideas, though confused and changeable like everybody else's, were always brilliant, and, like all good journalists' ideas, ready-made for a sparkling quick column. The wife was, like most wives of distinguished traveling correspondents, silent, patient, and resigned. When Father had started his newspaper in New York, they had taken him in hand, encouraged him to buy a house, helped him pick one not too far from their own, and now wanted to see how we liked it and to welcome us to our new country.

"Welcome to the United States!" the man shouted as he came in waving a bottle of real bourbon. "There are many things wrong with this country, I'm ashamed to admit, but it's the goddamnedest best country in the world and improving all the time." We all sat around him on trunks and packing cases and listened. He drank most of his own liquor. He delivered a long and humorous speech, which I can reconstruct from old notes. Nobody could interrupt him. At one point he turned to the four young Barzinis and told us: "You are lucky. You'll never regret having come to

28

the United States at such an early age. This is a young country, a young people's country." And, to his wife: "Isn't it so, darling?" Then, without waiting for her answer, continued: "This country is bound to dominate the world, believe me, not in a stupid imperial way, not by defeating its rivals in wars, which we always win anyway, but are a wasteful method which ends in catastrophe in the long run, but by making friends, by showing everybody how to make more and better things, and how to run railroads." He reassured us we would easily make our way. "There is plenty of room at the top," he said. "I envy you. Oh, to be sixteen again in these wonderful times! Everything is possible here from now on. You'll see wonders we older people cannot even imagine." He downed more glasses of his bourbon, each at one swallow, turning his face to the ceiling like a drinking hen, as I had seen cowboys do in the movies, and, as time went by, he got more than a little drunk.

"This," he explained, "is a high-minded, hopeful, optimistic country, the first of its kind in history. We work not for ourselves alone but for all humanity. Look at President Wilson. Think of what he did for the world. Two cars in every garage, we say, but we do not say 'in every American garage.' Oh no, it's two cars one day for every man, for the poor Chinese and the Indians and the Italians, too." He went on: "It's a tough life, but worth the effort. You have to be on your toes all the time, deliver the goods, keep your nose to the grindstone, never let the other man get ahead of you. Any Saturday you may get a letter of dismissal in your pay envelope without even a thank you. That's the way it should be. The fittest must survive and the hell with the old and feeble. There are iron laws and regulations here, none of that happy-go-lucky sloppiness, none of that charming cheating and artful lying and compassion which brought your country to ruin. Do you realize every one of us is happy to pay his taxes?"

His wife interrupted him at this point. She said patiently: "Edgar, don't lie. You know damned well you don't like paying taxes at all and you curse the government whenever you have to."

"Well," he went on. "We may not like it, as we don't like to die at war, darling, but we do it anyway. We sure do. Of course, all this makes it a hell of a country for old people. But it's nature's way. Look at the old stags in the herd. Your own children abandon you. My wife and I know it. We are prepared. We'll put ourselves out to pasture. We'll leave the herd before it's too late. Maybe we'll get a farm in Tuscany or something, out of the squirrel cage, where I can write a good book or two without deadlines, read all the books I bought and never read, a place where the climate is mild, the wine good, the olive oil tasty, and the people still honor the elderly and the peasants treat landlords with respect." By this time he had tears in his eyes and was talking at random. "I like the harmony of the countryside in Tuscany, the beautiful old villages, the feeling that nobody is out to screw you, and nobody around you is trying hard to get anywhere fast."

When he left, he waved his hand enthusiastically from the car and shouted what I thought was a witty remark: "It's a great life, boys, if you don't weaken!"

Chapter 2

THE REASONS WHY I ended up with the rest of my family an involuntary adolescent immigrant in America naturally have little to do with me. The decision was Father's. His reasons were many and tangled, related to his personal life, the waning of his fame, the world around him, and the moment in history. They were, however, not dissimilar to those that had driven millions of humbler men down the generations to the same country, which, in the end was nothing more than the sum of all their different and sometimes impossible hopes. This is why it may be interesting to reconstruct the influences that inspired one immigrant, not a typical one, to be sure, yet not as exceptional as he might have appeared.

Luigi Barzini *padre* was the greatest Italian journalist of his time. He was so well known that people recognized and stared at him on trains, in theaters, restaurants, and side-walk cafés. Nature had made him unmistakable. He was about six feet tall, one head taller than the average Italian of his generation, slim, elegantly dressed like an English clubman, with the small head of an El Greco figure, curly hair brushed close to the cranium, and a conspicuous nose, an incredibly long, bony, thin, arched Roman nose, which delighted cartoonists. His eyes, like those of an El Greco saint, were black, piercing, and burned like live coals. Headwaiters called him "Maestro"; shopkeepers, to have him as a client, treated him like an impecunious royal prince and offered him large discounts as a matter of course. He was unaware of the extent of his popularity, and thought it embarrassing and annoying, as well as vaguely unmerited, the product of blind chance, somewhat like winning a sweepstake, rather than the reward of merit.

Once, in 1905, in Japan, while covering the Russo-Japanese War, hearing from a newly arrived Italian friend that he had become some sort of a national hero back home, he suspected it was only a stupid joke. He asked doubtfully: "Are you sure?" He actually believed that his work had been so bad he would be fired with ignominy on his return. As he doubted his gifts and disliked his fame, he was also particularly repelled by the Luigi Barzini of popular imagination. He was a man of modest origins, born in Orvieto, an ancient sleepy town, famous for its wine, in 1874, the son of *Sor* Ettore, a tailor who became a small entrepreneur supplying uniforms to the Italian Army. *Sor* Ettore was a radical of sorts. His father, Luigi, a tailor too, as all Barzinis had been for generations, had been considered a dangerous revolutionary by the Papal police. The pride in craftsmanship and the remnants of libertarian and progressive ferments were inherited from his ancestors by my father, who was otherwise by no means subversive in his outlook. (I suppose I inherited some of the same traits, a preoccupation with impossible perfection in my work and a stubborn attachment to independent ideas.)

To be sure, the term "journalist" is now misleading. Like most of his celebrated contemporary colleagues in France, England, and the United States, my father really was a gifted writer under contract to a newspaper. In those years in Italy, books seldom fed families and paid rent, plays took a long time to write and could be flops. (My father's first attempt at playwriting was a memorable fiasco. The play lasted one evening, submerged by a storm of whistles.) Brilliant and talented young men, who did not have an income of their own, like Giovanni Verga, or a wealthy wife, or did not want to bury themselves, like d'Annunzio, under avalanches of debts and be pursued by creditors, adapted their art to the needs of the daily press. Barzini *padre* would sketch a complex political panorama in a foreign nation with the clarity and grace of a novelist outlining the background for a novel set in a distant country. He could describe a historic event, the particular color of an hour, an apparently insignificant incident, the fleeting expression on a man's face, a battle involving half a million men and tens of thousands of horses, or a famous personage with fastidious accuracy (some of his eyewitness reports have been used by historians as documentation; his book on the Battle of Mukden was obligatory reading at the Japanese Imperial Staff College), and at the same time in a vivid, transparent, enticing, spare, humorous, ironic, or occasionally moving prose.

This took a great deal of painful work. He was a slow and

tormented writer, always vaguely disappointed and sometimes disgusted by his prose. In the end his articles looked so effortless and simple that readers thought anybody who was where my father had been could have done what he did by merely jotting down what he saw or heard. The métier, which was a tough one for all his famous colleagues from other countries, was tougher for an Italian. He and other good Italian journalists had to invent a language. Italian had been for centuries a written, erudite, difficult language, used by an élite of literati, scholars, or lawyers, and never a familiar spoken one. People mostly used dialects, at home or at work. As a result, the most admired Italian prose at the end of the last century and the beginning of this one was flowery and tangled, like wrought-iron grillwork, with leaves, bunches of grapes, and curlicues, adorned with archaic, unfamiliar, iridescent words, proudly placed here and there like gems. It was prose designed to provoke the stupefied admiration of onlookers but scarcely to communicate information or emotions. The best journalists of my father's generation were the first to experiment with a living, spoken, and less pompous language. Barzini *padre* was recognized as one of the most successful. He managed to write an Italian almost as simple, flowing, and limpid as the French or English of his colleagues. The literati of the old school naturally despised him and never officially considered him a real writer. His success was with the masses of middle-class readers. (The aristocracy and the lower classes did not read.)

A great journalist of his time did not have to study political science, psychology, Marxism, economics, sociology, syndicalism, and anthropology. In fact, those disciplines interested my father very little, nor was he always aware of their influence on world events. He never saw himself as a political journalist. He merely tried to be an honest mirror. What he understood, what fascinated him, and what he reproduced magically was the spectacle of man's adventures, the indecipherable mystery of his erratic destiny, his unfathomable capacity for heroism and endurance. D'Annunzio (whom my father knew well but did not like because of his baroque, ornate, theatrical, ormolu style of writing and living) once called him *pittor di battaglie*, "painter of battles," like Paolo Uccello. The definition came near the truth. Some of his best writing was about war. War obsessed him. All his life he dreamed the same dream, guns being pulled uphill into position, the horses straining, the drivers shouting and cracking whips, gunners putting their shoulders to the wheels. But Barzini *padre* was more than that. He was a painter with words. The *Daily Telegraph* invited him to London in 1910 to describe Edward VII's funeral to its readership. This was almost unbelievable at the time, a proud English newspaper asking a Continental writer, a Catholic, and an Italian to boot to depict, for proud English newspaper readers, the sacred burying of their King.

He could be a painter with words because, of course, he was a gifted writer. Among his memorable pieces is one which describes the agony and death of the young Peruvian flier, Geo Chavez, the first man to fly across the Alps in 1910, from Brig to Domodossola, where he crashed on landing. Barzini, who had become a good friend of Chavez at Brig during the weeks of training and preparation before the flight, sat in the little country hospital room almost continually, for days and nights, a notebook on his knee, and jotted down everything that happened and was said,

the description of the people who visited the dying hero—
the weeping veiled French lady without a name, his
brother, friends, competitors, doctors—and diligently recorded the disconnected words the young man mumbled in
his delirium. At times he thought he was still flying over the
Simplon Pass, the motor was humming happily, the air was
clear, but then something went wrong, the earth rushed at
him with terrifying speed. Words came out pell-mell in
French and Spanish, childhood memories, dear names, invocations mixed with altimeter readings and technical details. In what Barzini wrote (an article so long it was printed
later as a small book) he showed no emotion, never raised
his voice, and unknowingly used the impassive camera-eye
and tape-recorder technique of future generations. The
result was devastating. The tale of Chavez's death has been
often compared to another memorable description by a
great Italian writer of the death of another hero, a dear
friend of his, the classic recording of the agony at Mantua
of Giovanni dalle Bande Nere, the *condottiero,* written at his
bedside by l'Aretino in 1526.

Barzini's many adventurous feats convinced people he
was a fearless swashbuckling desperado. In reality he was
a shy, silent, intense, impractical man, inept in business
affairs, embarrassed by all human contacts, even those with
his own children. He disliked the company of other writers,
society characters, artists. He was *à son aise* only with old
provincial friends, possibly around a country dinner table
in front of a fire. Above all, he loved solitude and silence.
He had gone with the Italian contingent of the international expeditionary force to the relief of the Peking lega-
tions besieged by the Boxers in 1900; interviewed the
Wright brothers at Kitty Hawk; described the ruins of San

Francisco after the earthquake; miraculously saved himself in a Zeppelin wreck over the Black Forest. . . . He had been with the Japanese Army at Mukden in 1905, one of the only two Western correspondents on the spot (the other was an agency man, who could not leave headquarters, the source of news). Barzini *padre* wandered on horseback along the hundred-mile battle line, at −22° Fahrenheit, without once changing his clothes, for about thirty days, eating the soldiers' food, taking notes and drawing sketches. He sent short dispatches from the field in English, the only foreign language the Japanese military censors could read, but when the battle was over, he wrote a description of it, perhaps the best and at that time the longest in Italian journalism, about fourteen thousand words, and rode day and night on horseback over the cold Manchurian plain to the nearest Chinese telegraph office, so as to be free from the Japanese censors. After that he collapsed. News of the thirty-one-year-old wonder journalist dying alone in a Japanese hospital moved Italy. Eleonora Duse started a subscription among rich American friends to send a doctor to him. . . . In 1907 he and Prince Scipione Borghese went from Peking to Paris in an automobile, winning a purse put up by *Le Matin,* the great French newspaper. In 1911 he landed with the first Italian troops in Tripoli and followed their conquest of Libya. Then came the Balkan wars, the Mexican Revolution, the Great War, the Versailles Conference, and the Washington disarmament conference.

Exactly what my father, who lacked most qualities that made a proverbial American, believed had attracted him to the United States, I never discovered. We never talked about it. It surely was not because one of his ancestors, Antonio Barzini, also a tailor, had died fighting for the

Republic of Texas at the Brazos River. (This my father never knew, and it was found out by my brother Ugo many years later.) Whatever the reasons, he was fascinated by the United States and visited it as often as he could. He made many American friends, some of them eminent. Among the Italian historian Guglielmo Ferrero's papers at Columbia University, I have been told, is a long letter to him by my father describing and analyzing Theodore Roosevelt, whom he had known well. Ferrero, who had been invited to the White House, had asked my father's impression of the President before going.

It was during the Washington disarmament conference that Barzini *padre,* now forty-seven years of age, conceived the idea of starting his own newspaper, the dream of all traveling journalists. It was to be published in New York, an Italian daily. Millions of potential readers had been landing for decades and were still arriving by the hundreds of thousands every year. Most of them, certainly, could not read, and those who could were not inclined to; nevertheless, the project looked fabulous on paper, a real gold mine. As soon as the daily, called the *Corriere d'America,* came out, the stream of potential readers dwindled to a trickle, drastically reduced by the new Immigration Law. The paper never flourished.

One of the compelling reasons (though possibly not the main one) which actually drove Father to America was the usual one. He had never been paid enough, certainly not in proportion to his popularity, his contribution to the *Corriere della Sera* circulation, and its owners' wealth. His modest salary had not risen, after the war, at the vertiginous rate of all prices. We felt the pinch badly. This humiliated and saddened him for years before the war and embittered him after it. We were not really poor, of course. We were as well off as the family of an obscure middle-echelon bureaucrat. Father, to be sure, did not expect to become a millionaire in the United States. All he wanted was a little more independence for himself, a house of his own, a car, a little more comfort and ease for us all, luxuries like an extra pair of shoes for his children, an occasional good dress for his wife, a few more books, a trip or two for the family, and possibly to set aside some safe investments for his old age.

The decision to change continents was, as usual, a last resort. For years he had idly hoped something would magically turn up and solve his financial problems without the trouble of moving, perhaps a great international success in the theater, like Luigi Pirandello's, a world-wide best-selling book, or a fabulously lucky adventure in the business world. These were all improbable. He had no knack for the theater and publishers always got the better of him. His most successful book, translated into eleven languages and published simultaneously in many more countries (English, Spanish, and Portuguese serving for more than one), made practically no money for him. It was the movingly well-written account of the 1907 automobile race from Peking to Paris, which the whole world had followed. He had been convinced by a Milan publisher, a shrewd *Schweitzer,* to sell him the manuscript outright for a tiny sum. Another famous book of his, written for children, *Fiammiferino* (second only in popularity to *Pinocchio* among little Italian readers), has been reprinted over more than half a century by a publisher who could not afford to pay one cent of royalties for the simple technical reason that he was always broke.

Father at times also idly dreamed of opening a great international restaurant in Milan or Rome, or perhaps an

Italian restaurant in one of the great foreign capitals. As he was an excellent cook but a bad organizer and administrator, his establishment would have been one of the world's best but would also surely have gone bankrupt in a few months. Among his other impossible schemes was the idea of importing Oriental rugs. He knew something about them, too, but certainly not enough to best Levantine carpet merchants, notoriously more cunning than horse traders. Fortunately, moneyed businessmen, often fascinated by Father's vast imagination, also recognized his childlike incapacity for running any practical enterprise. Nobody ever backed him. Instead, a few businessmen got him to back them in clearly ruinous enterprises with what little money he managed to save from time to time. He always lost his shirt.

All this Balzacian building of *castelli in aria* was not for himself but for us, his family, whom he loved dearly. Personally he needed nothing. He had no problems. He lived like a prince. He traveled most of the time; his expense account was unlimited. His publisher, Luigi Albertini, who was one of the owners of the paper and, incidentally, my godfather, insisted that his star writers travel only on famous trains, the Orient Express, the Trans-Siberian, the *Flèche d'Or,* and on great liners; carry only expensive English leather luggage; stay at the most celebrated hotels; wear clothes made by one of the three or four good tailors in Europe; and eat in stately restaurants. Father was for us a little-known personage, the character in a popular novel, an American millionaire, a Russian grand duke, or an Indian maharaja. Almost always he came home unexpectedly and, on our return from school, we knew he was there before we saw him. We smelled his presence, the odor of good leathers, the Turkish tobacco smoke of his gold-tipped cigarettes, the eau de Cologne with which he rinsed his face after shaving. His arrivals were memorable and exciting events. One day my sister Emma, who must have been eight or nine at the time, blurted out in class to her teacher: "*Signorina,* guess who I found in Mother's bed this morning!" The teacher, fearing an indiscreet revelation, tried to shut her up. "You can tell me later, dear. Now let's get on with our work," she said hurriedly. She was relieved when Emma continued: "My father!"

Mother was a shrewd and rigorous administrator of our limited resources. She managed to protect our European middle-class dignity; we had a cook and a maid, the least one could have at the time, and lived in a comfortable apartment. She watched the *centesimi,* had suits and over-coats turned inside out before passing them on to the next son, Father's discarded clothes cut down to my size, her old dresses freshened up by a seamstress, read mostly books borrowed from a library, and was a wizard at obtaining discounts, wholesale prices, free tickets for the theater and concerts. She made extra money occasionally writing for magazines and translating an endless number of cheap serial novels from the French. In reality we could not even pity ourselves. Many wealthy people lived like us in those parsimonious times. It was then considered prudent to conceal one's means. We lacked nothing essential. To be sure, I dreamed of a bicycle throughout my youth but without really missing it, just as, I suppose, boys today dream of owning a supersonic plane. And our life was pleasant in many inexpensive ways. Every summer we made use of the free ticket, granted once a year by the State railway to all journalists' families and their servants, to travel to a small and beautiful village by the sea, unknown to wealthy and noisy tourists, Levanto on the Eastern Riviera, where we had many friends. And we read a lot, sometimes a book a day each, all the year round.

What money Mother could spare went mainly to prepare us for the future. We all took French lessons very early and English a few years later. Since it was an accepted fact that I was to follow in my father's footsteps, possibly because I had been given his name, which would have been wasted in any other profession, like dentistry or accounting, and because I was considered good at composition, I was also taught the two skills absolutely necessary to a journalist, fencing and riding. A journalist had to be prepared to fight duels all the time. A good knowledge of fencing, acquired at an early age, gave him confidence and a bolder writing style. He could more easily call a spade a spade and call corrupt people by their real names. A war correspondent followed battles on horseback and his riding skill sometimes helped him best his competitors. Incidentally, this money was unwisely spent. I never fought a duel in my life (nor had father ever fought one, for that matter), although I was asked a few times to act as second for other people. I followed battles sitting in automobiles.

Mother's efforts to prepare us for the future did not meet with the approval of the publisher. In fact, he resented them. He was a nineteenth-century, benevolent, fatherly, and frugal *padrone,* who felt it his duty to run the family life of his staff as if they were all irresponsible minors. Some of them, of course, were. He was helpful and resourceful. He set aside part of everybody's salary, knowing that it would be wasted thoughtlessly if made available. The amount was kept secret. Nobody knew how much he really earned and how much had been saved in his name. Albertini was invaluable in emergencies. He produced good doctors, specialists, surgeons, lawyers, and also reliable plumbers, electricians, masons, or carpenters. He provided loans or advances when absolutely necessary. He pacified outraged wives who had discovered perfumed letters in their husbands' pockets (as Mother did once or twice) and severely scolded unfaithful husbands.

It was he who saved d'Annunzio from financial catastrophe in 1910. The poet more or less belonged to the *Corriere* family. He wrote occasional patriotic poems for it which set Italians afire. He was declared bankrupt, his belongings were sold at auction, including his priceless books, clerical bric-a-brac, hunting horses, and a pack of borzois. He fled to Paris and later to Arcachon so as not to be distracted by legal persecutions. Albertini organized the gradual payment of some of his debts, utilizing his future royalties, granted him modest advances, and wrote him stern letters on the necessity of not basking in princely splendor, of living within one's means, and never borrowing from cutthroat moneylenders. The great poet, of course, paid no attention whatever to all this nonsense.

What the publisher disliked above all about d'Annunzio and other members of his staff was that they all wanted to live in a style above their station. People, according to him, had to keep their allotted place in society. He once fired Paolo Monelli, a young veteran of the First World War who had written a book of war memoirs as good as Erich Maria Remarque's novel (better in my view), because he had bought an automobile. Only the publisher and the *amministratore,* Albertini believed, were eminent enough to own automobiles. All the others, no matter how well they wrote, what great books they published, and how much money they made, should walk, travel on trams, in fiacres, on bicycles, or, in emergencies, in taxis. He thought it appropriate that his star writers live splendidly but only when they were representing the newspaper abroad. Their families at home were to be kept at a proper modest level.

Among the things he deplored was Mother's grandiose idea that we should learn superfluous foreign languages. He thought it his duty to make her understand how wasteful it all was. The matter, however, was a delicate one, to be handled with tact. He did not want to write her a letter, which would have been left in the files. (Father was as usual traveling abroad.) He sent his son instead, to conduct a diplomatic *démarche*, and explain that language lessons were, like automobiles, or, I suppose, yachts and racing stables, luxuries people in our station should avoid. Mother listened politely and answered simply: "Please thank your father and tell him that his own sons can well do without French and English, as they will always have an ample income. My sons will have to make a living. For them languages will be absolutely necessary."

There was another reason why my father decided to emigrate, a reason which had been equally common to most settlers in the United States for three centuries, the desire to flee the corruption and decay of Europe in general and those of his country in particular. Barzini *padre*, like many men of his generation, did not even suspect he had political views. He thought he was only a good citizen, a patriot, preoccupied solely with the welfare and good name of his country. In reality, he was a nineteenth-century bourgeois liberal, the heir of Risorgimento ideals, who wanted to see Italy modernized, tidily and honestly run, its prestige

44

abroad defended, its economy expanded, and the liberty of the people preserved at all cost under an impartial law. He favored a great fleet, an efficient army, and a well-run bureaucracy. He was proud that the quotation of the paper lira had been higher than that of the gold lira for years before the war. His ideal model was Victorian Britain at the end of the century (the first country to which he had been posted as a young correspondent), little and heroic Japan defeating the Russian giant, or the patriotism, loyalty, tenacity, and compactness of the American people, which had produced military victories, an amazing progress, and a miraculous industrial prosperity. Poor and chaotic Italy, of course, could not possibly be compared to these admirable models.

He wanted Italy to become a respected, powerful, efficient, law-abiding, prosperous, industrialized nation, but, like Alexander Herzen and John Ruskin, felt a stranger in the countries he envied because he could not bear their shoddiness, uniformity, vulgarity, and diffused stupidity, the boredom of their life and the lack of *joie de vivre.* "Countries without salt," he called them. Once, in 1907, when he was walking up Fifth Avenue, the sight of a beautiful old bronze brazier in an antique dealer's shop window stopped him abruptly. It rested on capriciously draped red velvet. He looked at its dents and at the two brass handles shaped like two angels. There was absolutely no doubt. It had been his family's, in Orvieto, made by a local artisan when Father was a child. Each dent corresponded to a well-remembered incident. He entered the shop and made some polite inquiries. The clerk told him haughtily that it was Italian, of course, made in the sixteenth century, a rare specimen. The price was very high. Father gave a last look at the old brazier and walked slowly away. He could not afford to buy it and what would he do with it? He realized then that he and it belonged to another world, strangers in New York, a world in which one ordered one's brazier from the local craftsman, an old friend, discussed at length over a glass of wine its shape and design, the handles made like little angels, and would not consider buying one ready-made like millions of others.

He always lamented the national defects which, in his view, prevented Italy from becoming his impossible-dream country. He had seen Italian soldiers in action in China in 1900, in Libya in 1911, and in the Great War. He had wept (mostly privately, in letters to his wife and lengthy reports to his publisher, which were published only a few years ago and are now widely quoted by historians), contemplating the capacity to suffer, the incredible courage, intelligence, resourcefulness, and occasional heroism of little men, soldiers and subalterns, a treasure wasted by the incapacity and insouciance of most generals and politicians. He literally wept once (the only time I saw him weep), after Caporetto. When the front broke, he rushed to Milan by car, to report and write what he surely could not have transmitted. In the evening, still dressed in the crumpled muddy clothes he had worn at the front, he told his wife about the débâcle. She held him in her arms as if he were a boy. Tears streamed down his brown cheeks.

What grieved him most, in war and peace, was the wasted excellence of many obscure single and solitary Italians. They were artists, writers, musicians, philosophers, economists, entrepreneurs, inventors, strategists, financial experts, bureaucrats, who managed somehow to keep Italy afloat. He undoubtedly was (but did not consider himself) one of them. Nobody thanked them. They were *antipatici,* as rigorous and eminent people often are, and isolated. Some of them had to emigrate to find recognition. They were not prophets *in patria.* The postwar years finally broke his heart. The feeble and ineffectual behavior of the Italian delegation at the peace conference, the evident amused contempt of the Allies for Italy, the disarray and impotence of successive governments in Rome, the disorderly and dangerous condition of everyday life, embittered him further. He despised the trickery, cheap political subterfuges, slick smartness, and the resigned and hopeless pessimism of many politicians. He resented the lack of frankness, punctuality, and precision of most of the people around him, the national reliance on charm instead of virtue, ornamentation in lieu of substance, Italy's aged courtesan's display of decayed beauty to entertain paying foreign visitors. He despised the Italian habit (which he thought of almost as a symbol) of placing the best oranges on the top of the crate and the bad ones at the bottom, until the buyers became aware of the trick, turned the crate upside down to open it, whereupon the best oranges were put at the bottom. His spare, almost Anglo-Saxon, prose proves his innate repugnance for frills, fretwork, and arabesques, often concealing a moral vacuum or dark despair. In those years he avoided writing about Italy. He preferred traveling abroad.

The country was torn by violent, bloody, and apparently senseless political strife, tumults, and street riots. Father, of course, was acutely aware of the desperate conditions of the poor, coming as he did from their class, the hunger and misery of the exploited workers, the medieval life in the countryside. He knew the number of unemployed was enormous and growing (they received no State subsidy to speak of) and that there was no immediate hope for them. He knew that most of the wealthy bourgeoisie were ignorant, overbearing, and obtuse. He never liked such people; "cretins who know only how to make money," he called them. But he also knew that bloody street fighting was no solution. The socialists were not able to carry through a real revolution to its Leninist conclusion, which would have been a way out, because they did not have the men, the ideas, and the courage. But they were also unable to stop preaching revolution, calm the frightened and angry workers, share the responsibilities of government to restore some sort of order, get things moving again, and solve some of the more urgent problems.

The result of all this was Fascism, a regime of half-cultivated, muscular, and pragmatic war veterans. In the beginning Father, as well as his publisher, Benedetto Croce, Arturo Toscanini, and many other honorable men, reluctantly welcomed it. He was disconcerted by the illiteracy and coarseness of most of the leaders, their contempt for liberty, and their belief that they were above all laws. Two things, however, he did not dislike. These men seemed to want (or so they said) the kind of Italy he had desired all his life, from the defeat at Aduwa in 1896 by the Abyssinians, to Caporetto in 1917, to the *brutta figura* at Versailles two years later and the disorders after the war. And—the second—most of them had fought well in the war, as brave unknown subalterns who had led their men against the enemy barbed wire and machine-gun fire, and had earned medals. Like Albertini, Croce, Toscanini, and the others, he hoped against hope they would clean up the Augean stables, re-establish the rule of law, and the authority of the

48

State, then retire like Cincinnatus. It was a desperate and impossible hope.

The socialists had disappointed him. They had been among the few who had taken seriously Lenin's Zimmerwald appeal to sabotage the bourgeois imperialistic war. The French, the German, and the British working-class parties had loyally supported their countries. The Italian socialists had preached defeatism and desertion among the troops and applauded each national defeat. All these were mortal crimes in the eyes of a solid, old-fashioned patriot, and incomprehensible too. The flabby politicians of the center had also disappointed him. What else was there but the Fascists? They were being admired, praised, and envied by foreign observers, by all conservatives, to be sure, but also by American liberal journalists, who believed Mussolini was the only alternative to Lenin. (They changed their minds only after Hitler came to power in 1933.) The Fascist leaders honored Father practically as a national hero and flattered him. Nevertheless, he never had a Fascist friend. They did not speak his language. He could not understand them, was deeply suspicious of them, and often frightened at the thought of what the final outcome of the desperate experiment might be. At the same time, he was not openly anti-Fascist. His newspaper, published abroad for émigrés, cautiously supported the government of the time, trying at the same time to avoid rhetoric and demagogy. It would have been almost impossible to do otherwise and retain the readers' loyalty. When Mussolini sent him an unrequested photograph with a flattering dedication, Father thanked him but did not publish it in his paper. He thought it was a private matter, and a slightly embarrassing one.

There was a third reason, I suppose, that made Father decide to emigrate. His prestige in Italian journalism was still very high but no longer what it had been only a few years before. Since the beginning of the century, when he had been practically the only one, the number of journalists enriched by his example or simply imitating him had increased enormously. In fact, in the early twenties, all Italian newspapers were filled with younger and less talented sham Barzinis. They missed his real secret, of course, which was the painstaking observation of reality's details and colors. They wrote fiction, sitting comfortably in their studies. They did not waste time going and seeing, investigating, meeting people, or gathering facts. The exact truth is contradictory, untidy, illogical, and embarrassing for anyone trying to write an elegant article. Inevitably, the style lost credibility. It was called *"barzinismo"* in those years. (The term was contemptuously coined by Mussolini himself.) Then, of course, the red-hot political atmosphere in Italy after the war was not ideal for Father. He found himself attacked from extreme right and extreme left for what he had not written but had been read between the lines by his critics. Ideologies, like theology during religious wars, had become supreme. There was no longer a place for simple honorable men, nineteenth-century bourgeois, who merely wanted to observe the world and prod their country toward a gradual progress. He never wrote about politics with pleasure and found himself increasingly unable to avoid it. Finally, for all these reasons, his supremacy in the *Corriere* was waning. He had begun to disagree with his publisher during the peace conference and the two men gradually grew apart. He found himself shoved aside by younger and more politically adroit men. When in 1921 he proposed the founding of an Italian newspaper in New York, Albertini enthusiastically encouraged him, and promised financial and editorial backing, like that the New York *Herald* provided its Paris edition (promises which he was not able to maintain, leaving Father in the lurch).

The main reasons which had always driven Europeans to the United States were therefore present: the need for autonomy and a higher standard of living, the hope of a better future for his children, the disgust with the demented and cynical corruption of the Old World, and finally the dawning awareness that he was no longer adapted to cope with the postwar life in Italy. His decision (like millions of similar decisions) was an affirmation of hope, to be sure, but also an implicit admission of (as well as a flight from) failure.

Like the America of all immigrants before and after him, his was not entirely a real country. It was mostly imaginary, a mosaic composed of all the virtues he believed Italy lacked, the perfections and improvements he had dreamed for his native land. He said to me, once, when he was old: "I wanted my children to grow up where their future depended not on family connections, political factions, powerful friends, intrigue, or camarillas, but on their talent, capacity for hard work, and real worth." He saw the United States as from a distance, out of focus and beautified, like a movie star of the twenties photographed through a veil of gauze. American expatriates like Henry James, Edith Wharton, and, later, Gertrude Stein, Hemingway, and all the other refugees from America saw France, Italy, and other countries similarly composed of what they longed for and could not find at home. The United States, of course, while not entirely the country my father imagined, was nevertheless closer to his ideal than Italy in 1922.

Father put a proud motto on the masthead of his paper, elegantly written on a scroll around the engraving of a caravel, presumably one of Columbus's, which said: *"Seguendo il sol lasciammo il vecchio mondo,"* or "Following the sun, we left the old world." The motto made a lovely hendecasyllable and sounded like a well-known line by a great poet, something well-read men should remember. All great Italian poets wrote hendecasyllables. I could not trace it. Surely father made it up himself, an imitation antique. He was good at writing doggerel. *"Il vecchio mondo,"* of course, evoked the image of an impotent, decrepit, toothless, driveling, iniquitous world, run to seed, torn by senseless strifes, tangled in its own intrigues, swept by hurricanes of fanaticism, lost in Byzantine controversies, resigned to its sores, condemned to self-destruction. Evidently, it could be forgotten only by those who traveled in one direction, westward, toward the dying sun. Westward, in America alone, could life be renewed. Only in America, where industry was rewarded, could one find prosperity. In America stock prices rose magically, at that time, like leavened dough, without cease, every day, and banknotes could always be redeemed in gold coins. America was the abode of the righteous, where honesty, justice, virtue, liberty, and reason prevailed, in the long run anyway. *"Seguendo il sol"* probably seemed to him all the explanation and justification needed.

Surely the myth of the West was born with man. Adam and Eve themselves must have trudged toward the setting sun after the Fall. This is not certain, of course. It can only be inferred from the Bible's words that God had built Eden "to the east." Where else could they go out of the East? Milton takes the direction of their voyage for granted. He explicitly describes them "marching from Eden towards the West" without a doubt. Since then, all wandering men had left their native soil and moved toward the setting sun as a matter of course, as if the flat earth were tilted: the legendary tribes from Asia at the dawn of history, the Huns and Teutons from Scythia, the Mongols and the Tatars across the Russian plains, the Turks from Turkestan to Constantinople, the Arabs to Spain, the Saxons from Jutland, the Normans to Normandy. There are only a few small exceptions, but they are only apparent exceptions. The Jews marched east from Egypt but they were going home; the Venetians went to the Orient, the Russians to Siberia and the Eastern coast of Asia, the English south to Africa and east to India and the Far East, et cetera. However, these people were not migrating en masse with women, children, and cattle, but adventuring, extending their power, conquering and robbing weaker populations. The first and principal hope for all men moving west was gold, to be sure, the gold Columbus promised Queen Isabella, the gold he was reproached for not bringing back from the New World in sufficient quantity. They also sought other kinds of wealth: richer and vaster pastures where fatter flocks would multiply, a more fertile soil in which to grow larger crops and grapes as big as watermelons, and docile slaves.

But the quest was not only a grossly material one. Men sought peace too, a miraculous return to the golden age, and wisdom. The sun had been the symbol of the deity from the beginning, the divine source of life, but its light was also believed to be the light of Reason. Men went west to find enlightenment, knowledge, the dangerous and forbidden knowledge which would help them change their own very nature and their fate, Adam's curse, and devise new rules for governing themselves. Without knowledge, without wresting some of its secrets from Nature, how could man build the wonderful future for himself and his progeny he had always dreamed of? Dante himself firmly believed this myth. In the twenty-sixth canto of the *Inferno,* Ulysses urges his companions to dare go west, beyond the gates of the known world, through the Pillars of Hercules, on to what would be later known as America, with these words:

> "O frati," dissi, "che per cento milia
> perigli siete giunti all'occidente,
> a questa tanto piccola vigilia
> de' nostri sensi ch' è del rimanente
> non vogliate negare l'esperienza,
> di retro al sol, del mondo senza gente.
> Considerate la vostra semenza;
> fatti non foste a viver come bruti
> ma per seguir virtute e conoscenza."

("O brothers," I said, "who through a hundred thousand perils have reached the West, to this so brief vigil of the senses that remains to us choose not to deny experience, in the sun's track, of the unpeopled world. Take thought of the seed from which you spring. You were not born to live like brutes, but to follow virtue and knowledge.")

To go west, in short, was to abandon a brute's life, to leave the corrupt and tragic past behind, with its vices and delusions, in order to build a new and happy future, which would not be new or happy unless man could be changed into "the new man," who would finally conquer his evil penchants and cultivate his small gift for goodness, a man who would follow unswervingly Dante's *"virtute e conoscenza."*

Chapter 3

To BE SURE, none of us young Barzinis then bothered to analyze the reasons which drove Father to the United States. We young Barzinis were four: Emma, eighteen, the oldest, the only girl, who painted and loved the theater; Luigi *figlio;* Ettore, a poetic and dreamy boy two years younger than I, who was killed by the Germans in 1945, a few days before the Americans arrived, at Mauthausen, where he had been interned as one of the first organizers of the Italian Resistance; and Ugo, five years old, a child prodigy with a tenacious memory. Like most Europeans, we assumed placidly (as one takes for granted the existence of seas and mountains) that our life in America would surely be infinitely better in many if not all ways than in Italy, and that the trip was not merely a geographical adventure, but a chronological one, a short cut to the future, the liner on which our passage had been booked as freeloading guests being really a time machine. Were not the Americans already living one generation or more ahead of us? Had they not bravely discarded consoling old superstitions, abolished comfortable old injustices, and discovered daring solutions to the dusty problems that made Europe uninhabitable? Who would not prefer spring to winter, youth to old age, wealth to poverty, health to disease, the rule of law to tyranny, a brand-new house fitted out with impeccable plumbing to an ivy-clad and ghost-ridden hovel?

All this was amply confirmed by all we knew of the United States. There was little we did not know. To begin with, Mother had lived there with Father in 1908, when expecting me (she got back in time, thus unfortunately preventing me from aspiring one day to the Presidency of the United States).

Mother was an unusually beautiful and intelligent woman. Barzini *padre,* just back from the Russo-Japanese War, had been introduced to her in a Milan theater box, during a performance by Georgette Leblanc, Maurice Maeterlinck's wife. Father looked fit, healthy, after a long rest in a sanatorium, and (as he did till the end) very young for his age. Mother looked incredulously at the lanky youngster and said: "Barzini? So young and . . ." He finished her sentence: ". . . and already so Barzini? Yes." They fell in love that evening and were married a few months later. That she was beautiful is easily proved by old photographs. That she was not only intelligent but also cultivated, a fastidious reader, a minor private poet, and a polished writer is proved by her library and the few books and the few poems she left behind. She finished the *liceo* in Milan (eight tough years of it), a rare performance for Italian girls at that time, and, what was even rarer, went on to the Sorbonne in Paris. Few of her friends, however, were allowed to discover she was a latent *bas-bleu.* Her rare essays, fairy tales, and short stories were published under a pseudonym. She showed her knowledge of literature and history only when absolutely necessary, and then with hesitation in her voice, as if not quite sure of what she knew well. Her conversation was pungent, unobtrusively witty, ironic, and wise.

For some reason, she never felt happy in the United States. She had few friends and it was difficult for her to meet the well-traveled, well-read, well-mannered Americans with whom she could have exchanged *mots d'esprit,* obscure quotations, rare kitchen recipes, reminiscences, and anecdotes. She thought such Americans did not exist. She had a group of European lady friends who, when they gathered around the tea table, talked of nothing but the barbaric habits of the natives. What disturbed her about the Americans she happened to meet was their lack of interest in the things that filled her life—books, poetry, history, and well-turned phrases—their indifference to the virtues she cultivated: moderation, discipline, skepticism, prudence, thrift, patience, and understanding. She was frightened by their noisy and indiscriminate enthusiasms. She lived in the United States eight months a year (she went back to Italy every summer) as resignedly and courageously as the wife of a missionary in an incomprehensible and practically uninhabitable country.

Our childhood had been filled with amazing stories of her adventurous stay in America. Americans, she told us, never mended holes in old socks. They recklessly put them, still good for a few more years, in the garbage can, and bought new ones. (Like all European women, she slipped a wooden egg inside our old openwork socks and spent hours patiently filling the empty spots with delicate tracery.) She explained that the Americans pretended they did this to keep production flowing and factories humming. In reality they were only rich, spoiled, and impatient. That they were impatient (impatience being, for some reason, their main national characteristic) was proved also, Father once pointed out, by the fact that they raced horses one year younger and over much shorter distances than in Europe. They could not wait. They uniquely consumed salted butter in 1908, forced to do so by the obscure powers that governed such things, probably because it kept forever and could be shipped long distances. Father, Mother told us, refused to adapt himself to such commercial constrictions. He wanted his Italian sweet butter. Mother had to churn it for him. (She brought the American hand churn back to Milan as a memento of what she had had to go through.) She also told us that most American houses were quickly and cheaply built, not with durable bricks and stone for future generations but with wood. Perpetuity in houses interested these people as much as in socks. The wooden houses burned as easily as matchboxes and the city of New York was deafened day and night by the firemen's clanging bells and roaring engines. It was, according to Mother, the sound of New York, as that of church bells was the sound of Italian cities.

Americans, she told us, not only restlessly changed wives, parties, homes, jobs, and sometimes their names, more frequently and with greater ease than Europeans, but fanatically embraced new religions, cults, political utopias, miraculous diets, rejuvenating cures, revolutionary medicines or cosmetics, and forms of physical exercise, and tried hard to convert all their friends to their new faiths. This was but one aspect of their eternal quest for improvements in all fields, which incidentally had also filled the country with inventors. New machines, gadgets, contrivances, and scientific discoveries that would transform the world for the comfort and delight of humanity were announced every day. Where else could the famous King C. Gillette have been born, who freed man from cheeks perennially crisscrossed with bloody cuts? Where else could Thomas Alva Edison have flourished, who gave the world the stock ticker, the dynamo, the incandescent lamp, the cinema, the gramophone, and was now trying to communicate with the souls of the dead? Who in Europe could have thought of the disappearing bed, a bed during the night, a handsome wardrobe during the day? Where else could the rocking chair have been invented, in which a man could move and sit still at the same time?

We knew that obscure geniuses, thousands of them, were at work all over the country developing wonderful new contraptions and devising the applications of new scientific discoveries that would liberate man from more drudgeries and needs, and transform his life, first in the United States and later, gradually, inevitably, all over the world. In fact, Americans went so far as to think up many needs of which men had never been aware in order to satisfy them. Furthermore, they rarely failed in their undertakings. Success in every field was almost always inevitable and produced wealth, prodigious wealth such as Europe had never dreamed of. Almost all Americans were rich, some fabulously rich, as rich as only Croesus and Midas had been.

Years before, during the war (I was nine), I often accompanied Mother to the "American Rest House," a makeshift wooden structure built by the YMCA at the Milan railway station to comfort American and other soldiers on their way to the front. (The few local ladies who spoke English had been drafted as hostesses.) I observed these khaki men with great attention. (I am sorry I do not remember the only American I should remember, a lame young man from Illinois, a journalist and writer with thoughtful eyes, clipped mustaches, and white shiny teeth, named Ernest Hemingway, who was convalescing in Milan at about that time. I should have noticed him as he unaccountably wore the uniform of an Italian ambulance driver.) These American soldiers were all tremendously healthy, big—bigger than the gray-green Italian or the sky-blue French soldiers —and strong, dressed in expensive woolen uniforms, provided by their government with splendid raincoats, as well as with solid boots, leggings, and belts made of thick leather. They ate ample and substantial meals (not the watery pasta and cabbage of the Italian soldiers), traveled not on weary feet and worn-out boots but mostly in cars and trucks, and drank vast quantities of coffee, beer, and wine. They had plenty of money.

They were generous, bought worthless souvenirs to send home, and distributed gifts all around, even to the English-speaking ladies of Milan, who were chagrined, as they themselves had prepared less expensive gifts, of which they were ashamed, for the American soldiers. They gave me candy, biscuits, chewing gum (which I had heard described but had never seen), one new silver half-dollar, several overseas caps, and one large khaki felt hat like those the Boy Scouts then wore. They were not shy and never intimidated by their officers. They teased each other, joked, laughed loudly, sang songs in chorus, slapped each other's backs, and wrestled. They seemed not to be aware that war was a dismal tragedy. To them, I suppose, it seemed above all a stupid mess from which they alone could extricate the Europeans who had got themselves tangled up in it. They thought it was an easy job, a wonderful picnic. They surely were a different race of men, freer, happier, younger, more confident and generous than the old, weary, miserly, and resigned Europeans.

It was definitely impossible to forget America even after the war. Wild American dance tunes were in the air, generally played on American Victrolas. On Father's desk was a brand-new American typewriter, whose keys he ponderously and slowly hit with two fingers. Americans often came to our house, for lunch or dinner, journalists mostly, friends of Father on their way through Milan. They wore new clothes, so well pressed they appeared to be made of plywood, mad neckties, and shining new shoes. They drank a lot, smoked thick cigars, wanted to know all about Fascism, and compared Mussolini to Theodore Roosevelt.

Then there were the dentists' showcases. Here and there in the city were small glass cases, hung during office hours by the street entrances of the dentists' rooms. They were filled with rows of splendid laughing dentures. The sign in gold letters said "DENTISTA AMERICANO" and an American flag in the background showed that the national pride covered, among many other, more tremendous achievements, the minute perfection of dental prostheses, so perfect, in fact, they could not conceivably have been created anywhere else. They were a minor illustration of the Americans' unrelenting war against man's destiny, the fatal decay of old age, one more proof of their capacity to invent better materials than those made by God on the day of Creation. God, in fact, rarely bothered to make teeth as even, incorruptible, and resplendent.

Then there were weekly installments of Buffalo Bill's adventures (pronounced "Boofalo Beel" in Italy), displayed on newsstands, with wonderfully colored covers showing the white-haired Colonel Cody, on his white horse like the Archangel Gabriel, massacring evil and ugly Indians who wanted to stop the march of progress and civilization. American cars could occasionally be seen in the city streets, long, sleek, visibly expensive, or ugly, black, practical, spider-like, and cheap. . . .

In those years the adjective "American," added to any noun, indicated something naturally excellent, a drastic improved version of a dreary Old World article, or a diabolical new invention. *"L'oeil américain,"* said my old French dictionary, was *"l'oeil scrutateur, auquel rien n'échappe,"* the all-seeing eye. *"Cose fatte all'americana,"* or "the American way," meant the quick, forthright, straight-to-the-point, pragmatic way. People were shaved *all'americana,* like butlers or coachmen, or had American mustaches (the toothbrush kind). There were American bars in hotels; the *"truffa all'americana,"* a wonderful new foolproof swindle invented by clever Americans; mechanized, sanitary, shining American barbers' chairs; revolutionary American fountain pens, typewriters, cash registers, bootjacks; there were American shoes in which the feet were free and happy, shoes shaped with bulging toes and inset invisible rubber heels.

When visiting the American Consulate in Milan, I was

particularly impressed by the shape of the wooden chairs. They looked like ordinary chairs, perhaps a little bigger, sturdier, and more expensive than Italian office chairs. What made them unmistakably American was one single feature. The bottom was not flat but carefully sculpted in the shape of two concave buttocks. Who but an American would have thought of that? The chairs showed not only the people's ingenuity and obstinate rejection of stale precedents but also a hospitable and humanitarian approach, a restless search for improvements that would add to the comfort and happiness of man, and, incidentally, to the wealth of their inventor.

Then, of course, there were the movies, which allowed us to live the everyday life of ordinary Americans for a few hours. Movies could not lie. I was literally transported across the ocean when sitting on the Italian flat-bottomed wooden chairs of my favorite cinema (half-price for students and soldiers). It was called *Silenzioso* but was by no means noiseless. The public loudly cursed and insulted the bad guys; the single usher tried to eject by force the boys who sat through the film two or three times; occasionally girls screamed when somebody pinched them or put a hand under their skirts. The picture was drowned in deafening music, produced by an amazing automatic machine, which looked like a tall glass showcase, lit from inside. It was filled with many upright violins from which fast bows traveling in a circle drew a stream of melodies, surely an American invention. The films depicted the heroic struggle of American men and horses against hostile Nature, against evil characters with black hair and shoe-polish-black mustaches (bankers or gamblers), and against the crafty and cruel Indians. They also described life among ordinary middle-class Americans, surrounded by liveried Negro flunkies, in stately and ornate houses full of potted palms and marble pillars. The great incredible beauty of the young women mesmerized me, the beauty of the simple farm girls defending their homes from greedy and cruel bankers, and of the splendidly gowned and coiffed girls in the stately mansions. I had to admit there were no such beauties in Europe. If there were any that healthy and indestructible, I had never seen them.

America was, in my adolescent eyes, a sunny country (if you dismissed the torrential rains which seemed to pour on every scene, indoors or out, in the worn-out films) where victory and pretty women smiled on brave men, and success allowed them all to live like Oriental potentates or simple feudal princes.

All this could not help but confirm our idea of the generally blissful life awaiting us, give or take a few inconveniences and deficiencies. Yet we were also worried. Americans (as seen from a distance) were known to get things done, ruthlessly, meticulously, quickly, against all obstacles. They were hard workers, efficient, punctual, law-abiding, truthful, earnest. They were justly proud of their achievements, their philanthropies, their immense suspended bridges, their trains (always on time, immaculate, served by benevolent black porters), their skyscrapers; proud, too, of their wealth-generating industries, their free government, their laws, the honesty of their politicians (most of them anyway), and the genius of their scientists. They skillfully blended races and nationalities into a new homogenized model people, with more or less uniform tastes, beliefs, clothes, principles, and habits, if not skin color. They knew they were way ahead of Europe and did not hide their feeling of superiority.

What perturbed us, above all, was this: Could we, the Barzinis, easily be turned into Americans? Would not the homogenizing be painful? Would we submit to the process? Would we not suffer when shedding our old personalities? Could we survive the rigorous separation between right and wrong that seemed to obsess all Americans, the characters in their movies and magazine stories as well as their austere statesmen at international meetings who looked like Protestant ministers? Would we not long for the human, shabby, undisciplined, wise, compassionate life in Italy, where the border line between right and wrong was so often conveniently blurred? Were we made of the stuff from which Americans could be fashioned? And, after all, were they really as different as they thought they were? Had they changed as much as they proclaimed themselves to have? Were they New Men? *"Coelum non animum mutant qui trans mare currunt,"* warned prudent Horace, whom I had read that very year, or "Men change the sky over their heads but not their spirit when they cross the ocean." Even Walt Whitman, the optimistic patriot, had complained: "General humanity has always been full of perverse maleficence, and is so yet." Obviously in the United States, too.

In fact, we were secretly scared not by the possible shortcomings of the country awaiting us but by its very perfections. There were also moments when the excitement of the approaching departure, the foretaste of the new wonderful life, and the relief at leaving behind troubled and unhappy Italy were marred by another secret doubt gnawing at our entrails. Were we the eager heroes of a new

66

adventure or cowards slinking off the European field of battle to a safe and sheltered place? How much was America the country of courageous adventurers building a happier life for man and how much a deserters' paradise? Maybe Nature, the Indians, and the wild animals had been easier to fight than the human enemies of all kinds in Europe. This doubt or secret remorse, I discovered years later, is a perennially unasked and unanswered question hovering over American history.

We had to visit the American Consulate, where I observed the convenient shape of the wooden chair, to obtain our immigrants' visas. This firsthand contact with the power and majesty of the United States Government impressed us greatly, but, strangely enough, it also left us vaguely uneasy and perplexed. We were asked by a clerk to fill out official blanks under oath in order to obtain the necessary visas. Similar forms in Europe were, and still are, contemptuously couched in cryptic bureaucratic jargon, smudgily printed on grayish pulp paper. No oath is ever requested, as the authorities wisely think people always lie when necessary. We were pleased to see the American blanks were richly and elegantly printed on durable white paper; the language (and its Italian translation) was peremptory and meticulous, but courteous and clear. The questions to be answered proved the United States Government definitely to be what we expected: impartial, stern, motherly, nosy, fussy, and efficient. It rightly wanted to know a lot of things about us before making up its mind whether to admit us among the happy inhabitants of God's own country.

On closer examination, however, some of the official

preoccupations seemed to reveal a puzzling suspiciousness on the part of the authorities concerned, a sign of weakness so unexpected that we tried to dismiss and forget it as absurd, attributing it to our crooked and wary Italian minds. Surely the government of the richest, most powerful, safest, best-regulated, and biggest country in the Western world, led by laconic and sagacious Mr. Calvin Coolidge, could not be as insecure, naïve, inept, and transparently astute as a back-country peasant. It asked, among other things, whether we had means of subsistence in the United States. Obviously, if we had not, we would not be allowed in. This puzzled us. Was not America the country where the tired, the poor, the wretched refuse of Europe, the homeless and tempest-tossed, could start a new life? What kind of a refuge could it be if only self-sustaining affluent immigrants could be admitted? At the same time, the blank went on to warn us, we would be excluded if, before leaving, we had signed a contract for work in the United States. Evidently, America preferred to lift her lamp beside the golden door for rentiers, who did not really need her help. Then the blank tactlessly asked us whether we were Northern or Southern Italians, with the clear intention of weeding out the latter as less desirable. Why the racial discrimination? And why ask anyway? Was not the indication of our birthplaces enough? Did American officials not know geography?

What was even more bizarre was the last question. The blank wanted to know from us, under oath, whether we—all of us youngsters, the child Ugo, and our staid and virtuous mother—believed in the overthrow of the American Government by force. Did it think itself so vulnerable? Did it expect Anarchists, Blanquists, Social Revolutionaries,

Maximalists, terrorists, dynamitards, desperadoes, Bolsheviks to be intimidated by an oath? Had any of them ever answered "Yes," in a fit of boastful folly, absent-mindedness, or self-defeating honesty? And hadn't the United States been the proud refuge of heretics of all kinds, including political heretics? We honestly answered "No," to be sure, as we had neither the intention nor the capacity to overthrow any government by force, least of all the seemingly indestructible American Government. As nobody surely had ever answered "Yes" down the years, since the day the blank had been formulated, why was that particular question kept on it?

Not all the hopes that drove Father to the New World were strictly American. Like all wanderers to the West, he sought above all a nonpareil land replete almost exclusively with the particular virtues, gifts, blessings he longed for. Once there he (like all of us, for that matter) inevitably concentrated his benevolent attention on whatever confirmed him in his belief that he had made the right choice and considered everything else irrelevant. His America, to be sure, was only partially that of his sons. We happened to be in revolt against the manners and morals of his generation as much as our American contemporaries were against those of their own parents. I was particularly obsessed by and ashamed of what I believed were ineradicable Italian national defects. I despised above all the sordid and corrosive concentration on the individual's and his family's survival, come what may, at all cost, what Guicciardini calls *il particolare,* which made Italy a crumbly nation at all times.

In Italy, I often had to dodge street battles when going

to school. I would know there was one ahead of me from the noise of the *saracinesche,* the iron shutters, being slammed down by frightened shopkeepers, the shouting, the scurrying of frightened feet, the hail of cavalry horses' hooves, and the sound of shots. It was unconvincing to attribute the endemic disorder merely to the undeniably wretched conditions of the oppressed proletariat; the revolutionary trade unions and parties managed to make the people's conditions even worse. In reality, once the Fascist dictatorship was established, problems were still dealt with in the old Italian way. The rot was hidden at the bottom to deceive naïve foreigners and trusting Italians. Behind the flags, the colored show, the uniforms, the medals, the parades, and the bands, behind the rigid and brutal police control, the spies, and the censorship, behind the theatrical gesturing and oratory of the leader, the old decrepit Italy remained almost intact, its old sores festering, some of which were gradually becoming incurable. Most of them are with us still.

I also knew the rest of Europe was not much better off. General strikes and riots were almost as frequent and as frightening elsewhere as in Italy. Demented parties of the right and left, agitators, demagogues, and rabble-rousers kept people in turmoil. There was, to be sure, the postwar economic crisis, with its millions of unemployed, starving and desperate masses. Yet the *désarroi* in Europe could not be attributed solely to economic factors. It was deeper and older. Long before, the élite had stopped believing in itself and its own principles, and the people no longer placidly accepted its leadership. It was terrified by the people's blind and bloody rage and the people were afraid of its hysterical and bloody contortions to preserve power. In a way, Europe no longer had faith in the things that had made it great, civilized, powerful, magnanimous, wise, and unbeatable. It had forgotten the secret that had allowed the *optimates* and the common people together to traverse historical vicissitudes, to win glorious victories, suffer defeats and humiliations, disasters and famine, and rise again, always together. What Guglielmo Ferrero called *"la grande peur"* gripped the Old World. You read it on people's faces. New men, mostly raw and ruthless (or, sometimes, the old and tired élite in fancy new uniforms, with new titles and new fanatical ideas dictated by *la peur*), emerged from the confusion and conquered power, promising a new Spartan order. People had to accept it, keep their mouths shut, or go to jail.

The horror of *la peur* and disorder was perhaps one of the main reasons why I was happy to be in the United States in the years before 1929 and saw in it only a tidy, disciplined, moral, earnest country, an honest country where the oranges were all invariably good from the top to the bottom; a self-satisfied country, to be sure, a little arrogant and proud, predictable and boring at times, as all virtuous and wealthy countries are, nevertheless one in which one could hope to live in peace and, even if one did not become rich and famous, be justly rewarded for work well done. My America, the America I saw enhanced by distance and from outside, was by no means entirely imaginary. It existed at the same time with several others. Not being particularly stupid, I was well aware of the dark shadows in the landscape. As a student, an avid reader, and a reporter, I knew the squalor of the slums, the poor people's suffering, the corruption, the injustice, the oppression, the persecutions, the fear of the future which still tormented many people's lives. But what really counted in my eyes was the people's vigorous reaction to their ills. To be sure, I took a vociferous part in demonstrations to save the lives of Sacco and Vanzetti, the two Italian-American Anarchists perhaps unjustly condemned to death, but the tragedy of my countrymen was to me a glaring exception, the remnant of a fear of foreigners and romantic revolutionaries which real Americans were doing all they could to correct. What was perhaps important was not the two Italians' death but the mobilization of all honorable Americans in their defense. In this America of mine, liberty and respect for the law were synonymous: political decisions were peacefully reached through elections and not demented street riots; harmony between the races, the old and new immigrants, and the different classes reigned most of the time reasonably well. The majority of the descendants of foreigners looked American anyway; it was difficult for me to distinguish one class from another, everybody looked middle-class in European eyes, including the black students in the university and the beggars in the street.

The country seemed to me, as a whole, give or take a conspicuous crook or two, miraculously governed by honest and reliable leaders. They were probably dull men, a few of them insufferable stuffed shirts with narrow fixed ideas, but, not knowing them personally and at close quarters, I was grateful they lacked the disreputable and elastic sophistication of eel-like European politicians. The American leaders looked to me (as I admired their faces in newspapers and magazines) a little stupid sometimes, but prudent, firm, solid men of their word, solicitous of their country's welfare and good name. I liked Calvin Coolidge (even when he wore his Indian feather headdress), who seemed to chew perennial wormwood, the bitter scorn of a Yankee for weakness, sin, and man's frailty. I considered Herbert Hoover's high collars, carved in Carrara marble, the white piping on Mellon's waistcoat, and Dawes's up-side-down pipe as decorous guarantees of solidity. Charles Evans Hughes or Henry Cabot Lodge looked like kings of old to me, Henry IV of France or Frederick III of Germany, bewhiskered fathers of their people. Who would not trust his future to such dignified wise men as Elihu Root or Henry Stimson, who looked like benign lawyers who took scrupulous care of widows' and orphans' interests? Who would not entrust his savings and future security to the austerely dressed bankers or financial wizards whose portraits appeared frequently on the business pages? They looked pensively into the distance, some of them supporting the excessive weight of their ivory foreheads with one hand, at the unsolved problems of humanity.

These people's physiognomies reassured me also because, at the time, I had not yet discovered one of the many gifts a generous God had bestowed on the United States at its birth, that of producing, in almost every generation, leaders who looked like the best possible character actors cast by the best possible casting director for the roles of themselves. Who better than George Washington, who even before his death looked like the larger-than-life statue of George Washington, could impersonate George Washington? Was not Abraham Lincoln the only Lincoln imaginable? And what else could Theodore Roosevelt look like? The contemplation of the America of my choice gave me infinite pleasure. I trusted every word in the *New York Times,* with its immutable graphic style as uncondescending as the model T Ford, filled to the brim with boring but authentic facts. I particularly admired the pages dedicated to the verbatim reproduction of verbose, obscure, surely historical documents. I was impressed by gentlemen in morning coats and top hats solemnly walking up Fifth Avenue, chest out, to meet their God in church on Sunday, together with their elegant wives and well-washed children. I loved to look at pretty little girls with ribbons in their hair and fluffy white dresses politely skipping rope, and their bigger sisters as spick-and-span as dolls just out of the box. I loved the healthy, steady, untroubled, humorous look of many American faces, like that of Charles Lindbergh, the Lone Eagle, or John J. Pershing, familiarly known as Black Jack. Once, when drinking with two big blond American friends of my age, I studied the image of the three of us in the mirror behind the bartender. The other two looked like extra-large muscular angels and I like a small, dark, watchful, nervous, tortured infernal creature.

I envied the simplicity and solidity of everything: the majestic battleships strung like beads at anchor along the Hudson, the shining red and brass fire trucks, the well-fed and well-groomed policemen's horses, the impeccably spotless Long Island trains always on time, the fatherly conductors dressed in silver-buttoned Prince Albert coats with silver chains across their ample bellies, the vast and well-shorn lawns, the Greek temples which religiously housed the banks, the solid-brass spittoons, the immense libraries, the cavernous clubs filled with shining woodwork, dark paintings, solemn sleepy gentlemen, and attentive black servants. Everything in my America was clean, spotless, immaculately kept up, tidy, freshly polished or varnished. I admired the meticulous, firm, and sometimes incomprehensible regulations presiding over every activity, regulations which were never enforced because nobody ever thought of disobeying them, like the warning not to spit in subway cars, printed in gold classic Roman letters, which threatened violators with a fabulous five-hundred-dollar fine which, I am sure, had never been exacted. All these minute rules (often irksome and incomprehensible to an Italian) prevented conflicts, misunderstandings, confusion, and made everything in American life apparently run as smoothly as if on roller bearings.

I liked the friendly simplicity and lack of arrogance of the rich and the lack of servility of the poor; the commodious and unpretentious wooden houses; the Americans' shirt-sleeves hospitality, glass in hand, on the back porches; the neighbors walking across summer lawns to visit each other; the lack of malice and envy in their conversation; the candid readiness with which Americans saw the good points in anyone. I liked their concern for animals, red Indians, Negroes, the poor, the illiterate, the heathen Chinese, the drunks. I liked the people's honesty—the fact, inconceivable anywhere else, which made everybody pay his taxes to the last penny without cheating, or close deals for millions of dollars on the telephone, on trust. "I never speak evil of dead men or living women," a courtly old gentleman told me once.

The wonderful stability and harmony of it all warmed my heart. Everybody seemed to believe fundamentally the same things, cherish identical ideals, just as everybody wore more or less the same clothes, or as the men put on and took off straw hats on the same two days in spring and autumn, and all behaved more or less according to the same code. The two political parties were twins, practically indistinguishable one from the other. There were (or there seemed to be) no mortal hatreds among the people as I saw them. I even enjoyed the absurd moralism inspiring their guileless foreign policy, the noble and innocent hopes in their futile official pronouncements. I was even pleased by the cruel rudeness of honest people, who unhesitatingly spoke the truth, went straight to their targets, and played no games, come what may. "How do you like my article?" I would anxiously ask a friend. "Lousy," would be the answer. "Doesn't make sense, badly written, and boring to boot. Anything else?" There was no substitute for truth, was there? Honesty was not only the best policy; it saved time, cleared the air of obnoxious delusions, and, in the end, was most advantageous for all concerned, particularly for those who were hurt by it.

All this, the discipline, the solidity, the common sense, the reliability, the stability, the honesty, the simple unquestioned ideas, the tranquil consciences, the harmony, the friendliness, I cherished above all because such things were not make-believe, a put-up show, the smooth contrived result of invisible coercion. All this, in America, was not the preservation of dead and embalmed ways and privileges. Americans were free men. They were progressing steadily and peacefully en masse, like a river toward the sea. They improved things, solved problems, and maybe—who knows?—would really succeed one day in building a better future for everybody. Why should they not? They had always succeeded in all tasks, after all. Perhaps the slow, almost imperceptible advance of these steady people toward their unpredictable tomorrow, the multiplication of the good things of life, the maniacal improvement of everything, all this could be the real revolution of our times and not the hysterical and bloody convulsions of impatient rebels in other countries. Americans followed the leaders they chose, not those given to them by God or imposed by screaming and violent crowds. The leaders they freely chose, most of them anyway, who looked to me like Roman senators or Renaissance princes, were born on small farms, the sons of humble people. This free and easy flow of a whole nation toward the future seemed to me to be the enviable secret of America, a country where it was still possible to hope. But was that all there was, was it real or a creation of my imagination?

Chapter 4

THE INSIDE OF our new American house, in 1925, was reassuringly Italian. There were the Italian smells from the kitchen (above all the aroma of coffee, which father bought fresh-roasted at De Rosa's in Mulberry Street, near his office); there were Italian voices and occasional Victrola music; there were books, prints, our familiar paintings and old furniture. The *terra incognita* began beyond the front door, which, we learned, did not have to be locked and bolted as in Europe, for the same reason that there were no forbidding walls and grilled gates around the garden, our lawn merging with our neighbors' without visible markings. Apparently, there were no thieves in America, or they were too rich to bother with petty pilfering, too rich also to steal small change in the wooden cup beside the unguarded piles of morning papers on the station platform. Each customer picked up his copy, scrupulously dropped the right number of pennies (two for the *Daily News,* three for the *Times* and the *Herald*), or left a bigger coin and gave himself the correct change. We never tired of admiring the whole impossible procedure with the same amazement with which, later, I watched staunch and gallant American students fearlessly take examinations under the honor system without even considering the shabby but seductive possibility of cheating. I could not believe my eyes.

The first few weeks I spent in my room studying English or reading American books and magazines, to prepare for the imminent school term, and, feet on the window sill, raised my eyes from time to time to peer at the United States outside as an explorer prudently spies from a safe vantage point on a strange and possibly hostile territory before advancing into it. I had to admit it did not look like the efficient, inhuman, and pitiless country I had expected, where the future had already arrived. It did not look particularly hostile either: no Indians or gangsters lurked behind tree trunks, no shooting or galloping horses could be heard in the distance. In fact, the scene was sleepy and peaceful, vaguely boring, but then it was very limited, a couple of quiet suburban blocks and five or six houses. In the tremulous speckled shadow of the immense trees I saw an occasional car or truck slowly travel the lonely road; the milkman's white wagon drawn by an old horse stop, patiently, at every door (as a devout Catholic stops at the stations of the Via Crucis); the postman in his sky-blue uniform and with his leather bag go from house to house twice a day; children in baseball uniforms going to play in some empty lot or running with their dogs; the cart of a Negro junkman on which the iron scraps bounced noisily to the rhythm of the trotting horse. In the late afternoon I could see collarless elderly men in unbuttoned waistcoats watering flowers, and old ladies with hairnets over their pale blue hair rocking themselves on their porches. My reading was desultory and intermittent; sometimes I was completely distracted by the blonde dancer in her one-piece bathing suit (a girl as unreal as the movie actresses I thought could not exist), who once in a while practiced on the lawn next door. I dreamed of her at night.

The light was definitely American, the clean transparent light of a mountain plateau in which all details were sharp and clean-cut. The fat birds and the squirrels, which would have been shot at sight and cooked succulently in the old country, were also American. The sounds were American, too: the clanking of iron garbage cans thrown around in the early morning; the elegiac lament of lawnmowers close by, distant, or very distant; the songs of the unknown appetizing birds; and the thumps of the afternoon paper pitched accurately against each front door by a boy on a bicycle. Definitely American, to be seen nowhere else, was the procession of dignified men in stiff collars and straw hats who walked to the station in the morning, swinging briefcases, and came back in the late afternoon. American, too, were the workingmen in Larry Semon overalls who were covering the road with a thick coat of new asphalt without bothering first to remove the old tram rails, further proof of American impatience and wasteful wealth.

Very American to my eyes was the enchanting wood we discovered a few minutes' walk to the north. It looked to us exactly as the Indians, the *coureurs de bois,* and the trappers must have left it, a place for Leatherstockings. We often went there, my brother Ettore and I (we had no other place to go). We never found out how large it was. We never walked to its end. It looked immense. It was filled with tall trees, moss-covered dead trunks, unknown flowers, squirrels, and the same mouth-watering fat birds. There was a large and deep pond in the wood, a Walden Pond of our own, which froze solid the following winter. We skated on it then and made friends with young people from the neighborhood. Particularly American was, later in the fall, the tang of burning leaves, so American in fact that when I smell it anywhere in the world it always brings me back, like the taste of synthetic vanilla, to my first months in the United States. It was a strange world, as seen from my window, but it looked safe, friendly, and hospitable.

One of the few things that disturbed us was our address. It went something like 158–04 35th Avenue. The postman explained that it meant our house was the 04th on the block between 158th and 159th Streets on 35th Avenue. We could not help but admit it was a rational, tidy, convenient, timesaving classification. Friends and taxi drivers could find our address with no hesitation. We admired it but did not like it. We had been accustomed to tortuous streets named after forgotten saints, illustrious artists, obscure kings, or obsolete crafts, like the streets of the swordsmiths (Via Spadari), the trunkmakers (Via dei Baullari), the arrowmakers (la Frezzeria), et cetera, streets in which we could imagine historic events had taken place, picturesque conquering armies had marched with drums rolling and flags unfurled or defeated armies had fled in disorder. The perfect network of inexorably straight streets crossing at right angles, designed by obtuse geometricians with a wooden rule, as well as the rigorous numbering of streets, avenues, and houses, gave us the uncomfortable feeling of having irreverently been catalogued and cased for easy location in a hurry, like books in a library or corpses in an ossuary. Some of the numbers corresponded to ghost streets, anyway; they existed only on maps and covered swamps, woods, or wild meadows. Would the map of the whole world, we asked ourselves, be overlaid one day with one continuous Fourierist network of numbered roads at right angles, a nightmarish grid over everything, the Sahara and Amazonia, the Indian jungles and the Siberian tundra? Would the whole world one day, if these Americans had their way, be turned into one spherical city plan, imprisoned in a dull arithmetical net in which men would feel treated not like human beings but contemptuously like things?

Soon enough, certain incomprehensible complications of American life caught up with us inside our jealously preserved Italian stronghold.

We had brought our old cook and maid from Italy. Decorously dressed like ladies, they had traveled second class on the *Duilio,* and visited us every day in the more expensive class. Each evening the maid, Ida, had laid out Mother's evening dress before dinner and tidied up our messy staterooms. The cook collected the recipes of some of the *Duilio*'s tastier dishes. They loved us like their own family, loved Mother almost more than her own children did. They had known us since our births. They always said they wanted to die in our house. Within a few weeks in the United States they had both disappeared.

The maid had met a portly Italo-American widower on the boat. He was bald and middle-aged, with a pasta-filled silhouette, and many rings on his fingers; he had a good business of sorts (probably a funeral parlor), owned a beautiful house with a garden somewhere in New Jersey and a resplendent car. The temptation was too much for her. She was no longer young. She married him suddenly without warning us. She came to announce her new status, wept, begged to be forgiven, and kissed us all as if we or she were shortly to die. During the next few years we saw her once in a long while, mostly at Christmas time. She came in a funeral-black, chauffeur-driven limousine, all dressed up in dowdy American clothes and wearing incredible hats precariously perched on her permanently waved hair. She sat with hands crossed over her belly, fingers spread out to show off her rings. She brought us little gifts and told us endless tales of life in darkest New Jersey in the midst of a complicated and emotional Italo-American family. She wept copiously.

The cook left us only a little later. She had been stalked and captured by a neighboring American lady, who had first seen her at the Italian grocery store. The American lady spoke a little Italian and was rich, perhaps not really rich but richer than we anyway, which was not difficult. She had patiently cultivated Maria's friendship, taken her to the movies on her days off, and translated the subtitles; asked her to her home for tea, and finally made her an offer she could not refuse. The cook, too, wept copiously when she announced she was leaving, kissed all our cheeks, kissed Mother's hands, promised to be back as soon as she had saved a little money. We never saw her again. Probably an even richer American lady had taken her farther away.

Mother resolutely faced the domestic crisis. She remembered that her first cook, the one she had hired in Milan just after her marriage, a peasant woman named Palmira, had come to the United States with her husband and must live not far from us. She traced her. Palmira came, driving her own car. She was now a widow with two sons; she was much fatter than Mother remembered her, and had smartly bobbed hair. She wore a dirty diamond ring. She told us she was doing well, making and selling bootleg wine, beginning to distill *grappa* and experimenting with whisky. She left her home, sons, vats, and customers for a few days, for old times' sake, only to help Mother in her emergency, but could not stay. Her affairs needed constant attention. She had to defend herself from competitors, pay bribes to policemen and Prohibition agents, as well as protection money to her protectors. She had to produce and deliver cases and cases of her brew. (The wine was barely drinkable, the raw *grappa* not bad, the whisky poisonous.)

Then father did what he could. He knew the former head of the Italian squad in the New York Police Department, the legendary Michele Fiaschetti, the successor of Joe Petrosino, the squad's founder. Fiaschetti was a herculean six-footer from Abruzzi, the terror of the Black Hand, who was now running a detective agency of his own. He was so strong he extracted confessions from suspected men merely by holding them out of the window with one arm while questioning them. Fiaschetti promised help. Within a few days he brought us a middle-aged Sicilian woman, Rosalia, who had to be hidden where nobody would find her because her husband had sworn to kill her. She was easy to hide, as she was as thin and small as a child. She had large frightened black eyes in a little wrinkled-apple face, never went out, kept all windows closed, the curtains drawn, and tremulously peered out at the road through the side of the curtains. Her cooking was spicy and unfamiliar, her dialect, to us Milanesi, almost incomprehensible.

She told us endless tales of her native village, most of which we did not follow clearly. Her husband had been her only love, she said. He had raped her against the cemetery wall when she was fourteen and she could never forget such a romantic proof of affection. Why he now wanted to kill her we could not fathom. She did not explain. It must have been for some complicated reason out of Pirandello. We could not believe it was to avenge the family's honor, one of the imperative island reasons. I thought she was not young, fat, or appetizing enough, too scrawny. But then I was not an old Sicilian peasant. Or maybe she had betrayed a secret, had unwittingly revealed something to Fiaschetti himself, who had to save her. When I was occasionally left alone with her, I made tours of the house clutching Father's automatic revolver from World War I in my pocket, feeling like Tom Mix or Nick Carter. I never saw anybody resembling a grim Sicilian killer or *cornuto* husband lurking in the placid suburban neighborhood.

Some weeks later Fiaschetti came to fetch her in his car. For equally mysterious reasons she could no longer stay with us. She disappeared. We learned later she had been killed. Why, by whom, we never found out. For a while we had to make our own beds and wash our own dishes.

I went to the local high school for a few months to practice my English and possibly learn something more about the United States than what I could pick up at the movies, at the family dinner table, or by reading newspapers. I studied American history, among other things, wondering how these ingenious people, with then only a century and a half to go on, managed to fill books as thick, unreadable, and complicated, as rich with memorable dates, legendary events, and famous men, as the Italian textbooks, which dealt with thousands of years, the rise and fall of entire civilizations, invasions, and innumerable wars. "History is like a gas," my Spanish brother-in-law says. "No matter how little there is, it fills the space available." But the language was what interested me most. Learning it was a vital necessity. It had not seemed particularly difficult on paper, back in Milan. It was spelled in a demented and unpredictable way, to be sure, but it had the grammar of a *lingua franca,* that is practically no grammar at all, which was a great advantage. I managed to read it easily with only the occasional use of a dictionary. The real thing living people spoke was, I found out, something entirely different.

There was a multitude of American English languages and two main written ones, a dignified American (somewhat similar to what I had been taught, which I read with relative ease) and *demotikos,* some of which, like the monologues of baseball players and petty crooks, could be understood only through a native interpreter. The varieties of spoken American could not be counted, and most of them were incomprehensible to me, used as I was to the clean-cut pronunciation of Italian. Words were usually ejected in lumps, at enormous speed, groups of them strung together like rushing railroad cars without perceptible separations. (The people surely did not speak as fast as I thought in those first few months. One always believes a foreigner speaks whatever his language is at vertiginous speed.) The enunciation seemed to me thick-tongued and gelatinous. "Butter" sounded to my ears something like "burrow," "Baltimore, Maryland," like "Balmer, Murlin." Voices often emanated, like that of a ventriloquist, from unexpected parts of the anatomy, the nose, the depth of the throat, the belly, the top of the head, and, in the case of many middle-aged men, the side of the face from which a cigar did not protrude. These spoken languages changed from region to region (in New York from borough to borough), and from class to class. Sometimes, in the same person, the language changed according to the hour of the day, the circumstances, the interlocutors, and the amount of drink absorbed. (All these impressions changed as my ears became more attuned to the people's speech. I still do not understand every word pronounced by many provincial Americans, but generally in the East and among friends, any conversation sounds to me as clear as running water from a mountain brook.)

And then there was the cryptic slang. "So's your old man!" said the girls derisively. Why my father? The whole thing was disconcerting and frightening. Would I ever be able to recognize, separate, and interpret all these languages? Would I ever be able to emit imitation American sounds good enough to be understood? In the beginning, I remember, I would diligently compose a simple sentence in my mind, asking for information or directions, pronounce it as clearly as possible, and wait. If the answer was plain yes or no, I was safe. More often it was a smile accompanied by a rush of gurgling rumbling sounds. What had the person said? Not always daring to ask for an encore, I meekly thanked him or her, and sadly went away unenlightened. How often in lunchrooms I ate not what I wanted but resignedly whatever repellent dish the waitress decided I had asked for! Frequently, too, my requests met with insolent and obstinate incomprehension. "What the hell do you want?" a shop clerk would say impatiently and turn to another customer.

For some reason Americans (the inhabitants of the country peopled by a steady flow of the foreign tempest-tossed) did not seem willing to make the charitable effort necessary to understand a poor foreigner's slightly distorted pronunciation. They were too easily defeated by a mere displaced accent in an otherwise perfectly enunciated word. This puzzled me. In Italy, of course, people have patiently been listening without surprise for centuries to Goths, Visigoths, Longobards, Germans, Saracens, Englishmen, Frenchmen, Americans, Turks, and Italians from other provinces murdering their native vernacular, and have almost always managed to interpret what the barbarians were trying to say. I supposed the Americans' pretended incapacity was due to their national impatience or repugnance to the irregular and unfamiliar. It was also probably connected with the hostility older immigrants always felt for the more recent ones. "What the hell do you want?" said the Indians to the Pilgrims, the English to the Scotch-Irish, the English and Scotch-Irish to the Germans, Irish, Jews, Italians, Greeks, Armenians, and all other newly arrived foreigners. And I patently was newly arrived.

Another pitfall to avoid was the wrong use of an English word which, while almost identical to an Italian word, had a different meaning. There are many: "to support" does not mean *"sopportare"*; "inclined" does not mean *"inclinato"*; "fastidious" does not mean *"fastidioso"*; "ruffian" is not *"ruffiano"*; "to annoy" is not the same as *"annoiare"*; "to demand" does not mean *"domandare"*; et cetera. The confusion could occasionally be embarrassing. One night

Beniamino Gigli and I happened to be sitting in a gilded box at the Metropolitan, surrounded by dignified matrons covered with brocade and diamonds, his devoted admirers. He was in evening clothes because he was not singing but had come to watch the performance. One of the ladies tapped his arm with her fan and asked graciously: "How do you feel tonight, *Signor* Gigli?" (*Signor,* incidentally, was the wrong title. It should have been *Commendatore.*) He cleared his throat and said: "Not very well. I am a little constipated." The ladies looked at him and at each other with astonished horror. I hurried to explain that by "constipated" he did not mean what they thought but only that he had a slight cold.

My stay in the local high school was short but grueling. It tested my fortitude. The students derided me, played practical jokes, called me strange names, made fun of my accent and my strange clothes. I was dressed *all'italiana* and did not wear the long plus-fours, sweaters, and saddle shoes in two colors the others wore. As long as we lived in the United States my brother and I, as well as Father, of course, always wore Italian clothes, made by ear by our old Milan tailor. They were cheaper and fitted us well. The American ready-made clothes, besides being more expensive, made us look like flood victims clothed by public charity. Evidently, we Barzinis did not have the bodies scientifically foreseen by the manufacturers. Our suits were ordered by mail and smuggled into the United States by a sailor, Lazzarino, the grandson of our boatman at Levanto. He wore them all when going ashore from his ship, one over the other, three or four trousers, waistcoats, coats, and overcoats. He came to our house for dinner and shed them. The customs men were never puzzled by the fact that this young man went out fat and came in lean.

Later I had to defend this habit of mine in interminable discussions with fellow university students. It was, I admitted, a deplorable attachment to a previous historic era, the age of craftsmanship and artisans, an attachment which, however, could be justified, as the survival of craftsmanship was vital in particular fields where mass production could not yet approach its perfections. The Americans answered that trying to look different from the rest of them was antidemocratic, antiegalitarian, offensive to the country whose guest I was; furthermore, it was antisocial, because by consuming one more factory-made suit, I would increase production by one unit and help lower costs by an infinitesimal fraction, thus contributing to the general welfare. These discussions, of course, never arrived at any conclusion.

The high school students made fun of my language, my pronunciation, my inadequate mastery of American idioms. They occasionally also made fun of what they thought was my pretentious use of rare words. Those, of course, were the words of Latin origin which came more readily to me. "May I accompany you home?" I once asked a pert girl with porcelain skin. She guffawed. "What odd foreign words you use," she said. She explained that I should have said, "May I walk you home?" They also made fun of my ignorance of things familiar to them (American history, the rules of baseball and football) and of my knowledge of things they knew nothing about.

It was a relief, in the spring, to move to the College of the City of New York. Father had a friend there, Professor Arbib-Costa, who taught Italian literature, and, being a spare-time journalist, considered Barzini *padre* a maestro who could be refused nothing. Almost certainly, my admission had not been rigorously determined by what Father thought was the enviable American respect for impartial law, come what may. I suspect it had been an operation *all'italiana,* the conquest of a privilege under the protection of a friend. I took a series of easy exams in Latin, Greek, Italian, French, and English, and was questioned by a few professors. One of them, an American luminary in philosophy, after a few simple questions, to test what I knew (I did not know much as I had studied only the history of philosophy, back in Milan, without taking sides), asked me: "Do you think all this will be of any use to you in everyday life?"

I was baffled. Did one read potted Plato, Aristotle, Spinoza, Hegel, Kant, and all the others as guides to solve practical problems? All I knew was that they were necessary to pass exams and to acquire diplomas, which surely were a help in everyday life. Perhaps they also supplied you with a general framework of ideas, which aided you in knowing yourself and clarified the world around you, but that was true of all humanistic studies in general. I tentatively answered: "Well, I don't know. I haven't thought about it." The professor smiled a very bright American smile (the kind politicians and actors smiled in front of cameras) and affirmed, perhaps with excessive certitude: "Young man, you'll discover that philosophy will actually be of great help to you in the United States."

What did he mean? Maybe he possessed a new philosophy I had not yet heard of which was a key to worldly success. Maybe I should have paid more attention to the English utilitarians and the American pragmatists. But then he may have been desperately defending his own (and his colleagues') discipline in an environment which judged all knowledge strictly from the point of view of utility and possible profitable applications. (Only later did I discover that this was one of the puzzling mysteries of American life. The United States seemed to me, at the time, the twenties, fundamentally an eighteenth-century philosophic experiment, proudly based more on a few books and documents than on experience and reality. In fact, it often risked schizophrenia trying to be both a land immersed in history and a moral utopia. Nevertheless, Americans, a nation of philosophers if there ever was one, or I should say *philosophes,* mainly guided in all their historic decisions by a noble and vaguely obsolete set of ideas, curiously never lost a chance to express their utter mistrust and contempt for metaphysics. Evidently, they did not know they were *philosophes.*)

I found the College a relief. The architecture astounded me, a theatrical reproduction of English Gothic which had little to do with the United States or New York, a curious and timid homage to the Middle Ages and Europe offered by the world of the future, anti-Europe. This, I suppose, was merely one more symptom of the Americans' restless desire to escape in space and time from the ideal world they had created, as proved by the names and cuisine of restaurants—Alt Wien, Capri, Ye Olde Tea Shoppe, Le Trocadéro, El Chico, The Blue Grotto, La Grenouille, et cetera—or by the feudal names of apartment houses. But the students were easy to get along with. Gone at last was the constant derision of my accent, clothes, and knowledge. Everybody—or almost everybody—was vaguely foreign too, born abroad or the son of immigrants. Many spoke with a trace of an accent and wore weird clothes. They all studied tenaciously, read a lot, were well versed in subjects

I knew nothing about and eager to learn from me what little I knew that they did not. They loved to debate any subject whatever at any length. I am sure I learned more from them (mostly Jews), in the few months I spent at CCNY, than from the professors.

For some reason, I found the Jews more interesting than the boys of Italian blood. The Italians had shed what little *italianità* their parents had brought to the new country, and did not speak a word of the language, not even their original patois. They knew nothing much about Italy, in fact, little more than what they had been told in the American schools, and, as a result, were somewhat embarrassed by their origins and their names. The Jews, with their hunger for books and ideas, their wit, their capacity to spin webs of ingenious arguments, their compassion, their acceptance of reality and the nature of man, were nearer to me. It was easier to talk to them. One of my Jewish friends, David Davidson, took pity on me and offered to improve my English if I taught him a little Italian. We could meet only on Sunday, the one free day he had. We chose a convenient and heated place halfway between our houses, the Forty-second Street library. As it was forbidden to talk in the reading rooms, we sat on marble benches in busy corridors, with the books on our laps. I do not know if he learned Italian. I know I learned a lot from him, including one beautiful and rare adverb which I never found the occasion to use in my life. In fact, I write it here for the first time since 1926, as a testimonial of gratitude to a young man who sacrificed precious hours of leisure in an attempt to make me an American of sorts. The adverb is "needsmost."

Chapter 5

THE REASON WHY I was abnormally obsessed with mastering the fine points of an alien language was that I did not want merely to get along. I wanted to write. If I was to become a journalist, it obviously had to be in America. America offered many advantages. I was already there, for one thing. Then, one certainly found there more openings and better pay than in Europe, more ruthless and modern techniques, a larger market (the number of newspapers and glossy magazines was staggering). Above all, in the United States almost nobody realized I was the son and namesake of one of the great journalists of the time (only a few middle-aged foreign correspondents knew who my father was), which made the burden of the name easier to carry. The problem, therefore, was to learn English, the contemporary American usage of English, not the jocular and short-lived slang of students' bantering conversation, the limited and sugary vocabulary of love-making, the oversimplified and repetitive prose of newspapers, the intricately ornate language of some literati (there were a few d'Annunzios in the United States, too, I found out), but the powerful, spare, virile language of the best young contemporary American writers.

In the fall of 1926 (or was it the spring of 1927?), I went a few blocks downtown, moving from imitation Gothic to imitation English eighteenth-century, to Columbia, where I took a large number of Extension courses. I was told that the Extension could be a somewhat easier bridge to the celebrated School of Journalism, only a few yards away on the campus. It was then considered the best, perhaps the only, place in the country where one could learn the arcana of the profession. As every student in the United States with high marks in English composition was trying to enter the School, and as the number of candidates accepted was rigorously limited, I knew that, being a foreigner, my chances were very slim. I did not abandon myself to hope. I merely took as many courses as I could, according to a plan agreed upon by a professor who had been charged with my case. I naturally took all the obligatory courses like American History and English Literature, and added a lot of Latin on my own. I worked very hard, among a strange collection of idle middle-aged men, disenchanted housewives, bored Bovarys on leave from distant husbands, and young people trying to catch up with lost time or a neglected education, a varied and savory bunch of companions from whom I learned a lot more about Americans. But why Latin? It was considered a hard subject and was awarded more precious points than I thought it deserved; it was close to Italian; and I had had eight years of it and had already read most of the principal authors. The real reason, however, was that I always remembered what Dario Niccodemi had said one night at dinner in our house in Milan.

Dario Niccodemi was a playwright, the Ferenc Molnar of Italy, famous and replete with royalties. Born in Livorno in 1874, just eleven days before my father, he had been taken as a child to Argentina by his family. He grew up in Buenos Aires and, still in his teens, had become a literary and dramatic critic for local newspapers. Later, at the age of twenty or twenty-one, he began writing plays in Spanish with some success and became a minor celebrity. When Barzini *padre* was sent to Argentina to investigate the conditions of Italian immigrants, the two became great friends. They were vaguely similar, both tall, slim, with small heads and bony arched noses, fastidiously well dressed, bachelors and extremely pleasing to women. Back in Milan Father wrote some well-documented and scathing reportage. The Buenos Aires newspapers attacked him with vulgar insults and libelous insinuations. Niccodemi counterattacked in the press and fought a duel to defend the honor of his friend. That made his name dear to our family. A year or two later, bored with the provincial atmosphere of a great city lost at the edge of the world, he emigrated to Paris. He told us that, to pay for his lodgings and at least one meal a day, he manufactured visiting cards by hand. He wrote his customers' names and titles in beautiful Spencerian calligraphy on Bristol board (it was, at the time, considered vulgar to have one's cards mechanically and uniformly printed by a commercial establishment).

Niccodemi was lucky to be a good writer, in more ways than one. A few months later he met Réjane, who changed his life. Gabrielle-Charlotte Réju, *dite* Réjane, was one of the two rival queens of the Paris theater. She was also very beautiful and plump, something her rival Sarah Bernhardt was not, and very intelligent. An old French encyclopedia says of her: *"Possédant le talent le plus souple et le plus fin, elle excella dans les rôles les plus divers, se montrant tour à tour spirituelle et nerveuse, emportée et delicate, réaliste et subtile, portant avec elle une vie intense."* What more could a dull and sober encyclopedia say? Réjane dominated Europe like an autocrat. I remember the day my maternal grandmother came back from Paris and announced with consternation to all of us and her friends that she had actually seen Réjane eat grapes on the stage using a knife and fork. This was a small revolution. It meant that, from then on, anyone who did not use a knife and fork to eat grapes (an almost impossible feat) was no longer a well-bred person. One might as well be dead.

Réjane was twenty years older than Niccodemi. They had met before, in Buenos Aires, during one of her triumphant *tournées,* but she had forgotten him and it had taken him a few months to remind her of their first encounter. She officially named him her secretary, to dignify the continuous presence in her entourage of a handsome foreigner definitely too young for her. Niccodemi was very useful to her in more ways than one. He began translating classic Italian plays into French (Goldoni's *La Locandiera,* for instance, with which la Duse had gone to Paris a year or two before, and had had a memorable success). Then he wrote French plays of his own, always for Réjane, which filled the theater with mobs of paying customers. Rich and famous, he finally returned to Italy in 1914 and began writing Italian plays, all of them money-makers. He was not what is considered today a great playwright. His was the bourgeois theater, *le théâtre des boulevards*. It is now forgotten. But he undoubtedly was a talented and painstaking craftsman.

He was the sort of man a young boy who wanted to write admired and envied. His name was famous, he had beautiful women at his feet and in his bed, he was at home in Paris, in fact he belonged to *le tout Paris*, like Boldini, and he was rich. I watched him that evening at dinner, as a devout worshiper would watch a living saint with stigmata. I forgot nothing. Particularly his answer to Father's question about languages. How could Dario have shifted so easily from Spanish to French to Italian? Dario explained that Spanish had been the language of his studies, Italian the language of his family. He had them in his ears. They both came naturally to him. French had been the only tough challenge. He discovered that drawing-room and dinner conversation was not enough. Nor had it been enough practicing it in bed with the aging actress. To learn to write French, he took Latin courses at the Sorbonne. That was his secret. It was, he said, the only way. One had to construct sentences in a new unfamiliar language and could not circumvent difficulties by using *à peu près* periphrases as one did in conversation. It was as simple as that.

I remember little of all the Latin courses I took that year. They were not particularly difficult, most of them being at *liceo* level. Furthermore, I was not really interested in Latin but in the English translation. I recall the textbooks were up to German philological perfection, the teachers took the language extremely seriously, more than it deserved, the students were awed by it and worked hard. Working hard myself, I gradually learned to turn even Tacitus (the toughest of them all, who certainly wrote with a sneer on his face and rubbed his hands, thinking of the trouble he was giving to young people for centuries ahead) into a stilted, grammatical, and properly spelled English. As relaxation I sometimes translated choice bits of Catullus aloud in the soda fountain to some of the boys in my Latin classes. We laughed ourselves silly. Dirty words were rare in Academe at the time, and thought to be farcically funny.

There was one minor difference that I can remember between my Italian Latin and the American Latin. I read it casually and easily the way I had learned, more or less with the pronunciation of the Church, which unquestionably had spoken Latin without interruption since Roman days. I read it with feeling as if it were archaic Italian, which, after all, it is. I allowed the accents to fall where they naturally did. My reading produced agreeable sounds, hexameters following each other like breakers on a beach, all subtly different, each with its own inner rhythm. The old method was looked down upon as primitive and unscientific in America, where Latin was pronounced roughly as if it were German. (The old method is now looked down upon also in Italy.) Teachers often asked me to get up and read Virgil or Horace aloud to the class. Some of them listened to my reading of poetry with their eyes half-closed as if they were enjoying music, others with a slight contemptuous smile on their lips. Did they want to show the students how mistaken backward and untutored people could be who did not faithfully follow the imperative of science? Or did they want to prove that Latin could also be a warm, living, and live language and not merely an instrument of torture for the young? Both things were true, I believe. In America the ever-present contempt for the casual ways of old and the eagerness to be up to date are always flavored with an excessive dose of heartbroken nostalgia. In almost all fields Americans seem to be in love either with tomorrow or yesterday, seldom with today.

What impressed me most, more than anything else, more than the incredible number of students, the many buildings, the facilities, more even than the size of skyscrapers downtown and the wealth of Wall Street, was the Pharaonic magnificence of American libraries, and Columbia's in particular. It still staggers me. I never thought so many books could have been gathered together since the Arabs burned down the library at Alexandria. Doubtless the very material presence of such reservoirs of printed treasures must secretly influence all aspects of American life. How exactly I did not know. That accumulation of culture, intelligence, and historical records surely illuminated many isolated specialists, a few of them the best in the world. However, I saw no particular signs of the libraries' influence in everyday conversation, newspapers, magazines, political speeches, and international decisions. Maybe I was wrong. I knew little about science and was not much interested in it. I was born into a bookish family, pretentious cultural snobs who looked down on mathematics and the technical knowledge necessary to make money. We thought cryptic literary allusions, rare quotations, witty anecdotes in three or four languages, and acrobatic historical parallels ("New York, of course, is Venice, a republic of merchants built on islands. . . .") were to be admired more than the useful and dull bourgeois virtues. We thought history more important than current events, as it contained, generated, and explained them. Furthermore, I could only measure the cultural level of America by the things I knew best, which were by no means those in which Americans were interested (with the exception of the specialists, of course, who knew infinitely more than I). Almost everything I read in the United States about Italy, for instance, was wrong. The names were misspelled, the geography was awry, the history was ignored, the people's character imaginary ("childlike, happy Italians, in love with music, beauty and color, oblivious to the misery of their life"). How difficult it was also to trace, in American pronouncements about international affairs, the sobering influence of history, past experience, the wisdom gathered by men down the centuries.

Maybe the libraries were something more than what they appeared, more than imperial storehouses, kept up to the minute, of all the knowledge available, for the delectation of an isolated minority. They were possibly also monuments or temples erected by busy people to erudition, somewhat like the treasures of incunabula gathered by J. P. Morgan, or the many collections of beautifully bound unread books to be found both in Europe and America in the palaces of merchant princes, nostalgic and expensive homages of the ignorant to the learned. Maybe some people felt books were magic objects whose possession alone gave men and nations particular virtues.

The students surely did not consider books to be mere amulets. They filled reading rooms, read a lot, took piles home to read far into the night. I myself spent hours in the Columbia library as intimidated and embarrassed as a famished gourmet invited to a dream restaurant where every dish from all the world's cuisines, past and present, was available on request. I read a lot, almost always in search of the secrets of America. One little book illuminated me in particular. "Read this," said, with only a trace of irony, one of my teachers, a red-faced young man. "It's a bouillon cube of a book. When you reach the last page, you will know everything or almost everything about us. You can apply for your first citizenship papers."

The little book was *The Mind in the Making* by James Harvey Robinson, Harper & Brothers, 1921, ninety-five cents. My old copy is still in my library after half a century. Obviously, nobody was ever tempted to steal it. And rightly so, because it is by no means a good work of its kind (I have read dozens of more profound ones since). For years, as I grew older and more arrogant, I even thought it was sense-less bilge, which had impressed me and warmed my heart when I read it the first time only because it was as juvenile and guileless as I was then, its author as ready as I was to believe in the American future, or, should I say, as fright-ened as I was not to believe in the American future. Now I know it is a great little book, not for the reasons which Dr. Robinson thought had inspired him but as an involuntary exposé of America's greatness and fatal flaws, a *summa* of America's hopes, in short a definition of the very essence of America. It is dated, of course. It could have been written only at the dawn of the twenties. Americans have since become too circumspect, when expressing their old faith in public, to be as explicit as Dr. Robinson dared to be.

Au fond it is a candid "how to" book. It simply teaches, in the doctor's own words, "how to save the Nation and the rest of mankind from themselves." It imparts easy-to-follow instructions to solve all the problems which have beset man in general since the Creation, those that threaten his future, and those (much more frightening) which harass Americans in particular, most of which, incidentally, were generated by the Americans themselves. The author, however, being a wise and well-read historian, knew that men, the vast majority of men, are stubborn and blind fools, most often bent on self-destruction, and would listen to him only with great reluctance, if ever. He knew there was even a strong possibility they would not listen to him at all and go blindly to their doom. Nevertheless, he bravely wrote on, mainly, I suppose, to lighten his conscience. Whatever happened in the future, whatever world-wide catastrophe and cataclysm his countrymen got themselves embroiled in, possibly dragging the world down with them, he could always say to himself and his wife that he had warned them in time.

That he would not be writing in vain, while most improbable, was not entirely impossible. As his ideas were self-evident, convincing, and somewhat elementary, why should not young readers be persuaded to follow him? His disciples could grow numerous and powerful enough in time to slow the rushing train of human destiny ("The Locomotive of History," as Marx aptly called it), and to switch it to the safe track before it reached the collapsed bridge over the ultimate abyss. "If the majority of influential persons held the opinions and occupied the point of view that a few rather uninfluential people now share," he explains at the outset, obviously considering himself and his disciples the "few uninfluential people," "there would, for instance, be no likelihood of another great war; the whole problem of labor and capital would be transformed and attenuated; national arrogance, race animosity, political corruption, and inefficiency would all be reduced below the danger point. . . . No inconsiderable part of the evils which now afflict society would vanish or remedy themselves automatically." It is indeed a big order, and a noble one.

What must then be done so that the torrent of history (to change metaphors) comes out of the swirling mountain whirlpools and deadly rapids in which it has always run, finally slows down and spreads out like a mighty placid river on the vast peaceful plain of the future? There is only one way. "We must change the mind of men," he simply advises. It is, of course, one half of the old myth of the West, where one found gold and bred a New Man. If modern institutions are not adapted to man, we must transform man, or, at least, a sufficient number of men, to fit the institutions. This may not be easy, he admits: "There are tremendous difficulties that stand in the way of a beneficent change of mind." The possible consequences of failure are, however, so terrifying that we cannot afford not to try.

There are three traditional methods of transforming society, the doctor explains: changes in the rules of the game, spiritual exhortation, and education. He easily dismisses revolution, an example of "hasty readjustment," as well as fiddling with institutions. He also dismisses preaching: "Experience seems to teach that little is promoted by moral exhortation." What we need above all is education, he believes, not education somehow but education that would direct the young to the study of disciplines considered by the majority in America as "at best amenities which have little relation to the real purposes and success of life." He is right, of course, but, being American, expects too much.

His way is by no means a quick way. It is as if a king, to defend the shores of his realm from approaching enemy fleets, invited his subjects to plant oak seedlings from which one day to build the necessary ships. Nevertheless, no other way has been found to cultivate what Dr. Robinson calls "intelligent and independent thinking." First of all, man should free himself, through education, from the slavish acceptance of the accumulated weight of the past, from all the ideas conceived by his ancestors. "I have no reform to recommend," he concludes, "except the liberation of Intelligence."

Of course, the real problem of humanity is the fact that men do not listen to teachers like James Harvey Robinson and do not utilize their own intelligence. Reason has never become the supreme ruler of destiny. Men worship false gods and follow deleterious prophets. *"Vulgus vult decipi."* But would they be assured of avoiding catastrophes, hecatombs, ruination if they followed Dr. Robinson for once? This is a grave question. The doctor visibly struggles, like all his countrymen, with the hoary contradiction between the élite and the *demos;* between *liberté,* which allows only the best to emerge, and *égalité,* which pushes the best down to the mediocre level of the average man. His heart is with the *demos,* his mind with the élite. He knows only the élite is capable of inventing the future, a new improved future. The *demos* tends to stagnate blissfully in its egalitarian swamp, happy to see the eminent exceptions punished. Dr. Robinson, in fact, seems to be tempted by dangerous un-American ideas for the sake of attaining real American results. Like Plato he would like to see the Republic ultimately entrusted to philosophers, a minority of specialists, *optimates* fit for the job. This is, of course, a heresy in a country founded on the dogma (among others) that any honest and willing common man can hold the highest and most responsible position if he gets himself properly elected.

The doctor's is a desperate gamble. He wants to multiply the philosophers' élite and the flocks of their pupils in suitable cultural hothouses, fast enough to save the *demos,* the United States and the rest of the world before it is too late, for their own good, if necessary against their will. He sees it as a race between himself and Fate, a passionate competition. We know he lost, but it was a good sporting try. What philosophers does he want to cultivate exactly? Not any philosophers, certainly no black pessimists, no Spenglerian prophets of decadence, no worshipers of the past, no Hegelians resigned to actual reality, no matter how ugly. After they have freed themselves from an excessive regard for "the conventional chronicle of remote and irrelevant events which embittered the youthful years of many of us," they must look forward boldly and face decrepit problems with open minds, as if they had just appeared. But, on the other hand, they must accept some history, they must absolutely accept the main American historical beliefs as blindly as Neapolitans accept the miraculous liquefaction of San Gennaro's blood on the anniversary of his martyrdom. They must not dare question, among others, the national conception of man, the world, and the significance of the American experiment. They must believe that tomorrow will be a better day, that the new way is a better way. They must believe that man can be substantially transformed by indoctrination to improve the world in every generation but, at this point in history, to avoid catastrophe; and that it is imperative (and possible) to establish the knowledge of man and society on a solid, measurable, scientific basis. James Harvey Robinson's significant symbol is the village mechanic. How less terrifying the world would be if it obeyed known laws! How peaceful everything would be if it rigorously followed mathematical orbits easily calculated! How happy the Americans would be the day Chance was finally abolished!

The young Barzini was fascinated by James Harvey Robinson as he was (and still is in his old age) always fascinated by the learned, persuasive, and reassuring explanations to be found inside boxes full of pills. The young Barzini also longed to dismiss doubts and believe firmly that a few simple formulas had been developed to solve humanity's problems. It was not always easy to believe it. He had, of course, studied Machiavelli and Guicciardini, whose books are required reading in Italy, but it was neither Machiavelli nor Guicciardini who had taught him skepticism and a realistic view of man. He had absorbed these from his father, his teachers, and his countrymen, who had themselves taught them to Machiavelli and Guicciardini, and from his church, which had always had a warily pessimistic view of Man. He knew human events unfortunately did not always have happy endings. He was often at a loss to define a happy ending. He suspected (even if he probably could not find the arguments to prove it in an essay) that the senator mentioned by Dr. Robinson, who at best relied "on rhetoric and mere partisan animosity," and, at worst, on corruption, bribery, lies, and the ruthless manipulation of public opinion, was in reality as scientific in his own way as the village garage man. Fears, hopes, and emotions were, after all, the wires that permitted the puppeteer to move the puppets.

The young Barzini knew that collective man was almost never a rational being, and that science would never supply the great definitive solutions. (He has now learned that any so-called "final solution" can be a terrifying prospect.) He was aware of the fact that machines born of scientific knowledge were meaningless because what was important was what man made them for and how he used them. The search for certainty ultimately came back to the study of man. He also thought that history was invaluable. Without a critical knowledge of precedents, man would perennially be condemned to reinvent the umbrella, to discover and experiment with what had been discovered and experimented with before, and sometimes to make the same mistakes, with enormous waste of time and energy. Man could not perennially go back to the cave age and be his own Adam in every generation.

Finally, coming from Fascist Italy, he was aware of one danger the doctor probably did not yet suspect and would appreciate only a few years later, in 1933 to be exact. Unfortunately, there was only one way efficiently to impose the views of a minority on a whole people, even when the minority was (or believed itself to be) enlightened, progressive, and well intentioned. Universal education could help greatly, of course, but was not the ideal solution. People absorbed all sorts of dangerously different ideas from books. The results were beginning to disappoint even Americans at the time, possibly because for more than a century they had trusted education as a universal cure-all, an infallible panacea. The almost inevitable and unmentionable solution was, in the end, some form of authoritarian state, a benevolent one perhaps, ultimately implying the suspension of liberty and the abolition of dissenters, as

Plato himself had admitted. Similarly, if a powerful empire wanted to impose its views on the whole world, no matter how beneficent the views, indispensable for abolishing war, enforcing international good behavior, and encouraging prosperity, it had to arm, as the Romans and the British had done, be prepared to use force to achieve its aims, and resign itself to being hated for its arrogance. Words, both in internal politics and international affairs, were not enough, as the Italian motto of the State of Maryland aptly says: *"Fatti maschi, parole femmine."*

In spite of all these doubts, the young Barzini wanted desperately to believe that James Harvey Robinson was right; that only back in corrupt and resigned Europe were things and men still as Machiavelli, Guicciardini, and the Church thought they were. He wanted to believe that the United States had really discovered new miraculous ways of solving all problems; and that the quicker the young Barzini became an American, the better it would be for him and his descendants. In fact, he was so touched by the doctor's teachings that in spite of everything he subsequently learned and the skepticism of his maturity, some of them still live (like burning coals under ashes) within him. He knows, of course, as all elderly men more or less know, that the old pessimists were right, that man cannot easily be perfected, and can seldom be convinced he should act freely as a rational and enlightened creature in emergencies. Yet the older Barzini still hopes today that the doctor might be proved right in the end. What counts, for him, is to keep on trying. This is probably why his countrymen do not always consider him entirely Italian. Something in me is irremediably American.

Chapter 6

MY FATHER WAS SERIOUSLY UPSET and worried by my rash decision to follow in his footsteps. He thought it suicidal folly for many sound reasons. He never clearly enumerated them, but when he deplored the unfortunate destiny of young men we knew or heard about, something in his voice made me understand he was really talking about me. This he did as tactfully and guardedly as possible on many occasions. I never said anything. Only once, after I had gained admission to the School of Journalism but had not yet registered, when there was still time to save myself, did he bravely and openly plead with me to think twice before committing such an irreparable blunder and listed many reasons why it was essential that I choose another profession, any other profession or métier, possibly an obscure, safe, serious but profitable one, where mistakes and weaknesses would go unnoticed, where one was not always in the limelight.

This conversation took place on a warm summer afternoon of 1928 in his downtown office. His newspaper occupied, at 205 Lafayette Street, the old quarters of a defunct humorous magazine called *Puck*. A statue of laughing Puck could still be seen over the door. It had no relation to an Italian daily in New York, yet it was not entirely irrelevant. The old *Puck* had been founded by European intellectual immigrants, Germans, and at the outset had also been written in their own language. I went to the office daily, in the late afternoon. One of my duties was to translate the morning front-page editorial into English, for publication the next day on the last page. Father deluded himself that the English-speaking sons of Italian readers, possibly some of their American friends, or American journalists interested in Italian opinions might want to read the article.

It was usually written by him. He composed in pencil, slowly, standing up, as was his habit, at a tall lectern, on a yellow pad, in his shirtsleeves like an American. My job was easy. His prose was spare and limpid, his sentences were short and crisp, his arguments and vocabulary restricted to the modest capacities of his readers. I turned his editorial into passable English on a typewriter in a few minutes while thinking of my own affairs, girls of easy virtue, books, exams, money, the future. I did not really know what I was writing, just as a linotype operator quickly turns intricate prose into lines of lead without trying to understand it. Other people's articles were more difficult. I had to pay attention, play around with synonyms, and occasionally consult the dictionary. Sometimes I had to ask Beniamino de Ritis, the *caporedattore,* who usually was the author on father's rare days off, what some of his prose meant. He wrote clearly enough, but loved to drop in, here and there, chunks of poetic, ornate, literary, and involuted Italian. It was almost impossible to turn it into lifelike English, my English being then mostly a concrete and matter-of-fact language. Beniamino advised me confidentially: "Skip the whole thing. It means nothing really. This is the kind of *fregnacce* one writes for Italian readers. You know Italians. They like the tenor's *fioriture,* variations by the cornet player in the band, oratorical tirades, particularly if these bravura performances have nothing to do with the rest."

Once a week I had another job to do. Father bought one strip cartoon from a syndicate. It came in cardboard mats. After it had been turned into lead, the little puffs of smoke suspended in mid-air and containing the English conversation, had to be chiseled away by the printers, as presumably incomprehensible to most readers. To translate the words into Italian and write them in the place of the English ones would have taken time and money. It was cheaper to explain what was going on by printing Italian doggerel at the bottom of each frame. I wrote the doggerel. Like Father, I had a modest knack for it. Had I been born a hundred years earlier, I could probably have eked out a living writing opera librettos on marble café tables for obscure composers. I finished my weekly batch of strip cartoons in a short time, with ease, counting syllables by drumming fingers on my lips.

At the end of the afternoon I often left the office with Father and my sister Emma, who acted as his secretary and subeditor at large. Father thought proudly that keeping his son and daughter at work was, like taking his coat off in the office, a decisive step toward the American way of life. Emma and I did not mind making a few bucks. Usually, before heading home, we went shopping in the nearby Italian streets for what Mother needed, then took the subway to Pennsylvania Station and the Long Island train. Commuters around us often sniffed the air and sometimes commented aloud about the odd suspicious smells emanating from our packages. They were the odors of fresh-roasted Italian coffee (unknown at the time in the United States, where the coffee smelled of nothing at all), strange spices, a rare white truffle, or Gorgonzola. Once a portly gentleman with a gold chain festooned on his belly called the conductor to complain. "These foreigners stink," he said loudly. "I'm sure they are transporting pieces of a decaying corpse wrapped in their packages, a victim of the Black Hand, no doubt." The conductor asked us politely for explanations and placated the passenger, who got off at the next station anyway. He was almost right. We were taking home some good cheese, a very ripe *provola* or *robiola piccante.* This last actually smells like a summer battlefield revisited after a few days.

Father pulled a long-suffering face and we all laughed. Like most Continental Europeans, he had long since formed the opinion that Americans knew nothing about gastronomy and cuisine, not even their own. He used to say that "the best food in the United States was what the inhabitants must leave alone and do not cook, like milk and oysters." (Milk at the time was rich and full of natural milk flavor. Oysters, as well as clams, were and still are excellent. He loved them. Every time he landed in the United States, in the early part of the century, he made a dash for the oyster bar at Grand Central Station, sometimes even before registering in a hotel.) Next best in America, Father said, was food which must be cooked only a little, like steaks or lobsters. To be avoided were all dishes to which Americans dedicated a lot of care, because their compulsion to experiment and improve everything, not to leave simple and perfect things alone, ruined the best culinary inventions of man, including their own good dishes. He swore that American sea food was the best in the world, some of which, if it existed in France, would have been famous, deafeningly proclaimed all over the world as one more proof, with *la Comédie-Française, l'Armée, l'Académie,* and *la haute couture,* of French imperial supremacy. Among these unique American specialties, besides the shellfish and lobsters, father included Long Island scallops, soft-shell crabs, shad roe, and pompano. He thought the steaks, of which the Americans were greedy and proud, good but not as tasty as the English, the French, or the Tuscan. The fried potatoes that went with them he believed to be absolutely deadly; a little warning flag should be stuck on them with skull and crossbones, indicating a poison to be avoided. He was also wary of Italian food in the United States, as most of it was unknown back in Italy. It was monotonous, often consisting of tomato sauce and garlic indiscriminately spread over pasta, meat, fish, or vegetables; most of it was uneatable.

All this has changed, to be sure. Public and private food in America has become eatable, here and there extremely good. Only the fried potatoes go on unchanged, as deadly as before. People now buy millions of cookbooks and practice *la haute cuisine* or revive their own national recipes. Even so, the love of tinkering, improving, and experimenting, the irresistible passion for adding odd flavors or beneficial elements, vitamins, drugs, and minerals, so that a man can have the advantages of a week at Montecatini or in a Swiss clinic while eating a plate of pasta, a dish of soup, some pâté, or a simple slice of bread, often make eating the simplest things in the United States a hazardous experience for the unwary. Most cheeses are still as tasteless as wet chalk, while the meat is even better than before, though blander. To discover the reasons for this one would probably have to undertake a vast sociological survey on the general dislike of elementary emotions and sharp tastes among the newly affluent middle class in industrialized societies. All cheeses everywhere in Europe no longer taste as pungent as they did only a few decades ago. In Italy, Gorgonzola, *pecorino romano, taleggio, fontina, caciocavallo,* et cetera, have become genteel. None would startle commuters on a Long Island train.

That particular afternoon Father asked me to step into his office. He said he wanted to talk to me about my plans. A shy man, he postponed such solemn scenes as long as he could. When he finally had to face them, he unconsciously assumed an actor's pose and spoke like the father in a French nineteenth-century bourgeois play, say *Le gendre de Monsieur Poirier,* choosing his words carefully as if he were dictating. He composed well-rounded sentences, here and there broken by hesitant pauses and coughs. I, too, was embarrassed, intimidated by his timidity, and heard myself answering him like the son or aspiring son-in-law in the same sort of play.

After I had sat down in front of him he said anxiously: "You haven't registered in the School yet, have you?"

I reassured him that I had not.

"Thank God," he said with relief. "We still have time for reflection. It is a very important decision. All your life may depend on it."

A long silence followed. We looked at each other. Then he said:

"You have to protect yourself from a sort of *iettatura* [evil eye], as you well know. Most sons of famous men lead mediocre lives, particularly those who have their fathers' Christian names and follow in their footsteps. The only exceptions I can think of offhand are Alexandre Dumas's Alexandre or William Pitt's William. Sons of famous men are apparently obliged to conquer more difficult obstacles than the sons of obscure fathers. Look at Toscanini's Walter or at d'Annunzio's Gabriellino, nice boys, intelligent, who don't amount to much, unfortunate, insecure, ridiculed by everybody."

Toscanini's son, Walter, was his father's factotum, worked very hard, managed everything, and was taken seriously by only a few close friends. Agents and impresarios considered him an obnoxious busybody who wasted their time and patience as he had to be assuaged and persuaded before any decision could be taken. He was slowly becoming what I considered at the time to be middle-aged (his hair was beginning to fall out and his waistcoat to bulge slightly), yet everybody treated him still as a troublesome adolescent, a young man of no importance. Gabriellino d'Annunzio was a more frightening example. He was not only the son of a very famous father but also one of the only two Italians alive who had been given their famous father's first name. (The other was myself. First-born boys were never baptized with their fathers' names in Italy but with their paternal grandfathers'. To avoid confusing cases of homonymy a Fascist law later unnecessarily forbade what was considered a bizzare American fashion.) Furthermore, Gabriellino had also followed in his father's footsteps, as I intended to do. He wrote poetry and plays, staged plays (mostly his father's) and directed movies, with not even the modest success he would have had had he been called by any other name. He was undoubtedly *iettato*. Once, in a vast, ambitious, and expensive scene for a film about imperial Rome he was directing, the lions actually ate a few Christians. He was never entrusted with the direction of another film.

I knew Father was right. There are exceptions to the rule, for some reason mostly among musicians, but they are an exiguous and insignificant minority.

Father cleared his throat, lit a cigarette (he smoked straw-tipped Melachrinos made with Turkish tobacco), looked to see if he had frightened me sufficiently, and went on:

"What is more serious is that you want to become a journalist, of all things. Mine is not only a difficult métier but also a very hazardous one. It's one of those callings, like acting, in which there is no middle ground. You're either a great success, revered, honored, occupying rooms at the Ritz, or less than nothing, a little shabby man living in cheap pensions. And nobody really knows how to reach success. Take me. I turned to journalism because I had no money and could think of no other quick way to make a living. I became famous. Other men of my generation, more talented, cultured, intelligent, some of them better writers than I, got nowhere. It's a lottery. Fame probably depends on being born at the right historic time with the right qualities, on getting the right breaks, on unconsciously expressing the public's unconscious cravings. Who knows? . . . It's fascinating work, I admit, but only for a healthy and robust young man with a good digestion. Battles, catastrophes, international conferences, coronations, great personages, beautiful women, expensive restaurants, always on the move on trains and ships. Your dispatches are applauded. You get bags of fan mail. You make little money but you don't worry. You don't need much anyway. But then one day, as you approach (or pass) forty years of age, you begin to suspect you don't exist. During the last war, Marshal Foch often sent a staff car all the way to Milan to pick me up and bring me to the French front just before an offensive, endangering security, no doubt. General Cadorna asked my advice on future plans. I was flattered, of course. I discovered later what I should have known all the time, that these people did not want me but my readers. I was nothing to them. Some sleepless night you begin to worry seriously. The French rightly say that journalism *mène à tout pourvu qu'on en sorte.* Nothing is more pathetic than an old journalist youthfully scampering around, or an elderly actor playing Romeo in the provinces. At that point you start looking for an exit. You want to stop turning out hurried prose in strange hotel rooms about events you know almost nothing about.''

He was, of course, talking about *his* journalism, a good writer's resigned and often humiliating acceptance of a newspaper's technical exigencies and the editors' vagaries, in order to make a living. But I could have answered him that many had managed to escape, Ernest Hemingway, to mention only one. I said nothing. He continued:

"One day, you meet a school friend. It happened to me. A not very bright man. His name is unknown to the public.

He worked hard all his life, has a solid position, authority, a well-run house, a placid wife, good sons, servants, money, security. You discover he has matured and become wise and you haven't aged at all. Journalism has kept you an eternal adolescent, a sort of Peter Pan. And you wonder whether you made the right decision."

I was fully aware of all this, too. I was more afraid of failure than he thought, terrified in fact. And yet the mirage of twenty-odd years of international journalism was irresistible. What other profession offered such attractive prizes? Middle age and its insomniac doubts looked very distant, beyond the horizon. I would cross that bridge when I got to it, at the proper time, when rheumatism, indigestion, and weariness overtook me. The main problem was not the regrets of old age. The problem was the danger of mediocrity. I knew I had to have a go, reach the top and do it quickly, or not try at all, but I hoped my foreign upbringing and my knowledge of languages might give me some advantage over my American competitors, at the start anyway, and, at the age of twenty, one had the time to make mistakes and correct them. I could still become a lawyer.

Father went on, as if following an outline in his mind:

"And do you want to become an American journalist or an Italian journalist? Have you decided? The two are vastly different professions, as you well know. You must have realized by now you will never achieve success in America. The top people would never allow an Italian to reach the top. You know the hostility and suspicion surrounding all of us in this country. Even the best Americans think we are only good at singing opera, strumming mandolins, inspiring lonely women as poor Rudolph Valentino did, bootlegging, cooking, and cutting hair, but cannot be trusted with anything as serious as writing for newspapers. You might have to change your name. And even then you'll never be sure of making it. You'll never know the language well enough. You haven't got it in your bones. It will never flow freely from your pen. You'll always write with an accent. America, I'm afraid, is out. Italy, then? There you will be crushed by the weight of your name. Everybody will watch you carefully, anxiously looking forward to seeing you make a fool of yourself. As you know, work is now extremely difficult in Italy. The press is not only strictly controlled, but controlled by dull, incompetent, presumptuous people who know nothing of our métier. The men who get ahead and are entrusted with the glamorous assignments are naturally not the best, those who write the truth as they see it, but the most pliable, those who flatter the regime and obey orders. They are a miserable and mediocre and envious lot. You'll never make a good servant of the regime. I know you too well. You'll soon find yourself in exile or in jail, sure enough. What do you say?"

That was the end of his talk. There was little I could say. He was right. I was grateful he had not tried to play the role of the patriarchal autocrat, the Roman *pater familias,* which he loved to do on occasion. When we were small children, for instance, as we bade him good night before going to bed, he wanted us, one after another, to kiss his hand, which he then placed over each head in turn, saying solemnly: *"Dio ti benedica"* ("God bless you"). We thought it strange even then, as no other father in Milan that we knew of did that. Late he forgot all about the role of the patriarch and the ceremony. That day he did not tell me sternly, as most European fathers would have done, that, since the money would have to come from him, he had a divine right and duty to choose my school. He tried to influence me but left me free to decide, which I thought was an admirable American thing to do. I thanked him and promised I would think before I took the final step. He never mentioned the subject again. Neither did I. At the proper time I registered in the School of Journalism and told him. We were in his office. "Did you?" he asked. "Do you really want to become a journalist?" He then embraced me and kissed me with tears of joy in his eyes. I had made him happy by wanting to emulate him but, I think, also by proving that I was not frightened by the curse attached to my birth.

Acclimatizing Emma, incidentally, presented the most difficult problem of all. She was from Milan and not Sicily, a modern daughter of modern parents living in the United States. She was free. She went to the Art Students League and worked in Father's office. Nobody checked on her movements. The Americanization, however, ended at sundown. She was not allowed to go out with a boy on a date. That, according to the ancient Italian tradition, would have irremediably compromised her, destroyed her honor, and made her unfit to become somebody's wife, the wife of somebody worthwhile, that is, of an upstanding gentleman. She could go out only in groups which included a married couple, or with her brothers, or with Mother. Young men trying to court her had to do it on Sunday afternoons, in our house, sitting primly in the living room, under Mother's eyes. No wonder most of them disappeared after one or two sittings. Father was adamant. There could be no exceptions. Once I took Emma out dancing with a friend and another girl, my girl of the moment. Father was on the doorstep when we returned and ceremoniously slapped me on both cheeks, accusing me of dragging my sister into a life of dishonor and debauch. As usual he sounded embarrassed and not thoroughly convinced of the role he had to play. It was as if he had to preserve a dubious tradition at all cost.

In the end Emma fell in love with a young Spanish Air Force officer who boarded her liner at Gibraltar, on his way to the United States with an official mission. Liners or summer resort hotels were practically the only places where an Italian middle-class girl had a certain limited freedom in those years. Before leaving New York the Spaniard, who was also in love with her, invited her out to dinner, a show, and dancing, the two of them alone, as a proof of her love. Emma asked me for advice. I was twenty years old and totally without experience. What should she do? If she did not accept, she might lose him. He had intimated as much. She could have easily organized the evening by inventing an invitation to dinner at the house of some respectable friends. I was embarrassed. What should I say? I finally decided that, for many reasons, she should refuse.

To begin with, Alejandro, whom I had seen once and found handsome, intelligent, and *molto simpatico,* one of the few witty Spaniards I had ever met, was Andalusian. True, he had an English grandfather (his name is Gomez Spencer), but surely the Moorish strain would be predominant. I reasoned he would have been disappointed by Emma's refusal but would have loved her more. He would have considered her a sufficient guardian of her own honor to be entrusted with the defense of his family name or names. Emma refused as I told her to do. He vanished, went back to Spain, and did not write to her for weeks. I was devoured by remorse and anguished by her reproaches. Had I guessed wrong? Finally a letter came. More followed. She answered them. In the end he suggested a rendezvous at Gibraltar the following summer on the boat that would take mother and Emma to Italy for the holidays. He kissed her for the first time after he had officially asked Mother for her hand and given Emma a ring. The kiss took place in the swimming pool, a hurried wet kiss. It was the first time my sister had been kissed on her lips and the first time she had been kissed by a man who was not a very close relative. They were married the following year in Milan. Alejandro had a brilliant career, fought in the Civil War against Franco (he was neither a Marxist revolutionary nor an Anarchist, but, probably, also thanks to his English blood, an old-fashioned lover of liberty, like all of us). He was condemned to life imprisonment in a fortress, but amnestied after five years. He is very proud of his record.

Chapter 7

I<small>T WAS</small>, in those years, impossible for me to find sufficient interludes of inner stillness in which to think clearly, do some possibly enduring work, read ponderous books in multiple volumes like *Der Untergang des Abendlandes,* adequately contemplate the *Weltschmerz* and *la condition humaine,* and finally try to understand the bewildering United States and make plans for the future. I was distracted by many things, but above all by the girls, not this or that girl in particular, not only the visible and known girls, Betty, Shirley, Peggy, Ruth, or Vivien, the girls in the School of Journalism, but by girls in general, *girltum,* so to speak, the unseen and imaginary as well as the real; by the smell, feel, or vision of actual bodies, hair, lips, eyes, thighs, the twin domelike excrescences under their blouses, the happily swinging glutei, as well as the desire, anticipation, or remembrance of girls. They were all around like bees in an apiary and filled my brain with an unceasing roar.

The only refuge I found from this torment during the summer of 1929 was my work. The little paper I was working for was understaffed, some of the staff were often drunk, and, as if I were in a provincial stock company, I had to play one role after another, sometimes without warning, not only Hamlet, Polonius, and the Ghost, but occasionally also the Queen and Ophelia, in charge of society and fashions. Work kept me running all day like a whippet after the make-believe hare, breathlessly chasing one unimportant detail after another: exactly how many gunshots, ribs broken, eyes gouged out, or dollars stolen, how many fire alarms, how to spell some Polish or Czech name, and especially what were everybody's first name and middle initial (an American obsession), and write a complicated story against the tightest deadline. At the end of the day I was numb with fatigue. It was then that I began to suspect that Unflagging Work, in America, besides being a Moral Imperative, could also be the Opium of the Middle Class, nepenthe, the drug for people who wanted to forget who they were, what they were doing, where they were going, why they were born, as well as people like me who simply wanted to forget girls.

They could not be forgotten for long. I could not glance casually out of the office front window, catch a bus, buy a pack of cigarettes at Schultes', look at a wall calendar, eat a sandwich in a beanery, pass the stills posted outside the movies, without being struck dumb by the sight of a lithe goddess, a melancholic nymph, or a wild dryad. Most of them were as unaware of their breathtaking beauty as wild animals; they seemed as tranquil and unself-conscious as deer in a forest, but who chewed gum instead of grass.

Perhaps once a week, in the subway, a movie queue, or a soda fountain, I felt desperately that, by any possible legal or illegal means, one way or another, I had to capture this particularly splendid specimen, because there surely was no other like her in the whole world, and life without her would be an interminable sequence of dusty meaningless years. When she vanished (got off the bus or left the restaurant with a boy), I always felt bereaved as if I had really lost a dear one. Sometimes I could have cried. Once in a while, with a beating heart, I followed one of these dainty and airy sylphs, stopped her with a vacuous expression on my face, asked with a strangled voice some obvious information, which she would eagerly and innocently supply, and respectfully offered to walk her home. Having learned her name and her telephone number, during the following days I invited her to the movies and to the drugstore for a sundae, hoping something more would develop. Usually nothing much developed except vapid conversation.

A few of these undines could be as wily as the wild animals they reminded me of. Once, in my borrowed car, I picked up a startlingly delicious black-haired girl with violet eyes and a small waist. Her skin was like alabaster. She hid two small, hard half-cantaloupes in her blouse. I told her, in my studiously impersonal voice: "I would like to see you again. What is your telephone number?" She answered brightly: "Sure. Call me up. It's Newtown 1918. You'll remember the number because it's the year the war ended." The number did not exist. Evidently, the lack of hesitation and the freely offered mnemonic aid were old tricks of hers to disarm suspicions and avoid annoying insistence. One dance hall hostess one night gave me her address and the key to her flat, where she promised she would meet me at the end of her work. The address existed no more than the telephone number, and the key naturally fitted no door. She probably bought old keys by the hundredweight.

Pursuing girls filled every interstice of my life. I walked miles with them on beaches, in woods and gardens, and swam miles with them; saw more movies than I care to remember (choosing the back row so as not to have witnesses behind me); sat till all hours of the night on back-porch swings; roasted barrels of marshmallows (in the winter) and ate vast quantities of ice cream (in summer); curled up in hundreds of uncomfortable rumble seats; wrote square yards of love letters, loaned and borrowed barrow-loads of sugary sentimental books; cranked innumerable Victrolas; danced all kinds of fashionable dances (I preferred the slow waltzes which induced the languorous Latin mood I preferred, and not the wildly orgiastic Charleston); squeezed and held thousands of hands, kissed thousands of lips, and all the time tried, with beaver-like tenacity, gently to maneuver as many girls as possible into some convenient solitary dark spot. This took a lot of cunning. Having no money to speak of, I had only my fantasy with which to create inexpensive occasions. All this necessarily consumed an enormous amount of my time.

Were the American girls in the late twenties really as overwhelmingly beautiful as I remember them? When I look at old photographs or see an old movie, I sometimes wonder how such undeniably pretty but insipid adolescents with frizzy hair could have struck fear in my heart, treacherously stolen my inner peace, given me an occasional season of stupefying bliss, or kept me awake and howling at night like a lonesome dog. I try to tell myself that I was a deluded fool, they were only girls like any other, and that all girls have looked irresistible to twenty-year-old boys in every country and historical era. Yet I suspect there really was something disturbingly different about them. It could possibly be proved scientifically that girls like the American girls of the 1920s had not previously been seen on earth. I am sure a team of researchers suitably financed could easily demonstrate that the phenomenon was caused by widespread affluence, healthy living, soap and water, good orthodontics, open-air sports, the mixing of many bloods, and good food—all factors that had fully come together on a massive scale in the United States in those years, for the first time in history. The thesis could possibly be further confirmed by a comparative survey of the parallel growth of GNP and female shapes and allure in other continents. (For all I know, there may be entire libraries already dedicated to what is probably called comparative econo-euprepology.) Compare, for instance, the older Soviet leaders' broad wives with the contemporary Russian girl students, dancers, and gymnasts; the Neapolitan mamas, their noble ancient faces, proud and ample bellies, immense bosoms, majestic behinds, and piano legs, with their sylphlike granddaughters. It may be that the old photographs and films puzzle me today only because pretty girls like those are no longer startling rarities. You see them everywhere, even in Japan. Or it may also be that I have simply grown old and am no longer easily impressed.

The search for probable socioeconomic factors did not bother me at the time. Nor did I try to explain away my obsession with girls (and my occasional successes) because of my proverbially ebullient Mediterranean hot blood. I was always incredulous of the common myth that Italians are more generously endowed with hormones than other men. To be sure, it is a very old and widespread legend, older than the tale of Daisy Miller's seduction or Rudolph Valentino's fame. I sometimes benefited from it, but was also often enough one of its victims. Some girls brightened when they heard my name, but fellow students at the university provoked unnecessary defenses and complicated my life by crying out, amid guffaws: "Cross your knees, girls. Here comes Luigi." There must have been reasons for the myth, of course, as there are for all durable myths. I must admit that an exceptional number of Italians did (and probably still do) consecrate their lives (and shorten them) to astounding as many random women as possible, some of whom they would never see again, with their repetitive prowess. I always thought, however, that this insensate, stubborn, and selfless dedication to one single pleasurable activity might be due to other and more complex causes than mere hereditary endocrinology. In fact, I knew Nordic American boys, my contemporaries, as obsessed as I was, boys who successfully pursued the same quantitative and indiscriminate goals with the same tenacity as many Italians, boys who could have proudly marked their conquering weapon, if physically possible, with innumerable notches. They, too, behaved as if they had no other way in which to prove to themselves they were alive. *"Coeo, ergo sum,"* as Descartes should have said.

I do not know what provoked, at that time, my American friends' frenzied pursuit. They probably were a minority of rebels against their Puritan heritage or against boredom, the diffused boredom generated by a well-regulated life, with its insistent and tedious emphasis on virtue, duty, responsibility, and physical fitness. But I think I know what caused the Italians' omnivorous voracity in my youth (and possibly also today, even if in a more leisurely and vaguely bored manner). The origin of their hunting-dog eagerness, enthusiastic acceptance of all kinds, first come first served, young or old, pretty or plain, fat or lean, standing against a wall or lying down, on sofas, carpets, or beds, indoors or outdoors, in daylight or at night, was simply scarcity. Women in Italy had been, for centuries, indeed until only a few years ago, kept hermetically separate from men, as if all men were carriers of some mortal disease. As a result, women had always been seen as precious and rare treasures, to be snatched, if the opportunity arose, without wasting time, without looking them in the mouth or anywhere else.

There were always stupendous (and jealously guarded) beauties in Italy, Sienese Madonnas or Botticelli Venuses who were greeted with hushed silence and by the turning of men's heads when they walked down a busy street. Whole towns sometimes fell in love with one of them, from a distance. They were rare, there were never enough of them, in the old days anyway. The rest, just as well guarded from male contacts, looked vaguely unwashed, swollen by laziness, *tagliatelle,* pastry, and olive oil. Many had short hairy legs, dewy and bushy armpits, and often enough a vague dark shadow on the upper lip. Such shortcomings were considered so well established and immutable that old proverbs were designed to console men. *"Donna baffuta sempre piaciuta"* ("Everybody loves a lady with a mustache"), and another said, *"Donna pelosa donna virtuosa"* ("If nothing else, you can console yourself with the impregnable virtue of a hairy woman"), possibly because it is never seriously endangered.

As a result of Italian girls' aseptic isolation, their behavior in the presence of men was somewhat bizarre. I really became fully aware of it only after I returned to Italy in 1930, but even before my departure for the United States I was sufficiently familiar with it, having been exposed to girls in my *liceo* class for years (one called even the twelve-year-olds *signorina* then and spoke to them with the formal *lei*) and to my sister's friends. Most of them giggled and blushed inordinately when a boy addressed them. When he engaged them in conversation, he had to be very cautious, say nothing witty, subtle, or complicated, and choose every single word with the care of a jeweler handling precious stones. He knew everything he said could be interpreted as a cryptic signal, a secret declaration of love, an invitation, a repulse, or an insult. The girls sometimes confided their vague suspicions to their best friends, the best friends to their mothers, some mothers asked their confessor's advice, fathers would be dragged in, and, in a few days, the talk would grow like a summer storm cloud. The man in question could sometimes find himself engaged, for reasons he did not understand, to a girl he did not know well and did not want, ostracized as a cad, or forced to leave town.

All this, of course, made simple, everyday conversation halting and tedious, and casual friendship impossible. To be sure, some of these shy, religious, demure, well-guarded, and often hairy virgins occasionally became pregnant. Daring boys, in love with danger, invented subterfuges, heroic stratagems, and ingenious Renaissance intrigues, to get one of them alone somewhere for an adequate number of minutes in the appropriate wide-kneed position. One of the easier ruses was to get lost with her in the course of a walk in the mountains with a group of friends; another was to hide in the attic of the girl's house, ask her to join him as soon as possible, and wait through the night. Once they were beyond the surveillance of relatives and the external defenses, everything else became surprisingly easy, far easier than in the United States. The girl had not been trained to defend herself. She had always relied on others. The moment she found herself alone with a panting young man, feverishly trying to find the right buttons to unbutton, buckles to unbuckle, and elastic to loosen with trembling hands, she almost always resigned herself limply with a sigh to her fate. Her will to resist literally liquefied, so to speak. She relaxed. She even tried to collaborate. What else could a poor girl do?

The complicated defenses which, in the end, made Italian girls more vulnerable were increasingly indispensable just because the girls had been made so vulnerable. Having no brakes of their own, they had to be saved at all cost by parents, older brothers, or governesses from what could be a fatal and irresistible *dégringolade* into a life of indiscriminate debauch. Fortunately, the defenses were always there. Boys were relatively safe. Families would see to it that girls could not even go alone to church or to the grocery store around the corner for a can of tomatoes without a guard, as if they were all uncontrollable nymphomaniacs in a world teeming with half-blind satyrs. When, in New York, I thoughtlessly escorted some apparently emancipated and Americanized Italian girl home after a party, for the simple reason that she lived on my way, her father dramatically threw open the front door in his shirtsleeves, no collar and tie, braces dangling, with a terrifying scowl on his face, the well-known scowl of a man ready to avenge his family honor in the only two ways consecrated by immemorial usage, either marrying his daughter off as fast as possible to the man who had compromised her, or slaughtering him. I always mumbled a few words and fled in terror.

The first American girl I kissed was on board the *Duilio* —a charming blonde of my own age, sixteen, with an angelic face, thin arms, and a delicate bony bump on the back of her neck. Her name was Natalie. I considered myself an experienced roué at the time, having a few times illegally visited a pleasant family brothel (I was admitted because I looked older than, and was tall for, my age) in Milan. There I had been introduced to the mysteries of love by a motherly and compassionate woman with white silky skin. She was particularly devoted to the Holy Family, and, over the double bed on which she entertained her visitors, had hung a very large lithograph of bearded Joseph, pink-cheeked Mary, the dimpled Holy Child, the Ass and the Ox. It was embarrassing to undress and do the rest under their steady gaze. I had also spent a few feverish and sweaty nights in the room of a young maid of ours, that very summer while the rest of the family were at the seashore, when I had been left alone with her for three or four days, to prepare for an examination which I naturally flunked.

Therefore I behaved like an experienced and responsible man of the world when one night Natalie suggested a walk to the upper deck to look at the full moon. I was no fool. I smiled, took her by the hand, and said, "*Andiamo pure.* OK, let's go." I realized she was a flirt but also what was commonly known in Italy as *una ragazza per bene*—a nice family girl—therefore a dangerous girl, the American equivalent of the well-brought-up daughters of Mother's friends whom one avoided at all cost and did not risk fiddling with, for the fear of *histoires,* fuss, annoyances, family feuds, and possibly lifelong consequences. I knew how to keep them at arm's length all right and to avoid danger. So I went confidently into the night, holding Natalie's hand and humming a tune. What I did not know and was about to learn was that, with American girls, even the very young, a boy did not have to make up his mind which girl he liked best and exactly how far he would allow himself to go. It was all done for him.

Natalie led me to a dark corner behind a lifeboat, looked at the moon, sighed, quoted the lyrics of some contemporary song as if they were a poem by Shelley, clung close to me, then raised her white face with half-open lips, and shut her eyes. She smelled as good as a freshly baked cake and was as appetizingly tempting. Before I knew it I was kissing her. I kissed her once again, then a few more times, and held her as tight to me as the melted cheese on a *cotoletta alla bolognese.* I found this enchanting, infinitely better than wrestling with the maid. A few seconds later (or perhaps at the same time) I shivered in terror. What had I done, what insane passion had carried me away, why had I yielded to this adolescent bacchante, what would happen to me, to both of us, as a result of a brief moment of irresponsible forgetfulness? What would her mother say and do if she found out?

Her mother was definitely a lady, an imperious and awe-inspiring lady, all fluttering mauve and gray veils, white face powder and rouge, jangling bracelets, dangling strings of pearls, and a long gold cigarette holder. She would surely discover everything. In a moment of weakness or pride, Natalie would tell her what I had done. The next day or two I waited for my fate with Spartan fortitude. Nothing happened. At all hours of the day and night, Natalie and I hid in unknown and deserted corners of the ship to kiss and cuddle. We danced with each other endlessly and exclusively every night. Her mother did nothing. She said nothing. She did not even seem alarmed. She apparently suspected nothing or, if she did, could not care less. She beamed benevolently on us. She even called me "Dear Luigi." One morning, however, on the promenade deck, she waved to me and asked me to sit down on a chaise longue next to her. She said she wanted to talk to me. This naturally made me very nervous. I got even more nervous when she started, in a solemn and somewhat embarrassed voice, "There are a few things I must tell you, Luigi."

"Here we are," I thought, "this is it, I called it down on myself by my demented behavior. Whatever she says, whatever she asks of me, she will be right. I have behaved like a *mascalzone,* violated a trust, compromised her pure, trusting innocent Natalie. God help me."

"Luigi," her mother asked in a mellifluous voice, "you like Natalie?" I merely nodded enthusiastically but respectfully, as I could not speak. "Natalie likes you?" she went on. I modestly adopted a questioning look and waited. "I hope you speak Italian with her sometimes. She must get some practice. Italian is very useful in New York, don't you know, particularly with bootleggers and headwaiters in good restaurants. They give you a better table if you speak their language. They say that some people who know Italian can even understand the words of an opera and follow the plot, not that that makes much difference. . . ." I found the strength to assure her I often spoke Italian with Natalie. I promised I would speak more, although it was more vital for me to fortify my English.

She continued: "I love your language. I don't understand it, but it is so musical. It is the language of love. . . . There's nothing more charming than a shipboard flirtation like yours. You're only young once, I always say. But there is one thing I must absolutely tell you. When we're in New York, do not try to see Natalie again. She has plenty of beaux. You won't like it. And my husband, her father, disapproves of Italians. He dislikes having them around the house. They make him nervous. Italians, he says, are all right in Italy but even there he thinks there are far too many of them. So promise me not to call or write. You understand, don't you?"

I said I did, but, of course, I did not.

I could never become accustomed to American mothers' reckless disregard for their daughters' moral welfare. One evening in the early thirties, in Florence, I had a date with a beautiful nereid from somewhere in the United States whom I had met that morning in a glove shop. I promised to pick her up at eight in the lobby of the Grand Hotel, where she was staying. We were to go to dinner and on to dance. Later I secretly hoped to show her the fine collection of rare Cinquecento bronzes (four of them of dubious authenticity) belonging to a bachelor friend of mine who had lent me his flat for the night. Before going out, the girl proposed, perfectly correctly, to introduce me to her mother. The mother was playing bridge in the lobby with three other middle-aged American ladies wearing strange tiny hats, adorned with trembling flowers. She turned her head reluctantly from her cards and inspected me from head to foot. After a short pause she said to her daughter: "Darling, do be very careful." I felt ill at ease. Had she read my mind? Did she guess about the Renaissance bronzes? Was she worried about seeing her own flesh and blood disappear into the night escorted by a devious, dark-haired, and dark-eyed Latin, who, like all Latins, should not be trusted? "Be very, very careful," she repeated and looked at me. What dangerous temptation was she warning her daughter against? This: "Do not drink any tap water. Drink only San Pellegrino. You remember what happened to your Aunt Muriel the last time she was in Italy." Then she turned to me, probably to assuage my wounded national pride: "You know how dangerous tap water can be in these foreign countries." Her motherly duty done, she dismissed us. "Have a good time," she said, and turned back to her game. That was all. Tap water, indeed.

American girls definitely seemed a different breed in the late twenties, as different from the average Italian girls as prancing circus horses were from the weary animals harnessed to country carts. They were seldom as stupendously beautiful as the most beautiful Italian girls, to be sure, but, according to the law that, in all fields, the best in Europe is scarce but unequaled, and the good in America perhaps not as excellent but infinitely more abundant and available, many more American girls were or seemed beautiful. They were radiantly healthy, with porcelain skins, clean, delicately shaped, and always well groomed. They were as free as cattle on the range. Nobody seemed to keep watch over them. They came and went as they chose, often had dates and entanglements with boys their relatives did not know from Adam, boys whose families were not included in the certified acceptable circle of their friends.

The girls were not afraid. This was refreshing. You could talk to most of them about practically anything at all. They listened good-naturedly, laughed at the right moment, and answered intelligently. They could be witty too, at times, for some reason the not-so-pretty far wittier than the pretty ones. They seemed to have an unquenchable desire to know all about an insignificant boy's past, present, future, dreams, ambitions, and plans. He often found himself involuntarily confiding deep secrets to a practically unknown girl, secrets he had never dared tell to anybody else. It was as relaxing a pleasure just to be with them as lying in a hammock. They seemed to the unwary and inexperienced as easy to pluck as ripe pears at hand's reach, but they were not easy at all, not many anyway. They knew their own minds. They were stubborn. They might have looked like ripe pears, but many revealed themselves to be prickly pears. In fact, they had well-established frontiers in their heads which you could not easily convince them to cross. The frontiers were by no means rigid, always at the same spot, the elastic on their knickers or the clasp holding their brassières. They occasionally moved, but almost always unexpectedly. The whole thing was maddening.

The exact position of the frontier could be determined only by trying tactfully. It depended, on each particular night, on many unfathomable factors, a sudden caprice, a wave of sympathy, the compassion for the visible suffering of a boy, or a cold calculated decision. One inflexible rule was the number of previous dates. Apparently each additional date permitted (or justified) a certain limited progress. "How can I give you a kiss?" a girl would say on her doorstep after an evening out. "This is only our first date." This meant that her reluctance was not dictated by prejudice, dislike for the boy, religious scruples, but only by the inadequate duration of the pursuit. There were many other unpredictable criteria, of course, social, physical, intellectual, or moral. For some magic reason, as many discovered, all resistance could be pushed back more easily and quickly by the boy friend of a girl's best friend. The desire to do her best friend in the eye was stronger than virtue, love, or lust. There was also passion among the decisive factors. It was notoriously blind and swept every obstacle before it. It was stupendous, imperious, but rare.

When a boy approached the impassable line, not a word was spoken to warn him to stop. In fact, words of caution, entreaty, or pleading did not count. They were part of the ritual, meant to be ignored. They were also silly. "What are you doing?" the girl would ask anxiously when there was absolutely no doubt of what the boy was doing. The only message to be obeyed was a cold staccato "Uh-uh!" hummed in a boy's ear. That alone meant a categorical, absolute "No," with no appeals. It was somewhat confusing for an inexperienced young foreigner because a girl also hummed "Uh-uh" when she meant "Yes, go ahead," but it was an imperceptibly different "Uh-uh," which only a Sinologist, attuned to variations of monosyllabic tones, could possibly distinguish. One learned only by trial and error.

When my father saw me go out alone with a pretty girl into the night, he always thought I was a fortunate boy. The next morning, in his dressing gown, he would wink at me over the *caffè-latte,* smile wisely, and ask, man to man: "How was it?" He thought we were in Italy. I gave up explaining to him that things were not automatically easy in the United States, that being alone with a girl was not enough, that the course of events was seldom, very seldom in fact, in a boy's hands. In spite of all one read in the newspapers about the decadence of youth and the universal collapse of morals, a boy had to wait, work, scheme, sweat, plead, push gently and constantly, and talk interminably to drive the barriers back.

Manly and impatient brutality, considered irresistible in many Southern countries, was seldom useful. It could produce unexpected results. For one thing, the girls did not panic easily and were too robust anyway. I knew one who split a sturdy boy's forehead with a glass ashtray. She had to call an ambulance and wash the blood from the sofa and the carpet before her parents came home. Manly and impatient brutality could be employed, of course, but very rarely and opportunely, only as a pantomime, and with the girl's tacit consent. Like the influence of alcohol, it supplied, on occasion, her conscience with a satisfactory balm. "What else could I do?" she would say to herself or to her best friend the next day. "I was drunk." The night before she had probably had a glass or two of cooking sherry. Or: "He was too strong and impetuous for me. I was scared. He could have maimed me for life."

This does not mean that all American girls spurned the ultimate delights of love. There was a percentage, technically known as the fast girls, to whom all boys resorted in turn. They were the girls whom the authors of alarming articles on the sexual revolution of the twenties presumably studied with painstaking care. Others, not classed as fast, did not disdain the concession of their favors on particular occasions and to particular boys. This happened often enough, sometimes suddenly, unexpectedly, or after an interminable wait. It took a great deal of steady perseverance. Some of these teen-aged innocent angels were consummate experts in the diabolical arts of keeping a boy, or a number of boys at the same time, in a frenzied state of hopeful uncertainty. A girl would be available for one boy every evening for a period of days or weeks, give up other dates for him, and then suddenly vanish. "I was busy," she would explain later. Sometimes she would lead a boy maddeningly to the very dewy and slippery threshold of Paradise and then be seized by sudden qualms and scruples. It sometimes took him weeks to get back to the same point. Who had taught them at such an early age the ruses of veteran *demimondaines* in the Paris of the Second Empire I never could fathom.

Very experienced Italian men, well-tailored veterans to whom I always listened with rapt attention, irritably explained their intermittent successes with American women very simply. Those who resisted them were cold, cold as fish. Most American women, they said, were cold calculating monsters. They felt no emotion. They never lost their heads. They were seldom swept off their feet. The veterans agreed that the only enthusiastic ever-ready ones were the middle-aged, who were afraid life would pass them by, and believed that a missed opportunity was lost forever. Were the girls who rejected me irremediably cold? I could not tell. I remember one who, suddenly, one night, for no particular reason, as if carried away by strong emotions, was on the verge of yielding. She certainly was not cold.

She was sitting wide-legged on the sofa. I kneeled respect-fully in front of her, between her parted knees. Suddenly, at this supreme moment of rapture, I heard a buzzing sound in the silence behind my ears, "Zzzzz," and, after a tiny pause, "Zzzzz" again. She was winding her wristwatch. Maybe she was cold after all. Maybe she was only trying to control herself. Could the same girl be warm for some and cold for others, warm today and cold tomorrow? I never found the answer.

Chapter 8

IT SEEMED TO ME, in the twenties, that Americans could still hold on without difficulty to one of their favorite creeds, the reassuring certainty that in every, or almost every, field of endeavor all that was necessary for anybody to succeed, or at least to avoid failure, was a thorough mastery of the appropriate technique and a lot of hard work—more or less what Thomas Jefferson recommended for surmounting all difficulties: "resolution and contrivance." You studied the proper books, which taught you how to do everything, practice assiduously, and the rest would take care of itself. Naturally, the School of Journalism, which I entered in the fall of 1928, was solidly founded on this unshakable belief. In fact, it could not even have existed without it.

Americans must have doubts by now. Enough of them must know that the mere study of technique, even accompanied by relevant simplified theoretical explanations, may be all that is necessary in many fields, but not all, surely not in the arts and writing, in love-making, foreign affairs, gardening, cooking, making friends and influencing people, and politics, among others. Too many tens of thousands of eager country boys, to quote an example which was close to me, were taught, over the decades, absolutely foolproof ways of writing brilliant short stories, superb magazine articles, devastating novels and dazzling plays, and too few of them, in the end, probably only those who would have succeeded even without proper instruction, ever managed to be noticed at all or to make a modest living at their chosen trade, for the solid old certainty not eventually to have been weakened.

By this I do not mean, of course, that one can do without a knowledge of technique in one's chosen field, but only that it must be rigorously kept in its place. What one learns is usually the past generation's genial inventions diligently codified, just as staff officers are always taught to refight the previous war. Unfortunately, technique, while indispensable, is not sufficient. It has been compared to the art of sharpening pencils. Without a sharpened pencil a man who can write only with pencils, like Richard Nixon, clearly cannot write. He must therefore learn the art of sharpening his pencils. However, the essential comes immediately after. What he writes with his freshly sharpened pencil is what counts. In short, it can be affirmed without fear of contradiction that the invention of the automatic electric sharpener (or of the electric typewriter, for that matter) has not improved the quality of current literature, and that, analogously, the computer has not added to the wisdom of man.

This belief in technique and assiduity, "resolution and contrivance," dear to the hearts of Americans in the past and, in a way, still dear to many of them today, with its implicit disproportionate and tempting promises, annually produced a large quantity of competent, conscientious, and often dull professionals; some of the world's greatest scientists and engineers, the source of American strength and efficiency, without whom the United States would not be what it is today; but also an excessive number of deluded and unhappy misfits, who lead lives of quiet desperation, or turn to rebellion and hard liquor when they discover that they have wasted the best part of their lives pursuing an impossible Fata Morgana.

It is not difficult to see how this grew into a dominating and essential part of American life. To begin with, the United States was chronologically the first country which, more than a century ago, had to improvise in a great hurry a vast multiform élite, an élite that could somehow run a tumultuously expanding economy and proliferating institutions, as well as tackle unknown and frightening problems. Natural-born leaders, exceptionally gifted men, being as scarce in America as anywhere else, and no way having yet been found to breed them artificially, the country instinctively did what every country does in time of war. Easy handbooks, cramming courses, simple practical exercises, and the suggestion that a golden marshal's baton studded with diamonds might be found in many knapsacks (as prizes are found in an occasional box of breakfast cereal) quickly transform the ignorant, listless, inept, and timid into *strategoi* of sorts, officers who may never perform brilliantly in the field, never conceive Napoleonic maneuvers or Sherman's cavalry raids, but, it is hoped, might not commit fatally disastrous mistakes either.

It was this urgent necessity, incidentally, which a century

or so ago made American universities different from the European cathedrals of learning. Until recent years, until, that is, Europe was forced to face the problems the United States had tackled long before, Europeans did not have to worry about the training of instant leaders, specialists, and technicians. They needed relatively few anyway, and the scrambling and hungry middle class provided a sufficient number of them. Europeans concentrated instead on ideas, dead languages, poetry, theory, history, and fundamental principles. Technique could be learned on the job. As a result Europe produced a limited number of outstanding savants, illuminated by a vast and irrelevant culture, rather than multitudes of competent and efficient mediocrities. In Italy, in particular, the universities nurtured for more than a century an exiguous and inadequate number of brilliant and erudite sages, just enough for the needs of an archaic and stagnant agricultural country, and contemptuously neglected the rest. This, of course, is one of the causes of the Italian crisis today.

There has always been something vaguely un-American about eminently gifted men. This was suspected by, among others, Samuel Butler, a perceptive and touchy man, who wrote a long time ago: "I do not think America is a good place to be a genius." (He was probably not welcomed with the attention he thought he deserved.) "A genius cannot expect to have a good time anywhere, but America is about the last place in which life will be endurable at all for an inspired writer." He was only partly right, of course. Geniuses can flourish, and have flourished, in America since the beginning, provided they do not impersonate geniuses and try to be the symbols of what the average American believes himself to be, only more so. They must take care to look and behave like everybody else, men who put their pants on one leg at a time, occasionally make laughable mistakes, and show their homespun qualities. It helps if they are depicted in rumpled clothes and bedroom slippers. (Franklin at the court of Louis XVI, Jefferson in his later period when he abandoned fripperies and laces and stopped powdering his red hair, Abraham Lincoln in his long *pardessus* which looked as if he slept in them, are typical; conversely, George Washington, by punctiliously dressing and behaving as the English gentleman he was, dangerously threatened his prestige and authority among many of his countrymen.) Even today, when photographers arrive at the house of an eminent American writer or scientist, he takes off his necktie, if he is wearing one, ruffles his hair, and puts on an old shapeless sweater. American geniuses likewise learned long ago to refrain from delivering immortal lines of wisdom but mostly utter cracker-barrel jokes or laughable malapropisms which put their countrymen at their ease. (Sam Goldwyn, an intelligent man, is the most illustrious example of this ruse. He worked hard at appearing a cretin.) Above all, successful men must give the impression that their eminence is mainly the result of industry, the mastery of the proper rules, and not of luck or native gifts.

The belief is intimately connected with the basic American prejudice against inequality at birth, the egalitarian urge. "All men are created equal." To be sure, the country, like any other country at any time in history, has always been run, according to the law which Vilfredo Pareto and Gaetano Mosca formulated long ago, by a small minority of capable, ruthless, and ambitious men, abnormally endowed

147

with the qualities necessary to interpret the *Zeitgeist* and get to the top. This unassailable truth has, however, never been openly acknowledged. It cannot be. The hope had in the past to be maintained at all costs that anybody could become a millionaire or be elected President. The fact that apparently stupid men amassed fabulous fortunes, or were sometimes catapulted into the White House, confirmed this belief so repeatedly as to make it almost appear to be a law of nature. Genius must be the product of will power, industry, and tenacity, and not be capriciously bestowed at birth by God, otherwise the whole American experiment would have lost all significance and petered out. Without this myth the people would have become debilitated and paralyzed, though probably less restless and much happier.

An American writer (who was by no means a genius but only a prolific producer of well-machined prose) put the whole matter in a few well-known words, probably to encourage himself as well as to comfort his countrymen: "Genius is an infinite capacity for taking pains." He was, of course, paraphrasing Thomas A. Edison who had already said: "Genius is one percent inspiration and ninety-nine percent perspiration." Like most quintessentially American ideas, this, too, is not American at all and much older than the United States. Cicero wrote: *"Ingenium industria alitur"* ("Genius is generated [or fattened] by industry"). Buffon was once quoted as saying: *"Le génie n'est autre chose qu'une grande aptitude à la patience."* Even Matthew Arnold conceded: "Genius is mainly an affair of energy."

As the empty new continent was filled by foreign-born men, it was also animated by foreign-born ideas and symbols, some of them of venerable antiquity, which however immediately became brand-new and native-American on landing. "Yankee Doodle" is an old English folk song; the Statue of Liberty was conceived, made, and paid for by the French; and, I am sure, the apple pie, than which nothing is more American, has remote and alien origins. What is important is the instinctive infallibility with which Americans selected and adopted some foreign ideas as their own legitimate offspring, and their horrified rejection of others, those in which they could not see themselves reflected.

All this was, in the twenties, also inextricably connected with other American national traits, or traits which Americans liked to think were national: with pragmatism simplified, or the belief that only concrete results were important; with what was left of Calvinism, or the belief that hard work was the only way to salvation, and success a reward of virtue; with raw and vulgarized positivism; and finally with the Americans' curious abhorrence for abstract ideas. It was good to believe that greatness could be achieved by almost anyone who applied himself to the job at hand, with the proper technique and sufficient tenacity, without his having to waste time with vague theories. To be sure, in the United States, too, performance was always inflexibly governed by theories, but they could be left undefined and forgotten because everybody then, half a century or so ago, with the exception of cranks and eccentrics, most of them foreign-born anyway, implicitly believed the same things. Finally, in the late twenties, when I humbly entered the School of Journalism, the idea that technique and industry were sufficient keys for achievement, and possibly the main ones, was seldom questioned for the excellent reason that it had produced amazing results. It was rightly considered one of the decisive factors behind the stupefying success of the United States. It worked.

Whatever doubts I might still have entertained that, as Americans had invented new revolutionary ways of training their many-gaited horses, designing dentures, building automobiles, crossbreeding both chickens and corn, playing games, et cetera, they had also discovered perennial and fundamental laws governing the arts of good writing in general and of successful journalism in particular, would have been dispelled within days of entering the majestic portals of the School. In reality, my doubts were few and feeble. I impatiently silenced them as unworthy remnants of my corrupt, incredulous, and envious European nature, balm for my wounded European pride, ballast to be jettisoned lest it slow my ascent. It was evident that the United States was, in the writing trade, too, as Emerson said, "the country of beginnings, of projects, of vast designs and expectations. It has no past." As they had done in practically every sphere of operation, Americans had first of all thrown past superstitions into the garbage can and then approached the problem as if it were newly born. There was nothing arcane about their discoveries. They stubbornly and rigorously studied man's innate craving for news of the world around him and inside him; analyzed readers' moderate capacity to dedicate their attention to the printed page; measured, in fact, the minuscule percentage of intelligence even intelligent men deigned to give to printed words. They had established once and for all, apparently with the mathematical precision of astronomers, the order of readers' natural preferences. From these simple observations, as Galileo had done by watching the oscillations of a lamp in the cathedral of Pisa, Freud the vagaries of a few demented customers, and U.S. Army doctors the habits of yellow-fever mosquitoes, Americans had deduced durable rules, those which govern the writing of effective prose. Composed of a limited number of very simple and common words grouped in short crisp sentences, it was designed, as rigorously as the models of aircraft in a wind tunnel, to penetrate the opaque barrier of publishers', editors', and millions of readers' indifference, apathy, inattention, and obtuseness. The success of this (as well as that of other related techniques) was statistically proved by the steeply rising circulation and profits of magazines and newspapers at the time, the steady stream of best-sellers and their triumphant penetration of the pretentious, stagnant, and disheartened European book market.

The high priest of this new literary science, the man toward whose course all others in the School of Journalism harmoniously gravitated, was, at that time, a famous, almost legendary figure, Dr. Walter B. Pitkin. I knew, of course, all about him. Everybody at Columbia who wanted to write knew all about him. I had heard all about him from fellow students over malted milks with double floats in the soda-fountain-book-and-stationery-and-sporting-goods store in the basement of the School building. He had swept away, as easily as cobwebs, the accumulated wisdom of the ages, had cleared up mysteries that had baffled, retarded, and defeated writers since Aristotle or even earlier. Whatever had been said on the subject, by the European authorities I had read at the time, sounded obsolete, irrelevant, and laughably insignificant, as, for instance, Benedetto Croce's unserviceable definition of the best writing, *"una visione lirica della realtà"* ("a lyrical vision of reality") or Charles du Bos's dubious indication, *"La littérature c'est la pensée accédant à la beauté dans la lumière."* Undoubtedly, the doctor would have been contemptuously dismissed as a *cuistre,* a vulgar, pretentious, and ridiculous pedant, by Anatole France, who had once written: "Those who claim to give us rules for writing are *cuistres,* because there are no other rules than usage, taste and passion, our virtues and vices, all our weaknesses and all our strength." Undoubtedly also, the doctor would not have cared less. Dr. Pitkin not only had liberated man from ancient nonsense and taught him no longer to grope in the Cimmerian darkness of self-delusions, but, being a cold scientist, a psychologist, and an expert on the literary market, had almost entirely eliminated risk and guesswork, and indicated the way to chart a precise course toward a well-defined goal, avoiding disastrous detours.

All this, I was told, he not only taught anxious boys, terrified of failure, in the classroom, but proved daily in his own outside work. Hollywood, it seemed, sent for him periodically, as one calls a luminary for consultation in serious cases, to estimate exactly the propulsive quality of stories before they were made into expensive films, and to formulate suggestions which would make feeble subjects into memorable money-makers. New York publishers of magazines and books similarly paid him vast sums of money to overhaul their policies, draw up precise rules to keep their firms out of the red and allow them to hit an occasional jackpot. His diagnoses and advice depended on the evaluation of many factors, but one of the most important was an exact analysis of current events and moods.

One of his fundamental theories (my version of it may

not be reliable; after several decades I probably remember only an oversimplified version of what I, an eager and impatient student, had already oversimplified at the time) was that the public was hungry for emotions which life around it did not provide but which were necessary for its psychological equilibrium. Exhausted by the emotional orgies of wartime, frenetic patriotism and violence, many readers instinctively turned to idyllic tales of pastoral tranquillity, simple pleasures, and virtuous love; in times of stagnant peace, prosperity, prudence, and leaden boredom, they yearned instead for bloodcurdling stories of adventurers, crooks, international swindlers, massacres, dangers, tempestuous loves, et cetera. This principle was valid not only for light literature, novels, stories, and films, but also for the choice of real-life stories in newspapers. (When I studied with him, I had to correlate lending libraries' records at a given period with the front pages of newspapers at the same time, or to determine the reason for the fabulous sales of some unremarkable novel by defining the emotional mood of the public who bought and read it.)

To demonstrate (or test) the validity of his theory, he was manufacturing a synthetic best-seller, as alchemists of old tried to produce artificial men called *homunculi*. His laboratory was a well-organized office in the School building, filled with filing cabinets, typewriters, and laborious girls, as busy as workers on an assembly line. They gathered vast masses of superfluous material (as Americans always compulsively do when faced with any difficulty), ordered it, and wrote first drafts along his outlines for him to rewrite, polish, and edit. How primitive in contrast seemed the shops of great European writers of the past, who worked alone, slowly writing masterpieces in longhand by candlelight far into the night, in obedience to the random dictates of their inner demons! When the book finally came out, a few years later, it was indeed one of the largest sellers of the day. The *homunculus* lived as vigorously as if it were a real man. The contents were of no significance whatever, a *minestrone* of irrelevant facts. It was practically unreadable and did not have to be read. Its success had been determined solely by the title. It had been artfully devised by Dr. Pitkin irresistibly to attract one of the largest possible categories of people, in fact a majority of the population, most of whom had never before bought or read books. It appealed to one of their most powerful secret urges and placated one of their deepest fears. It proved that the frightening problem did not exist, but, in case it did exist, offered practical instructions on how it could be solved. Its message was hopeful, consolatory, and optimistic. The book guided readers securely toward the pursuit of happiness, challenged the inexorable fate of man, defied Adam's curse, and seemed destined to change the world for the best. In other words, it could not have been more quintessentially American. (The fact that the book also had a fabulous success abroad only proves that there is something American in all men or that Americans are almost as human as everybody else.) The magic title was *Life Begins at Forty*.

All this impressed me greatly at the time, not only for the gross though attractive reason that the doctor made a large amount of money (there was only a small income tax in the twenties, paper dollars could be exchanged at any time for bags of gold coins, wealth was real wealth not to be ashamed of, not to apologize for, not to hide, but to display and proudly hand down almost intact to one's heirs), nor because his successes proved he could possibly teach his students (and me, among them) how to wrest similar sums from the reading public, but because it proved once more that the best way to fortune was, after all, to satisfy the real spiritual needs of one's fellow men, an altruistic and noble thought. Dr. Pitkin was so logical, as logical as Euclid, incontrovertible, and irresistible that it took me years to suspect that his theories illuminated only a small portion of the darkness, possibly not the most important, and to try to free myself from them.

The Magician of 116th Street and Broadway, the Pied Piper of Morningside Heights, presumably responsible for more successful writers and competent professionals, but perhaps also for more insipid prose, mediocre careers, second-rate journalists, and alcoholic failures than any other individual in the country, was a slight man, with thin hair and dark and restless eyes. I observed him attentively during his first introductory lecture to the new class. He seemed in a controlled hurry most of the time, slightly impatient, not wasting a word, a gesture, or the fraction of a second, as if he were bored by the repetition of things that had become stale to him or were submitting to a tight Calvinistic schedule. I seemed also to detect something vaguely ecclesiastical about him. Maybe it was the black suit and white shirt he was wearing, his spare wooden gestures, the empty eyes and sober expression on his pale face when he occasionally fell silent and seemed to listen to inner voices. Maybe (as with many Americans) it was only the conception of his profession that was religious, a kind of priesthood, a mission. Later I discovered he had actually studied theology in his youth, probably to become a clergyman, before turning to other studies and gaining several different mundane degrees. In the end he had considered himself above all a psychologist, a specialist in the psychology of what today would be called mass communications, but his clerical disposition and early theological training had not vanished altogether. The bouquet was still there.

As he finished his first lecture, he asked me to come to his desk. He smiled benignly and reassuringly as he gathered his notes and put them in his leather briefcase. The other students, boys and girls, watched me over their shoulders with envious curiosity as they walked out.

Dr. Pitkin asked me: "You are Italian, aren't you? How is your English? Good enough?"

I replied apprehensively that I did not know how good my English was. I had worked hard at it and supposed it to be adequate for simple jobs.

"Don't be afraid," he reassured me. "The English of most of your colleagues is not as good as you think. In fact, some of them cannot spell. Nobody is perfect. Everybody makes mistakes. And don't forget you have a few advantages over your schoolmates."

"What advantages?" I asked diffidently.

"Well, you know Latin and you're a foreigner. You'll discover, if you haven't discovered it yet, that English is also a Romance language. All Italian words are to be found in the English dictionary too—well, almost all. When in doubt, make up a word. It's bound to exist."

He laughed. (In fact, his advice turned out to be useful. In emergencies I sometimes Anglicized Italian words which copyreaders and editors wanted to eliminate in a rage as they had never heard of them. I won several bets with the help of a good dictionary.) He went on:

"Your foreignness must not intimidate you. It may be an

advantage. . . . It will keep you on the *qui vive* when Americans doze. You're not a slave to colloquial clichés. Sentences will not come out of you ready-made. You'll have to build them up word by word. Think of Conrad."

As he walked to the door, he dropped a few more sentences over his shoulders in my direction. What he went on to tell me was more mysterious. He said:

"You know Dante well, of course. You may find Dante more useful, in the long run, than Dr. Pitkin. I never stop reading him. I discover more beauty, wisdom, and profundity of thought and feeling every time. And such economy of words, such capacity for compression . . . You don't know the Count of Aquino, Friar Thomas, the Angelic Doctor? You must read him someday. It takes years to get through the *Summa,* but it is time well spent. Goodbye."

All this was disturbing and incomprehensible. Did he not realize that I was in his class precisely in order to escape from Dante and Aquinas, as well as Petrarch, Boccaccio, Machiavelli, Leopardi, Manzoni, and hundreds of others? Why did he throw me back unfeelingly into the waters in which I had been drowning instead of dragging me onto safe and solid American ground? Was he joking? (Later I discovered Dante's old and sacred snob value in American culture and found out that Dr. Pitkin really loved and knew Dante, one of the few poets who cannot be understood without some grounding in Medieval theology, and was a great friend of Dino Bigongiari, who taught Italian literature at Columbia and was a *Dantista* of repute; the doctor's love for Aquinas must have been a leftover from his youthful studies or a new arcane hobby which a few professors of philosophy were beginning to pursue, Mortimer Adler of Chicago among them.) All this I understood later. That day

I was merely baffled by one of the perennial contradictions of American life, which exasperate foreigners who like to see Americans always behave as they are supposed to: a sign that America had never wholly become the country I thought and Americans hoped it was, the fact that the compulsive and impatient rush toward the West, the ever-retreating perfect future, always went with an aching and disproportionate yearning for the East, the past they did not have or had rejected. It was a yearning that drove so many of them to seek refuge, morally, culturally, or geographically, among the memories of Europe, at the time when millions of Europeans were flocking (or wanted to flock, if the laws allowed them) to the United States, or eagerly adopting back home American ideas and habits, which slowly corroded and destroyed their own old ways.

As he vanished through the doors, one of the boys asked me: "What did he tell you?"

"I don't know," I said. "He told me not to be afraid of English and advised me to read Dante."

"Dante?" said the boy incredulously. "Dante? He must have been joking."

We went to lunch together.

There was a good professor of English composition, who taught us rigorously to avoid frills, ornamentation, purple prose, verbiage, and obscurity, all the things young writers consider essential and pride themselves on. I remember his first lecture. He was young, wore tweeds and heavy brogues, and smoked a pipe, like an Englishman in the movies. His was a moral lesson straight from a New England pulpit. He said: "Read Genesis. It's a model. 'And God said, let there be light; and there was light.' One of the greatest events in the history of the world, a cosmic miracle, in just eleven words. Think of what a bad writer would have done." I also thought of what stupendous pages one of the two or three great writers of humanity would have left us.

Then there were old retired journalists who, a few days a week, organized a fascinating game. We were supposed to be the staff of a make-believe newspaper. Jobs were assigned in turn, a few of us were made editors in command for the day, all the others helot reporters. The editors scrutinized the morning papers, read miles of news agency tapes, and wrote assignments for the reporters. The reporters left in a hurry, roamed all over town, rushed to fires, funerals, weddings, scenes of murders, buttonholed eminent men, celebrities, movie stars, detectives, policemen, obscure passers-by, or weeping relatives, and tried to wrest last words from dying men in hospital wards. When asked what paper they represented, they usually mumbled inaudibly. Later in the day the editors surveyed what copy they had produced and what had arrived through the agencies' clattering Teletypes, and made up the front page. At this point we all went home. There was no shop to transform all our sweated work, our minor scoops, our iridescent descriptions, our cruel analyses of reality, our elegant metaphors, our distinguished choice of adjectives, into a printed newspaper that would, compatibly with the quality of the newsprint, last for many years. We all felt frustrated as, I imagine, the stallions must feel who are employed by breeders to excite mares for other stallions to fecundate and are pulled away before reaching the culminating and satisfying conclusion.

The old journalists introduced us to the inviolable sanctity of the lead, in which everything essential must be compressed clearly and in a way to titillate the reader's curiosity, and we became masters of it. We also learned to write stories constructed like chains of small sausages, each paragraph in descending degree of interest and importance, so that the whole could be cut at any point starting from the bottom. We were taught many other small but precious secrets of our trade. Practically the only thing about journalism nobody could teach us was how to get a job when we graduated.

The assignments I liked best were those which allowed me to do what I would have done had I been free: roam all over the city, stick my nose into strange milieux, meet odd people, possibly turn an insignificant story into a short feature in which I could stretch a little and write more at ease, freed from the Procrustean limitations of the School. The Bowery fascinated me. I tried to find forgotten celebrities of sorts among the bearded and grimy drunks and actually found a few, not very important, of course, but picturesque, an old conjurer, a violinist, an obscure opera tenor, and a small-town banker. I liked the School for Barbers, run by Italian immigrants to teach other Italian immigrants a better trade than ditchdigging. It was located in the Bowery because the raw material was there, the unshaven and long-haired bums on whom raw beginners could safely try their hand. The bums did not care if their cheeks were slashed and their hair cut in bizarre tufts, as long as they got a drink or two of rotgut.

I also liked Coney Island, where I made friends in a way with a nice compatriot of mine, the Man With Two Bodies. The tiny body of an unborn twin brother stuck out, ass-first, from his midriff, its head buried away in his stomach. It had small arms and legs, it was inert, pale, and disgusting. The

Man With Two Bodies kept it wrapped in wool when he was not showing it off. He was from Ravenna and had emigrated years before, first to France then to the United States, where he had hoped to make a lot of money. He had never married, probably because women were embarrassed by the silent presence of the small brother-in-law. We had a few talks (he was hungry to know all about life back in Italy), when there were no paying customers around, and once he invited me to lunch at a small Italian restaurant nearby, where we were treated like relatives.

I was enriched by my two years at the School, without a doubt. I learned many things. Many, I suppose, I was taught by the teachers, many more I picked up wandering through the immense city, a few others I learned trying to run our imaginary newspaper as one of the editors. Probably what good the School really did me was not envisaged in the curriculum. I had been herded with boys and girls from many parts of the United States all of whom wrote, wanted to write to make a living, dreamed of literary or journalistic success, read a lot, and talked of nothing else. We read all the good books that came out, the *American Mercury* religiously every month, and, of course, all the newspapers. The New York *World* was our dream model. It is almost impossible to discern whether the technique I was taught in so many months really helped me. I suspect I could have picked it up, and a fresher one, in a few weeks in any newspaper office. When I met old schoolmates later in life, we endlessly debated the unsolvable problem of whether we would have been better journalists and writers had we followed other studies and not specialized so soon. As I grew older, I began to suspect that, had I studied in depth one historical period, any historical period, the silver age of the Roman Empire, the early Church writers, the eighteenth century in England, the Age of Enlightenment, or the workers' movements in the nineteenth century, I would have turned out to be a more perspicacious writer.

But all this was idle speculation. I could not afford to do otherwise. I had to make a living as soon as possible, probably in the United States, and learn to apply Dr. Pitkin's patent rules without which there was no hope. And, should I have to return to Italy, how far ahead of all my competitors I would be, enriched by the technique which was then putting so many American writers ahead of every foreign competitor! Dr. Pitkin was, irresistibly, showing me the old path of the setting sun, the American road to wealth, success, and a freer life.

Chapter 9

I CAME TO KNOW New York well after a while, as well, anyway, as a penurious foreign college student, make-believe
reporter, and occasional real cub reporter could ever come
to know the immense, elusive, multiform metropolis—every city for everyman—in which, as in a cloud, a man could
always see the shapes that pleased him most. Later I also
got to know ribbon-narrow strips of the rest of the country,
as I drove several times to California and back. I remember
(to prove how Protean the city is) that when I returned from
European vacations New York always appeared to me the
quintessence of America, the world of tomorrow. My eyes
saw only daring bridges suspended on steel cobwebs, the
tumultuous traffic of boats, ferries, tugboats, smokestacks
vomiting clouds of smoke, barges loaded with railroad cars,
majestic liners moored in the comblike row of docks, clus-
ters of skyscrapers, immense imperious billboards which

could be seen many miles away, and, in the streets, the young, brisk, clean, healthy, efficient people, who, without looking right or left, hurried on their way as if driven by a divine wind. They sometimes stopped briefly, to eat with their hats on, standing up like horses. But when I arrived back from a trip to the West, New York looked to me like the first city of Europe. My eye saw with relief only the dingy little shops of secondhand dealers from Galicia or Hungary, bearded and bent men with cunning eyes, Italian or French restaurants, decrepit, decaying, ornate buildings, pushcart peddlers, old people sitting in the sun, idle loiterers, the Brevoort waiters with their long white aprons down to their feet, and fat smiling whores like those one saw in Naples or Paris.

I got to know New York well, but what I got to know best was the little Long Island town where we Barzinis had gone to live. I studied it avidly because I felt that only in such a place could I hope to surprise a more unguarded America, find out once and for all what Americans really were, capture the American secrets, and test my aptitude, if any, eventually to become myself an American of sorts.

In reality, I came to know the little town intimately only in the summer of 1929. I had then been working a few weeks on the New York *World,* covering boring routine matters and learning practically nothing new. My desk was in a cell with a Jewish and an Irish boy. We pecked at our typewriters in silence and tobacco smoke, writing little insignificant items which seldom got printed. Sometimes the Jewish boy impatiently tore a sheet from his machine and cried: "Christ!" The Irish boy raised his curly head and said quietly: "Moses for you!" One day I learned that the little afternoon newspaper in our town was looking for a young reporter. I immediately went to see the publisher, Mr. Clemens, a nephew of Mark Twain. He was an old, pale, bald man with watery eyes who spoke with what I took to be a Southern drawl. He wore a green eyeshade over his pince-nez eyeglasses, elastic bands on his shirtsleeves, a Hoover collar, a bow tie at half-mast, suspenders, and an acidulous expression. His roll-top desk was out front, under a large and lazily moving fan, by the street entrance, behind the empty display windows. On the grimy glass he could read the Gothic gold letters of the masthead written backward. He sat by the side of the low wooden swinging door through which everybody had to pass, near Judy, the telephone girl, receptionist, and secretary. His was (I discovered when I worked for him) a strategic observation post, the captain's deck. He could check on what time we went to work in the morning, see who went by in the street, who entered the office, know, too, which of us was going in, out, why and for how long, and, through the open door of the editorial room, whether we worked hard. He could see that every penny of his and every minute of our time were well spent.

Mr. Clemens looked me over with undisguised diffidence and disgust, and told me bluntly he could pay only fifteen dollars a week. I accepted eagerly. He looked surprised. He had probably been resigned to paying me more. He then described my duties. I was to start as a police reporter at 7:30 in the morning, become a copyreader, rewrite man, and headline writer later, and an assistant make-up editor around noon. I could then take time off for lunch, but was to become a feature writer and editor of sorts the rest of the afternoon, to prepare copy for the next day's inside pages that would keep the linotype operators busy. The only thing I did not have to do, apparently, was sweep the office. The night was my own.

"And, of course," he added incidentally, "you'll pitch in when needed and help the other men in their work from time to time. . . ."

In the end this proved to be my most time-consuming task. The three other men often drank themselves into a comatose state and I, who did not drink seriously, had to carry not only their burden but at times also their bodies home.

"What is your name?" then asked Mr. Clemens.

I told him.

"Luigi?" He looked startled and suspicious. "Are you Italian?"

I admitted it with some pride.

"And can you read and write?" he wanted to know.

I reassured him. There were (had always been, in fact) Italians who knew how to read and write. I was one of them.

I incessantly roamed the little town that summer and got to know many people and curious places. Every morning at the assigned time I dutifully turned up at the police station, wearing a cheap cotton suit and a straw hat on the back of my head, the livery of my trade. I asked the old fat sergeant, in my best brutal American from one side of my mouth: "Hey, sarge, anybody croaked last night?" He raised his eyes to the stamped-tin ceiling (one of the many revolutionary, timesaving, American inventions, democratically accessible to people of modest means, still unknown in Europe, where expensive craftsmen made similar elaborate things by hand, out of stucco, one at a time, only for the affluent élite), always said with a sneer, "You vulture, you," and turned the blotter around for me to copy. I then rushed back to the office with my notes and from that moment on never stopped. I wrote, rewrote, copyread, telephoned, invented headlines (perhaps I am the only non-English-speaking foreigner who mastered the challenging art of writing American headlines, which combines some of the difficulties of Japanese haiku with those of crossword puzzles), walked, ran, talked, lunched or ate a sandwich at my desk, cut columns of lead, made up pages, and wrote again till the end of the day.

The only sample of my 1929 newspaper prose that survives is a yellowed clipping, one silly little story which I found in an old trunk. (The rest of my work, which I thought brilliant, well researched, dramatic, and elegantly written, worthy to be preserved, has unfortunately all been lost.) Mr. Clemens told me one day that Mr. Weinbage, a jeweler and watchmaker in the neighboring village of W., had installed a stately street clock on an artistically elaborate iron pedestal, on the sidewalk in front of his store. Its face had a diameter of two feet. Mr. Weinbage was one of our faithful advertisers and it was *de rigueur* that we salute the memorable event with a two-column headline over a few paragraphs at the bottom of the front page that very day. I had no other information, no time to get more, just two or three minutes to the deadline. This is what I wrote:

> When the village of C.P. recently acquired its first street clock, W. felt suddenly bare. No public timekeeper adorned its streets. But now a new timepiece two feet in diameter stands in front of the well-known Weinbage jewelry store in 14th Avenue. The inhabitants of W. point out with pride that it can be easily seen two blocks away, and even farther with a pair of binoculars.

Commuters heaved a sigh of relief. The old way of telling how many minutes they had to make the 8:07 was by watching the other commuters going to the station. If they walked in a leisurely stroll, there were two full minutes to train time. If they trotted, one minute was all there was, and if they ran, they had only 30 seconds to reach the platform. If they broke into a furious gallop, the train had already left the station.

This way of telling time was primitive. It had something of the romance of scouting, to be sure, and made a commuter feel like one of the last of the Mohicans finding the time of the day by looking for the moss on one side of trees —or was that how to find the north?

Anyway, the method was unreliable. Sometimes an idle man jogging for his morning exercise would pass a group of commuters and stampede them. In a few minutes everybody in a radius of ten blocks would be running breathlessly toward the station. The platform would be filled with hundreds of panting men, ready to board a train that was not due for two or three minutes.

Now all this is changed. The machine age has destroyed one more romantic skill from this earth, and in a few years only old men will remember the days when the minutes one had to catch a train were guessed at by the rate of speed of commuters. "Grandpa," children will be saying, "tell us when there was no street clock in W. and you guessed what hour it was by the way people walked." And the toothless mouth of grandpa will grin as he tells them once again the ancient and by then almost incredible story.

At the end of the day I sometimes went to watch my colleagues drink their imitation whisky and talk about our work. Our speakeasy was across the street from the office. It was not glamorous, sinister, or difficult to spot. It was merely the old saloon boarded up, still reeking of stale beer, mildew, and damp sawdust, run by the old Irish bartender, Joseph. The town's two more notorious bootleggers did not hide either. They did not look like dangerous members of the underworld, shady characters out of a gangster movie. They could have been grocers or insurance salesmen. They were familiar and friendly men one said "Hi" to when passing them on the street.

I felt at home in the little town, as much anyway as a young foreigner born among stone and brick palazzi in tortuous treeless streets can feel at home among flimsy wooden dolls' houses in the liquid trembling shadow of foliage. People I had to see often asked me in for a friendly cup of coffee. Shop owners on their doorsteps and policemen greeted me. Some people ceremoniously called me "Mr. Barzini"; one old lady who had lived in Italy called me *"Signor* Barzini"; others, "Luigi" or "Louis"; the Italians, *"paesano";* a few friends, affectionately, "Lou the Wop"; truck drivers who gave me a lift called me "Mac" or "Butch"; and everybody in the office, "Mr. Smith-a." I had brought the last sobriquet on myself. When asking somebody's secretary or wife on the phone to tell her absent boss or husband to call me at my office as soon as he got back, I had quickly given up trying to spell my bizarre name. The effort took too much of my time. I soon decided to call myself something easy, Mr. Smith. There was no other Smith on the staff. Everybody in the office and the printing shop then started calling me "Mr. Smith-a," pronouncing the name with a heavy Italian burlesque-comedian accent, which was incorrect and showed the Americans' deplorable capacity for clinging to clichés. I did not speak that way at all. Being Milanese, I could easily terminate words with a consonant.

I obviously must have learned many things in those few

months. I probably would not be the man I am had I not worked in that small-town newspaper that summer. Who knows? Even taciturn Mr. Clemens taught me one American secret of success. He used to tell me cryptically, as I went by his desk: "Mr. Smith-a, you miss many things in life by not asking for them." Was I supposed to ask Judy, the Irish telephone girl and receptionist, for a night of love or him for a raise?

It was far from easy to understand how life around me really functioned. I watched the people, spied on their unguarded moments, listened to friends' boasts and adventurous tales, catalogued everybody's contradictory and confused beliefs and habits, questioned intelligent foreigners, and tried to formulate some sort of coherent general principles, in an effort to find clues, or The Clue. What I wanted was to discover a few simple and reliable rules, which evidently could not be those openly proclaimed for the advantage of adolescents and simple, docile people— honesty is the best policy, little strokes fell great oaks, don't watch the clock, and early to bed early to rise—but the real rules which would allow me to avoid unmarked shoals and sandbanks and eventually to ride a favorable current to fortune. But the more I observed, studied, and distilled deductions in my head, the more bewildered I became.

It was particularly disconcerting to realize that life in the United States seemed scandalously easy (easier than anywhere else) only for foreigners who did not read books, did not worry, did not study the American people's behavior in the light of their historical myths and sociology. The only foreigners who flourished took things as they came and went about their business as if the United States were more or less like any other country, inhabited by more or less ordinary human beings. They knew, of course, that the American natives were particularly odd and unpredictable, often inordinately stubborn or swept by emotional storms. These foreigners also knew the American natives were maniacally attached to their outlandish beliefs, superstitions, and fixations. But, after all, which natives were not? All one had to do to get along with Americans was simply to humor them and never contradict them. Such foreigners were at ease also because, *au fond,* as one of them who imported dubious antiques told me, Americans, at least the Americans he knew, were as a rule more reliable, candid, transparent, generous, friendly, and honorable than Europeans.

Among the Italians I met who found life in America easy, profitable, and pleasurable, far easier, more profitable and pleasurable than in Italy, were the ditchdiggers, hotel and restaurant people, Sicilians, wheeler-dealers, the Opera crowd, and the aristocrats.

The ditchdiggers were all called "Tony" (as Pullman porters were then called "George"). In spite of what seemed to some Americans their miserable and pitiable living conditions, they made more money, were less oppressed, and worked fewer hours than back home. They were happy and grateful. They were flattered when told they were brutally exploited. They sent money home, produced flocks of children, ate amply and succulently, made their own wine, and became very portly as soon as possible. The lucky ones were buying houses and automobiles by easy payments.

Hotel and restaurant people were in clover. They were dominating the market. New York was for them a conquered colony ("Colony" was, in fact, the name of one of their best restaurants). At the bottom of the ladder was the cheap one-family *trattoria,* where Mama cooked, Papa served, one always found homemade red wine served in coffee cups and homely advice on how to bear life's burden. At the top were Northern Italians, mostly from Lake Maggiore, who ran and sometimes owned some of the great "French" restaurants and managed the big hotels. They had usually arrived in New York after working in Switzerland, Paris, and London, learning languages and the métier. Once a year the manager of the Biltmore, the *doyen* of them all, gave a stag dinner for the Italian restaurant and hotel élite. Father was one of the few nonhotel guests, probably because he was known as a good cook and an expert and insatiable gourmet. It probably was the best dinner eaten in New York in the twelve months, accompanied by the best wines, and surely the best served. The top restaurant and hotel Italians did not concern themselves with the Americans' ideals, triumphs, technical progress, and political experiments. They considered their customers strictly from the *buona cucina* angle. They saw them as primitive, naïve, good-natured, and lovable barbarians, who ate anything set in front of them without complaining, people who could be awed into submission with one word or a raised eyebrow, grateful for a little attention, and wantonly generous with tips.

The Sicilian patriarchs spoke little Italian and little English. Few knew how to spell out simple headlines and street signs, or could write their own names. Like all unlettered people who make do without the prop of written words, they naturally were more sagacious, intuitive, and shrewd and had more infallible memories than the miserable people who were lost without paper and ink and printed words. The Sicilians did not need to learn anything about America, though they knew practically nothing about it. They carried on simply and imperturbably as if the street they lived on were their native village and the United States an immense Sicily. In fact, they soon discovered that the United States was a far better Sicily than Sicily itself. The trouble with their native land was that it was filled from shore to shore with nobody but Sicilians. Everywhere you turned, whatever business you were engaged in, you had to face another Sicilian. They all knew the same secrets, conducted themselves according to the same rules, were all terribly deft at managing complicated deals, legitimate or outside the law. They scented their opponents' concealed fears, anxieties, hopes, or confidence, and could also exactly measure their own. They were all equally secretive, incredibly brave, wary, honorable in their own particular way even when they were forced to play the slow and tense Sicilian chess game, sometimes a move or two a year, fully aware that death was the loser's penalty in the end. In Sicily one did not have to talk much (in fact, people were as laconic as Yankees), as everybody, friends and enemies alike, somehow knew without being told what everybody else was up to, thinking or planning, knew the exact weight to attribute to every word of flattery or implicit threat. They deduced all this from a single move, a tone of voice, an adjective, a superfluous word, a frown, or a sigh. This produced, back home, a kind of collective paralysis. It had frozen the island for centuries into its own peculiar immobility. Nothing much ever happened in Sicily, each inhabitant behaving like a wrestler wary of his opponent or tied to him in a knot of muscles impossible to unravel.

In the United States, on the other hand, where the Sicilians were few, everything was magically possible and many things happened happily all the time. Life in the new country was also infinitely easier for Sicilians because only a small number of Americans (mostly policemen) had heard of the Sicilians' crafty arts, and these ill-informed few coped with them as ineffectually as if trying to box with ghosts in a dark room. There was, to be sure, nothing arcane or exotic about such arts. In fact, there were many Americans, victorious powerful people, Irish, Jewish, German, or Anglo-Saxon, who, without realizing it, conducted their affairs more or less as the Sicilians did: impassive Wall Street financiers, ruthless bosses of political machines, implacable trade-union leaders, tough big-city mayors or state governors.

It must be noted that the Sicilian method was applied most of the time to the conduct of everyday legitimate business by the humble as well as by the successful, and only rarely (statistically speaking) to criminal affairs. It was indispensable for the weak and defenseless to protect himself from predatory bullies; for the hungry and illiterate pick-and-shovel workingman to get a job, the right wages due to him, and a better job later; for the pushcart peddler or small shopkeeper to defend himself from predatory rivals, racketeers, and corrupt policemen; and so on, up the social scale, as high as the wealthy businessman or politician.

The Sicilians, as they had done since the days of Homer, neatly divided human beings into friends, enemies, and neutrals. Their rule (which is also a Spanish proverb) was "To friends, everything; to enemies, the law." Enemies had to be intimidated, immobilized, or destroyed; friends protected, comforted, rewarded, and enriched. Power (everything depended on power) was artfully cultivated in many ways with great care. The family, first source of power, had to be made prosperous, respected, and feared with antlike tenacity; it was enlarged (like dynasties of old) by suitable marriages, strengthened by alliances with families of equal status, by negotiated submission to more powerful ones, or by establishing its domination over weaker ones. The gratitude of the humble was to be gained with gifts, loans, jobs, a good word to a judge; the gratitude of powerful personages, politicians, businessmen, judges, bankers (most of them non-Sicilians), with favors, pieces of precious information, gifts, money, or votes. All these people, high and low, at the right moment discovered they could not refuse a favor in return, sometimes but not always a vaguely illegal one. Certainly, the technique was invaluable in a crisis. The family and its allies then became a Macedonian phalanx going through American society as if through butter. The technique was also unique in its application to criminal life. Rival gangs who were not aware of the Sicilian code could be wiped out in a matter of days. Rival Sicilian gangs, of course, were more difficult. Then, technique was not enough since everybody shared it. What won the day was cunning, fortitude, courage, and discipline.

All this functioned smoothly in the United States, where free-for-all was the rule, everybody needed a favor, power and money were generally considered the proper goals of life, and few men in authority were reluctant to accept favors, sometimes a few thousand votes, more rarely a briefcase full of banknotes. If one of the Sicilian patriarchs had been told (I tried to tell one of them, once) that the United States was a very different country from his native island, a democracy dedicated to the equality of men and the protection, strictly by means of the law, of the defenseless and the meek from the rapacious and overbearing, a proper Protestant country where even the Catholics were Puritans, a Republic imbued with ethical prejudices, dedicated to liberty, truth, progress, the inflexible rule of law, where crime did not pay and blind justice would smite even an erring President, he, the Sicilian patriarch, would have risked death laughing himself into apoplexy. The one I tried to explain all this to looked at me as if I were demented but harmless, sympathetically tapped my knee, and said: *"Siete molto giovane"* ("You're very young").

Then, of course, the laws in America seemed to be expressly designed to make the Sicilians' lives easy. They did not know that the legal system was a sieve invented to defend humble and innocent seventeenth-century English peasants from the arbitrary despotism of aristocratic landlords, downtrodden city workingmen from overbearing *gendarmes,* innocent men from being framed by treacherous enemies, or political opponents of the king from *lettres de cachet.* All the Sicilians knew was that the police and judges were inexplicably paralyzed by a fine mesh of intricate legal precautions. In the United States, it was easy one way or another to prevent witnesses from appearing in court, or for some to appear and swear false statements contrived by skillful lawyers. The loyalty of the witnesses went first to the family, just as underground resistance fighters' loyalty goes to their cause and not to the enemy. (This, of course, is a fact also recognized outside Sicily. A wife cannot testify against her husband in many countries.) Without staunch and heroic witnesses not afraid to risk almost certain death for telling the truth, and with solidly contrived alibis, a defendant could rarely be found guilty.

The wheeler-dealers and smart operators, who were of course an infinitesimal minority among the hard-working honest Italians, proliferated at an abnormal and alarming rate. One got the impression, at times, that the percentage of crooks was somewhat higher among Italians than among different ethnic groups. It was, to be sure, a wrong impression, probably due to the fact that honest people are invisible while the picturesque adventurers (the Italian variety was as a rule excessively picturesque) stand out, that one knew the Italians more intimately, and that Northern operators usually preferred to look as dim and proper as clergymen. There was surely something in the American air that made such adventurous people flourish. It seemed to be the right, nutritious, and beneficent culture medium for them. They liked life in the United States, found it easy and comprehensible, and were as free as fish in water. They seldom went back home. On the other hand, worthy and capable people often withered in the obscurity, like one of father's friends, a talented musician and brilliant writer, the author of famous songs, Buzzi-Peccia, who lived on the verge of starvation, giving piano lessons in Brooklyn.

There were eloquent impresarios with diamond rings, white waistcoats, and dyed curly hair who assembled opera companies for distant music-starved provinces and vanished with the money before the season was over. There were agencies which sold steamship tickets home to returning immigrants, adding a substantial supplement if they wanted to sail over a smooth sea. There were go-betweens of all kinds, agents, organizers, herders of political votes, self-appointed bankers, dubious lawyers, all of them living on the poor trusting workingmen, their widows and orphans. For years some organizations had been collecting large sums of money from impecunious immigrants, who probably skipped a few meals to subscribe, in order to raise artistic monuments to the Italian great in New York. The monuments, like those of all *libertadores* on horseback throughout Latin America, were ordered in Italy, mother of Carrara marble, sculptors, and monuments for all occasions. They always cost far less than the funds collected. As the Italians in those years were despised, discriminated against, and frequently humiliated in the United States, and as Italy at the time seemed to be rich only in famous dead men, New York was gradually filled with marble demonstrations of national pride, stone and bronze answers to the barbarians' ignorant taunts.

Then there were the banquets. Whenever it was announced that a minor personage had arrived from the old country on a visit, a committee was formed, tickets were sold, a hotel ballroom hired and filled with eating and applauding Italians, a few Irish politicians who angled for their votes, flags of the two countries, and portraits of kings and Presidents. A number of prolix and flowery orators reminded the people present that Italy was the fatherland of a long list of great men, Dante, Michelangelo, Giuseppe Verdi, Antonio Meucci (Meucci is the obscure symbolic victim of American contempt for Italian immigrants' legal rights; he was a theatrical mechanic who at one time manufactured candles and salami on Staten Island and invented the telephone, an invention which Italians in the United States believe Alexander Graham Bell stole), Garibaldi (who lived at Meucci's house, when exiled in New York, and for a while helped him make the candles and the salami), and Marconi. Organizing such banquets (like the monuments, they cost far less than the money collected) was a hazardous operation. It was not easy to discourage rival committees with kind words. They often had to be intimidated with threats, some of which had to be made good.

I remember one singing teacher, an old man, who kept a vinaigrette filled with precious "Milan air" and allowed his pupils to breathe a little of it at a time for a few dollars. He explained that that particular air, which he imported at great expense, was what made the difference between a good singer and a great singer. It was the air that had made Milan the opera capital of the world and La Scala the greatest theater of all. There were self-made legal experts who drew up contracts, wills, bills of sale for remote olive groves in the mountains of Basilicata and Calabria, organized marriages by proxy with unseen and unknown peasant girls in Italy, and performed many other services for clients who could not read and write and knew nothing of the law.

There were then so many smart and ingenious Italians with obscure pasts that one could almost believe a surely apocryphal story that went the rounds in those years. The event was supposed to have taken place at the Metropolitan, on a gala evening, the opening of Pirandello's *La Giara,* which had been turned into an opera. Everybody was there because the performance was in aid of the Italian Hospital. The theater was packed, the more distinguished, affluent, and fatter Italians in evening clothes in the orchestra and boxes, and their leaner clients crowding the balconies. When the lights went out, the curtain slowly rose on a stupendous scene, a popular fiesta in a Sicilian village lovingly reconstructed with the meticulous care of nostalgic

179

exiles. All the details were painfully authentic. There were Venetian lanterns, flowers (the correct flowers for a Sicilian summer day), flags, the statue of the Virgin with a halo of electric bulbs, and triumphal arches made of laurel branches. There were foliage-festooned stalls loaded with roast suckling pigs, primitive toys, and sweets of all colors. There were priests in their vestments, peasants in their ancient costumes, and a brass band in admirals' uniforms with cocked hats adorned with ostrich feathers.

Most visible of all was, center stage, a substantial group of robust *carabinieri,* impeccably dressed in their black tail coats with red piping, silver buttons, white bandoleers, short swords, and Napoleonic hats. Within seconds, so the story goes, practically the entire audience rushed to the nearest exit as if the theater were on fire. The sudden unexpected sight, in such a realistic setting, of the policemen many of the guests had instinctively avoided for years in their youth, had unnerved them and triggered forgotten reflexes. They did not remember they had since become prominent, esteemed, prosperous, and *illibati.* The story is doubtless exaggerated. I am sure only a few hundred ran for the doors.

There was one Neapolitan financier of sorts, endowed with a fertile imagination, who founded a bank proudly called "Bank of United States." Obviously, he wanted the name to reassure his countrymen by analogy with the Bank of Italy in Rome and the famous one in San Francisco. Why he skipped the definite article I never found out. Maybe his knowledge of English was still faulty. Maybe it was a dodge. Some fussy American legal restriction possibly prevented anybody since Andrew Jackson's days from using the full historic title, "Bank of *the* United States." The financier's name was Ferrari. Once he invited all of us to a wedding banquet in his Brooklyn house. We were astounded by what we saw. Nothing like that ever happened in Milan. The feasting lasted from two in the afternoon till three o'clock the following morning. One course followed another with leisurely intervals in between; pasta, ice cream, roast chicken, fruit, fish, a different sort of pasta, turkey, cakes, shrimps, pasta again, soup, roast beef, *cassate,* boiled meats, and so on indefinitely without any discernible plan. Occasionally, musicians accompanied a singer on guitars and mandolins, an impromptu orator delivered a winy eulogy of the bride and groom or the host, or an amateur poet read an *ad hoc* composition with a few lame lines. The guests were not supposed to stay put in the same place. Some ambled around the house and the garden, took naps on sofas, sat in other rooms to chat, telephoned, sang choruses, washed their faces in the bathroom, came back to the table to taste the latest offering, a bit of fried fish, a *sfogliatella,* or a forkful of spaghetti with clam sauce. Some of them even left the house on errands of their own and came back after a while. Father enjoyed the whole thing immensely and thought it could be the twentieth-century version of a Roman banquet, on chairs instead of triclinia. Mother was bored, vaguely disgusted, and embarrassed. A few months after this unforgettable experience Ferrari's "Bank of United States" went bankrupt, he went flat broke, and avoided going to jail only by dying. I am sure that, had he enjoyed good health, with his unerring intuition about American ways, he would have prospered till extreme old age.

The Opera people lived in a mental cocoon of their own, as if they had never left their native land, as protected from the world surrounding them as the Victorian English in India. Arturo Toscanini lived at the Astor on Times Square. He had persisted in living there even after the neighborhood had become a noisy honky-tonk, because the owners (the Muschenheims) considered him a precious friend and treated him like a fragile premature baby.

At the Astor, too, lived a mysterious adjunct to the Toscanini family, who had also absolutely no contacts with American life. This gentleman arrived, separately, when they arrived. He left when they left. Nobody, or practically nobody, ever saw him in New York. Nobody mentioned his existence. Above all, the Maestro never found out he lived a few doors down the corridor or, sometimes, a floor away. The mysterious gentleman spent his days in seclusion, like the Man in the Iron Mask, ate in his room, never tried to contact his New York friends, and circulated circumspectly only at specified hours, in the afternoons or evenings of certain days, according to an exactly preordained schedule. He was a man in his forties, blond, elegant, handsome, rich, and unusually intelligent for an *homme du monde.* Women attributed to him a rare and effortless charm which many of them found irresistible. He was Count Emanuele Castelbarco from Milan (an uncle by marriage of Luchino Visconti). He shot, hunted, drove racing cars, gambled a little, courted handsome ladies, and fought a few duels, like all men of his station, but was also a dilettante of talent and a discriminating Maecenas. In the early twenties, he ran an avant-garde picture gallery in Milan, called Bottega di Poesia, and published numbered hand-set editions of rare new poets. He may have been the first to show Picasso in Italy and was certainly among the first publishers of Apollinaire, a friend of his. Castelbarco's edition of *Alcools* is now a rare bibliophile's treasure.

One day into his gallery wandered a beautiful sixteen-year-old girl. She had pale gardenia skin, splendid black eyes, a miniature Pinocchio nose, pointed and arrogant, a thin waist, and a beautiful décolletage. Castelbarco fell in love with her like a schoolboy. She fell desperately in love with him. She was Wally, eldest daughter of Toscanini. There were difficulties, besides the difference in their ages. He was married and had two sons. His wife would not let go of him and grant him one of those divorces wealthy Italians managed to obtain at the time, by changing nationality for the necessary length of time or by other ingenious means. The couple did not let such silly obstacles stand in their way for long. They became secret lovers. Theirs was one of those desperate affairs that can be found only in those nineteenth-century French or Russian novels which our mothers read during the summer. Toscanini soon heard about him and, famous for his irascible moods and for the violence of his rages, made a scene in front of his daughter which surpassed all the memorable scenes ever recorded by his biographers. He threatened to kill her or to kill him, told her she had dishonored his name, and ordered her to do the impossible, not to see Emanuele ever again. He swore he would not consent to allow her to marry him, if he ever managed to obtain for himself some sort of divorce. The reasons he gave in his wrath were that, besides being too old for her, a father, and the head of a family, he was rich, a count, and, of all impossible things, blond. The Maestro was a democrat, born in the popular quarter of

Parma, and proud of it. He apparently considered being blond an intolerable upper-class affront to the usually dark-haired middle class.

The result of all this was, of course, that Emanuele and Wally went on for years loving each other with the ardor and perseverance of few married couples. He followed her to New York every year and returned with her to Milan when the Toscaninis came back. In New York he could only go out or receive Wally in his room when the Maestro was rehearsing or giving concerts, according, as I have said, to an exactly preordained schedule. (In the end Emanuele became a Latvian citizen, or *Léttone* in Italian, got a Latvian divorce, was nicknamed *"Lettóne,"* or "Big Bed," by Milanese wits, and married Wally. They had a daughter, Emanuela. After a few years, marriage ties being notoriously less binding than those of forbidden loves, he left her for, of all people, a Swiss girl. People wondered. Swiss girls were, as they used to say many years ago, *comme les edelweiss, très difficiles à prendre et ça ne vaut pas la peine.*)

Giulio Gatti-Casazza, the Metropolitan manager, lived at the Plaza; most of the others at the Ansonia, at Broadway and Seventy-third Street; Beniamino Gigli had a princely apartment near Carnegie Hall, where he lived surrounded by a confusing retinue of familiar servants and courtiers who could not easily be told apart; the musicians and secondary singers lived in Italian boardinghouses scattered around the Opera House. They all knew little English. They did not need it. Gatti-Casazza, a portly patrician from Ferrara with Edward VII whiskers, lived for a few summer weeks in his stately family palazzo in Italy, completely staffed all the year round, which he considered his permanent residence, and for eight months in an anonymous New

York hotel suite, on the wing, possibly to prove to himself that America was a faraway exotic place, a quicksand society where a well-born person with means of his own did not put down roots. The only English he knew was the word (if it could be considered English) "Plaza," which he gave taxi drivers when going home from his office. He pronounced it "Pladza." He ran the opera speaking Italian (and occasionally French). His American employees had to learn the language to communicate with him. This could have been due to laziness, pride, and, as I have said, the idea that America was not a suitable resting place for a gentleman but only an adventurous way station. The only Americans these Opera people met were musical maniacs, fawning journalists who considered them immortal gods, millionaires who invited them to stupendous dinners or house parties in the country and solved many humble everyday problems for them, and crowds of cheering worshipers. The Opera people had a wonderful time.

Then there were the aristocrats. Most of them were beautifully dressed, handsome, and bored bachelors. They had high-sounding titles and several picturesque historic names strung together like beads. Only a few were impostors. Once I asked one of these why his visiting cards had a crown and a title in the United States but only his bare name in Italy. He said contemptuously: "You know well enough there's no freedom of the press in Italy." Most of them had little money, not enough to pay their Roman tailors and shirtmakers. Like penurious aristocrats from other countries, like distinguished Russian refugees, some had jobs. They disdainfully sold stocks and bonds to middle-aged American society women, champagne, or dubious old masters purportedly from their family castles. A few even had serious jobs. One, Ugo Veniero d'Annunzio, the son of Gabriele d'Annunzio and the Duchessa Hardouin di Gallese, his wife, had a degree in engineering and the future title (at his father's death) of Prince of Montenevoso. He efficiently sold Isotta Fraschini automobiles in New York, to millionaires and movie stars, each model designed especially for its buyer. They were as beautifully fashioned as Benvenuto Cellini's inkstands or Fabergé eggs.

These aristocratic bachelors were the pets of high society, more the pets of wives than their husbands, to be precise, apparently because of the curious fact (recorded by many foreign travelers and Henry James, too) that elegant women in the United States seemed at that time to belong to a different breed, to live in another continent and another century from their husbands. They spoke more foreign languages, read more books, listened to more music, knew more about food and wines, traveled more, encouraged more arts and artists, suffered from more delicate diseases, were more restive in a world of gross money-making, more lonely, and, for some reason, particularly sensitive to the fascination of titles and names which seemed to carry them into nineteenth-century romantic novels.

Strangely enough, these well-tailored and well-mannered young men seemed to be exempt from the Americans' diffidence and contempt for Italians. Once, on a date at Vassar, every girl who cut in on me asked me eagerly: "Are you the Count?" Evidently, my girl had tried to avoid the odium of having a simple Italian as her guest by ennobling me. I could not humiliate her by proclaiming my bourgeois origins and my single solitary family name without trailers. But I could not bring myself to lie. Why should

I masquerade as something I was not? I answered all of them affably: "Not officially. Not tonight. Just call me Luigi." They probably thought I was admirably democratic.

The aristocratic bachelors were considered, like exotic flowers, indispensable adornments for formal dinners, balls, house parties, and a perfect addition to a shooting party. They always appeared in wonderful *ad hoc* clothes, unpaid for. Their manners were suave and easy. They treated moneyed Americans with flattery, to be sure, but, like headwaiters, also with an amused contempt which somehow seemed to please their hosts even more than flattery. In the end most of these distinguished Italians married some rich widow or her daughter, for a few years anyway. They usually made good husbands. Having nothing much else to do, an aristocratic husband entertained his wife all day and all night, went with her to the dressmakers, traveled with her (and her maid) everywhere. These people, too, were not haunted by the problem of understanding American life.

Not being a ditchdigger, a Sicilian, a maître d'hôtel, an operator, a tenor, an aristocrat, I had a tough time. I was particularly bewildered by the Americans' unpredictable behavior. Were these people infantile and immature or the ultimate heirs to the wisdom of the ages? Were they, as so many Europeans secretly thought, really demented? Were they desperately interested in the welfare of the rest of the world or were they agoraphobic and narcissistic isolationists, jealously in love with their own perfection, which they had to defend from contamination at all cost? Did they believe all men were equal or were they really addicted to

187

separating them into almost imperceptible Neapolitan-ice-cream strata according to race, wealth, religion, and length of residence in America? One could easily prove that they were both the pathfinders of human progress and at the same time harbingers of decay and decadence; a violent, bloodthirsty, warlike nation which went to war at the drop of a hat, conquered other people's lands, and exterminated whoever stood in their path, and at the same time the champions of peace at any price, too proud to fight, champions of self-determination and human brotherhood. One day I believed they were greedy money-mad materialists and, another day or even a few minutes later, people animated above all by religious fervor, disinterested and sometimes indiscriminating crusaders in all kinds of humanitarian causes, some of them bizarre or daft. The common man was universally and vociferously proclaimed an omnipotent sovereign among them, but was also shown to be the perennial victim of economic oppression, exploitation, skulduggery, fraud, cynically manipulated by unscrupulous businessmen, and guided like sheep by advertisers. The answer, of course, which I was too young and inexperienced to discover, was, yes, they could be all these things at the same time, because in spite of all their efforts and brave pretentions Americans were still human beings.

The quality of their national pride seemed to me then the clue most worthy of attention. Most people, of course, are proud of their achievements, real or imaginary. Without some national pride even the most modest nation could not exist. Every self-respecting people fondly remembers the day when it more or less ruled the world, or believed it did: the Spaniards, the English, and the French, of course, but also the Greeks, the Persians, the Mesopotamians, the

Turks, the Chinese, the Arabs, the Mongols, the Egyptians. The Italians themselves were, at that time, officially and vociferously proud enough of their Roman imperial past to forget their present. There was no doubt that the Americans, too, had overwhelming and even better reasons of their own to be proud. Their experiment had turned out indeed to be the greatest success in history; the most incredible and unlikely success since the Creation. Within three or four generations, they had wiped a whole continent clean of wild men and beasts and quickly filled it with their own people; established elastic but solid political structures; miraculously pulled out of a hat the great or almost great leaders they needed at the proper time. They never lost a war, even though they did all the things necessary to lose the wars other nations would ignominiously have lost, built the Panama Canal when the French had given it up as impossible, wiped out yellow fever. . . . Particularly worthy of their pride and other people's envy was one of their unique gifts. They devised immediate practical applications of scientific discoveries, created out of nothing industrial monsters to produce their newly invented gadgets in vast quantities, and made them not only available but indispensable to the masses. See what happened in America to the electric toy of a young elegant *marchese* from Bologna, who played with it on the top of his father's barn; to the Lumière brothers' magic lantern; or to Dr. Gottlieb Daimler's self-propelling carriage.

But what especially puzzled me, what I thought was exclusively American, was the fact that they were proud not of their past alone, like everyone else, but, inordinately and prematurely, of their future, too. They considered the past and the present were modest *passaggi obbligati* on the road toward a wonderful tomorrow. The whole country seemed to live, plan, sacrifice itself, and work without respite only for the succeeding generation. In a way, the United States had to be man's best hope on earth, the masterpiece of all times, or nothing. And their sacrifice of the small pleasures of life dear to other, more leisurely people (peace of mind, good health, idleness, and serene old age) was not borne for themselves alone, nor solely for their still unborn descendants. They somehow knew that everybody's future on earth would sooner or later have to be imitation American, if only because they were developing what everybody everywhere would sooner or later be forced to recognize as a better world. No time could be lost.

Theirs had to be, as F. Scott Fitzgerald wrote, "a design for the whole human race, the last and greatest of all human dreams or nothing." In the meantime, they obeyed their inescapable historic duty, to discredit and weaken what was believed and had been done down the centuries by other men, as they pitilessly demolished their own old buildings, some of them dear to them, landmarks, architectural jewels, monuments of the past, to construct their spick-and-span new skyscrapers, or as they swept ancient forests clean of majestic trees so as to prepare the ground for rows of identical little houses, which they called homes. The lack of qualms and the sense of duty with which they went ahead with their revolutionary demolition work were but a reflection of their quiet belief that one had to suffer change because all change was progress, today did not count, and tomorrow was bound to be a better day.

The man who wrote the editorials on Father's day off, Beniamino de Ritis, in one of his lucid moments, explained it all to me one day. He was a classical scholar, a philosopher, and an essayist of note from Rome, who had become, in spite of his revulsion toward journalism, regular schedules, writing in particular and any kind of work in general, my father's right-hand man. He said:

"Life is hard labor. Hard labor is unpleasant drudgery. Man accepts it only under harsh compulsion. In Europe, in older days, men were compelled to toil by hunger and fear, by tyrants and their armed henchmen, and by laws made by the tyrants. To protect their self-esteem, men gradually convinced themselves they worked, as they fought, and occasionally died, for moral reasons, duty, God, King, country, and family. Then the Americans came. They performed a miracle. They are to be admired. They practically freed themselves from hunger, need, and all the old coercions, almost all anyway, but succeeded in not turning into loafing bums. In fact, they even managed to accept greater sacrifices, even to die in war with greater enthusiasm. They invented different and wonderful reasons to be slaves. The flag and the honor of their country, for instance, took the place of the ancient fear of the tyrant. For almost everything else, they discovered, avarice and emulation are almost enough.

"Americans now labor harder than the slaves of old, more than the men who built the pyramids or dug the canal of Corinth (and most of them meekly keep their place in society and obey the laws), because, for one thing, they hope to make money, more money, perhaps to buy a new house and a new automobile, and send their boys to a good university, possibly better houses, automobiles, and universities than those their neighbors can afford. To do this, most of them no longer have to be compelled like galley slaves by a man with a whip. Their docility is commanded from inside themselves. This is the great American discovery. They nobly call it the Puritan (or Calvinist) tradition, the work ethic, or something.

"All this, of course, is made easier by their horror of being different. Few of them ever abandon the race even on the verge of collapse. They die in harness. Then, we must not underestimate their idea of progress. Every sacrifice seems worthy to them because it brings them nearer to the perfect future. Have you noticed that everybody is progressive in this country? They would rather die than to be thought the enemies of progress. In the United States, even the imperialists and colonialists (who want to redeem lesser breeds from their own inefficiency, save them from the consequences of their mistaken concept of life), the militarists (who must preserve the peace of the world with their mighty fleets), the malefactors of great wealth, the wicked speculators, the owners of coal mines, steelworks, and railroads . . . all these are progressive. They are all working their asses off only to feed the hungry, clothe the naked, improve the world, and satisfy its needs. The American Bismarck, Theodore Roosevelt, was the leader of all progressives. So was the real Bismarck, for that matter. Americans now love Mussolini. They think he is progressive, too. He makes trains run on time, doesn't he? Progressive also are, *ça va sans dire,* by definition, the defenders of the workingman, the champions of inflation, the inventors of panaceas of all kinds, and the pacifists. One of the historic leaders of American progressives, curiously, seemed to believe in the Bible as the only acceptable explanation for the appearance of man on earth. The one indispensable magic word that automatically drives Americans to superhuman efforts and, when it is necessary, to the ultimate sacrifice, is 'progress.' Wasn't the last disastrous world war the progressive war *'par excellence'?"*

Beniamino's dislike for work was so strong that he wore a pair of blind man's dark glasses in the office so that my father could not tell when he was sleeping, which was most of the time. Exhausted by his long speech, he closed his eyes behind the dark lenses. I shook him and told him he was an envious European cynic. "Nothing would happen," I said, "even if [an absurd hypothesis] Americans' love of work, faith in the future and progress, pride in their country, avarice, and thirst for uniformity weakened."

"If all this happened one day," Beniamino answered, "America would go down the drain, *alla malora,* and maybe drag us all with her. After all, all forms of government have broken down sooner or later. But let's not worry about it, Luigi. It may not happen, and, if it does, you and I may be dead by then. What do you care?"

Chapter 10

THE LITTLE TOWN where I worked as a young reporter has since been devastated by a hurricane of ruthless demolitions and ugly improvements. A few forlorn relics survive here and there in the flood of shoddy little homes, advertising posters, neon lights, crummy supermarkets, and cement expressways. When I returned, many years later, I managed to recognize some of the old landmarks only with great difficulty. In 1929, however, the little town still preserved some of its identity, character, and provincial pride. It was still surrounded by dark primeval woods and vast empty meadows. On one side it faced a long and narrow inlet from the Sound, gray-green muddy waters often whipped by the howling wind to fine white watery dust. Screaming gulls darted hysterically or planed ecstatically over it. Across the creek was an ancient iron drawbridge, which was raised when a long slow train of barges, towed by a hissing tugboat and loaded with refuse, went by.

The town had a proper Main Street, like Zenith; a neo-classical pillared courthouse painted the color of Dijon mustard; a venerable gray wooden Quaker meeting house religiously preserved; a tiny red-brick military building of sorts which surely went back to the Civil War, designed like a toy castle with a crenellated tower. There were a couple of small department stores, movie houses (the newest, for some reason, in a preposterously splendid Alhambra Arabian style), one old and comfortable hotel, a small hospital, and some churches built in the best Walter Scott Medieval architecture.

There was also a monument to the Union dead, a bronze soldier with all the correct buttons correctly buttoned, proper regulation boots, the proper gun with proper bayonet at his side, a neat pack on his back, belts and cartridge cases, everything impeccably ready for inspection by General Grant. In a way, it was a pathetic show, because almost all the men who could have been comforted by such meticulous precision had died long before, and we contemporaries did not know the difference and could not care less. Near the Union soldier was a small cast-iron fountain decorated with leaping dolphins, surmounted, somewhat like the famous fountain in Bologna, by Neptune brandishing his trident. Around the Union soldier and Neptune a small park was laid out with benches, on which pale old men sat, munched peanuts, fed the birds, and read newspapers. Perhaps their melancholy idleness was cheered up by some of my finely wrought prose.

When you walked away from Main Street, as I had to do many times on my errands, you passed some very ancient Colonial houses, small and simple but noble in their chaste simplicity; then some merely ancient, the not-so-ancient, the just old, and, a few miles down the road, the not-very-new, the almost contemporary, and finally the brand-new. Evidently, the little town had grown like a pearl in successive layers and it would have been possible to trace the course of American society, its ideals and quality, by studying the gradual architectural variations. As you progressed from the eighteenth century to the twentieth, you noticed that the houses grew less plain, honest, and dignified, gradually becoming, block after block, more and more pretentious and ornate. The late-nineteenth-century specimens were definitely vulgar and ostentatious but in a happy way, as if designed for a laugh, full of fretwork, gimcrackery, domes, pepperbox turrets, bow windows, colored glass, gables, and unexpected mansards, sometimes with iron deer or colored plaster German dwarfs and toadstools on the lawn. Many of the newest specimens were not as happy. Many of them were small, crowded, flimsy imitations of the styles of other centuries and other countries, some as approximate as movie sets. There were American Colonial houses, miniature Scottish castles, Queen Anne or Regency manors, Italian Renaissance palazzi, Swiss chalets, Versailles pavilions, or Spanish Colonial structures which looked as if they were cut from cream cheese. You felt as if the restless dissatisfied owners for some reason dreamed of only one thing, to escape the present and their own country.

I looked at the oldest houses (an Italian was reluctant to call them ancient, as they were less than two centuries old) with pleasure. They had the dignity of handsome matrons who did not try to appear younger than they were. They had the style of genuine things, unself-consciously designed by honest people satisfied with their lot. They were always good for a short feature story. I remember, in one of the sitting rooms, among what could have been the original furniture, the portrait of an 1830s portly bespectacled gentleman with a yellow waistcoat and a tall collar hung over a roll-top desk, possibly his own, on which rested the very same square gold glasses he was wearing, and a young man vaguely resembling his great-grandfather pointing them out to me.

And everywhere majestic trees, higher than the church spires and the ugly water tanks on the commercial buildings, rose to the sky. They had been planted by Huguenot nurserymen two hundred years before. I hope I was not deceiving my readers when I copied from some book the fact that they were the ancestors of trees that later decorated gardens, parks, and malls all over America, first in the East and later, as one generation succeeded another, farther and farther West, to the Pacific shore. I had seldom the time to check interesting information. I also feared to discover it was not true.

It still appeared to be the kind of placid and friendly small American town foreigners seldom knew existed, or, if they knew, seldom bothered to visit and describe. Visitors from abroad were reluctant to discover that America was not all a tentacular glass-and-steel jungle, ruthless big men destroying little men, feverish and brutal money-making, inhuman efficiency, skyscrapers, grimy factories, stinking slaughterhouses, and Stock Exchange speculation; not all bootleg booze, instant wealth, violence, the rat-a-tat of machine guns, riveting machines, or pneumatic drills, fast cars, demented sex, gangsters' wars, rebellious youth, and jerky jazz. Visiting foreigners would have been disturbed to learn that many of the hard-working and taciturn robots they saw in the cities, many of the frenetic people who trampled on each other in trains and subways, the silent slaves who filled banks, office buildings, factories, and department stores as crawling bees fill beehives, went home in the evening to little wooden houses like those I knew well, to the old clothes, the children, the dogs, the neighbors, the lawnmowers, peace, and the rosebushes.

Nothing much seemed to happen in our little town that summer, not enough for my needs anyway. Sometimes I thought with rage that we were living in a pocket aseptically separated from the rest of the country. Tremendous events apparently always took place elsewhere, many of them tantalizingly only a few miles west, across the river. I read all about them on the news tickers: international intrigues, mysterious assassinations, romantic loves of movie stars, the rise and death of tragic underworld heroes, immense wealth striking poor people overnight, men beating the world record for sitting on flagpoles or blocks of ice, couples getting married at the top of Ferris wheels or spending their wedding nights in department store display windows, women giving birth to children under klieg lights, love nests raided, race riots. . . . I felt frustrated, like an eager soldier in battle, ready to accomplish feats that will make him a famous hero, who has to sit still with nothing to do, in a quiet sector, while guns roar and other soldiers die and kill and win medals all around him. The monotony of my days was broken at the most by little insignificant events which I tried hard to make complicated and mysterious, a piddling suicide, a banal automobile crash, a petty burglary.

The only story on which I could gratefully rely for a front-page column on any empty day was the saga of the dumps. To the south, at the end of the creek, stretched vast swamps which were being slowly filled with refuse brought from far away on barges. The contractors were pledged to bring only ashes but dishonestly brought mostly garbage. Some of it rotted or burned day and night. The landscape has an honored place in American literature. F. Scott Fitzgerald had just described it in *The Great Gatsby:* ". . . a desolate area of land . . . a valley of ashes—a fantastic farm where ashes grow like wheat into ridges and hills and grotesque gardens; where ashes take the forms of houses and chimneys and rising smoke, and, finally, with a transcendent effort, of ash-grey men who move dimly and already crumbling through the powdery air." It is where George B. Wilson's garage was, where his wife was killed by Tom Buchanan driving Gatsby's car. On good days, the stench of fermenting decay and greasy smoke was unbearable for miles around. Off and on I wrote, with subdued indignation and an eye for libel, about the corrupt contractors, the corrupt inspectors, the corrupt officials, the unhappiness of the people breathing the miasma, the mortal threat to public health of stench and smoke, the running court battles, and the drop in real estate values.

I often visited the dumps. A few poor and primitive Italian immigrants, all related and all from neighboring villages in Irpinia, lived there in shacks ingeniously made of tin cans, wood, and cardboard salvaged from the refuse. They had flattened some of the older ashes and garbage and turned the part of the stinking desert around them into luscious vegetable gardens. The rubbish made an extremely rich soil, and they had been making a living which seemed fabulous to them. They had produced a large number of black-eyed children, worked very hard from dawn to sunset. I occasionally stayed for dinner. I had to eat abundant helpings of the indigestible food which they piled on my plate and would have been an insult to refuse, drank the thick homemade red wine, and played *briscola* with the men in the summer twilight. The stench was overpowering, to be sure, but only for the first half-hour. After that one gradually got accustomed to it, to the point that one could taste the wine and the sauces, and smell the flowers.

While the women busied themselves washing dishes, the men played cards and talked. They kept their shotguns handy and, once in a while, killed a rat on the run in the twilight. The rats were as bold, big, and hairy as miniature wolves. I told these people that they literally had, as they say in Italy of anybody striking it rich anywhere, *trovato l'America*—found America in America itself—and congratulated them on their great luck. They reluctantly admitted that, yes, you could consider them lucky. The mad, frivolous, rich, wasteful, impatient Americans had not only overlooked the incredibly fertile land under their noses which gave the poor Irpinians their opulence, but also threw away bedsteads, old sewing machines, chairs, stoves, clothes, shoes, and many other useful and expensive things which needed only washing, small repairs, or a coat of paint to be as new. Why did the Irpinians not buy machinery to enlarge the extent of their cultivation? The men hesitatingly explained that their luck scared them a little. They were afraid it would not last. It was not natural. They were always ready for disaster to strike. Whose land was it? they wanted to know. Nobody collected rent. Was there no landlord who might exploit them but also guide them and give them some security? There were, of course, big, overbearing, and incomprehensible Americans, who appeared often enough, and extorted money. Possibly bribes or tributes. These Americans drank their wine, pinched the girls, shouted strange curses, and shook their fists under their noses. Who were they? Then gangs of neighborhood boys stole vegetables or fruit, made fun of the Irpinian children; threw stones at them, or beat them up. The men wanted the *signorino* who could read and write and spoke *americano* to explain. What real rights had they? Were they not wanted? If not, why did no one chase them away? Were they not useful? Why did people treat them with contempt and hostility? Did I know somebody, a landowner or a politician, to turn to who could defend them? Where could they find a powerful protector?

I did not know the answers, of course, but reassured them anyway. I told them I would look into the matter, but they had nothing to worry about, they did not really need a protector. This was not Irpinia. In the United States their rights were amply defended by the law. If they needed urgent help, why did they not turn to the nearest policeman, or a priest? (They explained the nearest priest was very far away, Irish, and could not understand them.) I promised that, if I came across a good man to protect them, possibly a sympathetic and generous man who would not want too much of a cut, I would recommend them to him. I warned them it was difficult for me to run across such a person, as I was from Milan, where these *combinazioni* were unnecessary and unknown.

I also told them to forget the precariousness of their situation. America was a mysterious country where things were not always easy to explain. Everything was precarious in America, here today gone tomorrow. Precariousness was the very nature of the country, what Americans probably meant by the pursuit of happiness. To be sure, they, the Irpinians, were, juridically speaking, illegal squatters. But the whole country was made up of illegal squatters. In fact, illegal squatting was what the United States was all about. It had grown by infiltrating brave illegal squatters into Indian country when it was forbidden by law to do so, and into neighboring countries like Florida, Louisiana, Texas, and other Mexican provinces, all the way to Los Angeles, before the American Army conquered those lands. Illegal squatters were, in fact, the heroes of the American epic. Why should the Irpinians be despised and persecuted for being foreigners, chased away from their flourishing vegetable gardens, when they were obviously doing the American thing, being more American than many Americans? I told them they should have been publicly honored by the President himself because they, like the pioneers in the West, had put up cabins in the empty wilderness, fought nature's discomforts and dangers, killed ferocious animals, worked themselves to the bone, and raised God-fearing religious families (there were colored lithographs of saints nailed to the walls, with tiny electric bulbs lit in front of them). Did they not, like the pioneers, preserve what graces they had brought from the old country, like *briscola,* the art of wine-making, seeds of unknown vegetables, and their appalling cooking recipes? I assured them that, no matter what other people thought, they, the Irpinians, were great Americans.

They always listened to me with rapt attention, as if I were telling them wonderful tales, and with silent respect.

To be sure, they did not believe one word of what I said. They thought the United States could not really be the country I described because, give or take a few details, *tutto il mondo è paese*—the whole world is the same sort of place and men are men everywhere. They also firmly believed that, if one behaved in America exactly as one did back in Irpinia, everything would turn out all right in the end. But they never contradicted me. They never explained to me what they really believed, probably because they thought I would not understand, being a foreigner from Milan, a man who read books, used difficult words, was young and enthusiastic. One never contradicted a *galantuomo*, anyway, a man of means, a bourgeois who wore a hat and a necktie, back in Irpinia. One did not disturb the candid illusions of youth either.

After a few weeks of work I began to suspect that appearances could be deceptive. While, of course, the peaceful and friendly story-book little town—the toy wooden houses, the children, the dogs, the rosebushes, the white wooden fences, the Huguenot trees—the place where nothing disreputable, unsavory, or vulgar ever seemed to happen, was everything it seemed to be, an exemplary American community where the middle-class virtues and proprieties were jealously preserved, it was also a deceptive screen behind which many other things were going on. It was definitely a part of the current American scene. For one thing, I got to know the ways of the young people, being one of them. Parents did not know what kind of parties were given in the stodgy family houses when they went away on trips, how many of their snow-white demure daughters got drunk on poisonous booze and were being kissed in the rumble seats of strange roadsters or on the back-porch swings, how many of them, as a result, were ineptly and joylessly made pregnant and, paralyzed with fear, had to look for back-street abortions. To be sure, upright commuters did not steal newspapers, thieves did not often rob unguarded houses, and students took exams under the honor system, but there was a lot of invisible skulduggery abroad and large amounts of protection money changed hands.

I explored the shady roadhouses and the few gambling joints which had sprung up here and there in the surrounding countryside. They, like many other things, were not always easy to fit mentally with the tidy, moral, and spotless little town, yet there was no doubt they were an intimate part of it. I was boisterously and affectionately welcomed by some of the Italian owners. They refused my money, put their arms affectionately around my shoulders, and volubly spoke their native dialects from the South or Sicily which I could barely understand. I was embarrassed and somewhat shamed by all this, but relieved to save some money and proud to show whatever American girl I was escorting that evening how well connected I was.

Visits to such spots were not always safe. While drinking and dancing cheek to cheek and hipbone to hipbone you had to keep your eyes wide open, darting in all directions, ready at any time to make a fast getaway. The danger did not come from Prohibition agents, who usually warned the owners politely before making a raid. It rarely came from rival gangs. More often, sometimes twice a week, the real danger to life and limb was that of free-for-alls among the paying customers. For some reason, they seemed always eager to fight after downing a few glasses of the powerful bootleg stuff.

A small limp quarrel between two drunks at the bar could quickly turn into a mild exchange of insults and of weakly aimed punches. A third drunk would come between the other two ("Cut it out, boys," he would say paternally), and get slapped in the face or punched in the belly for his meddling. A fourth would then try to avenge and protect the third. Then a fifth, a sixth, a seventh would join in. The big waiters tried at first to separate and pacify the contenders. At one point somebody would always shout out the drunk's war cry: "I can lick anybody in the joint." Within a minute or two every man in the place was punching everybody else, smashing chairs over the others' heads, and the women, looking not particularly afraid but annoyed and bored, retired to the cloakroom or the manager's office. Men wearing glasses took them off, before entering the battle, with a grim smile and a resolute gesture; some carefully shed their coats and folded them tidily over the back of a chair. The waiters pushed away the furniture, stowed away breakable things, bottles and glasses under the bar, with the automatic solicitude of sailors clearing the decks of warships. They had done it all so many times before. All the participants were so carried away by their fighting passion in the end that they forgot bleeding noses and half-closed eyes, and sometimes spat teeth and blood like cherrystones in cherry juice. Calling the police to placate the wild drunken fight was, of course, out of the question. The joint was illegal.

What frightened me most was not really the danger of getting hurt (I thought I was strong and sober enough to take care of myself and my girl) but the demented joy in the fighters' shining eyes, the anesthetized lack of feeling with which they took blows that would have stunned a dray horse, and the impenetrable gratuitousness and stupidity of it all. I never felt more of a stranger, a man from another world, than when I sneaked out, steering my girl in front of me, carefully moving at the right moment from behind the piano to behind the big waiter to behind the bar in the direction of the door and the open air. It was, of course, the only thing to do. The following day, drunk and beaten-up customers were sometimes found, asleep, without their wallets, on distant sidewalks.

I suspected at those times that it would be extremely difficult for me to become what I thought was a real American, one of the happy drinkers in roadhouses always ready to join in a fight. I had seen violence in Italy, of course, street fighting between political parties, left and right, or between the police and rioting strikers, but it seemed justified by political passion, a matter of them or us in the service of a cause, and the people involved, the rioting crowds and the policemen, obviously did not like it. They ran away when they could. Violence was, of course, endemic in Sicily, where men often disappeared as if by magic and corpses were found on lonely roads, but Sicilian violence was a cold and passionless ritual. For a Milanese boy the Mafia was a folkloristic and macabre tradition anyway, strictly limited to a distant and picturesque island, a tragic tyranny imposed *ab antiquo* on miserable, illiterate, primitive, and long-suffering peasants by miserable, illiterate, and primitive protectors, sheep thieves, blackmailers, and murderers. It had nothing to do with everyday life. In fact, I had never seen a live Mafioso, or a dead one for that matter, until I came to the United States.

There was something entirely different about violence in America. It broke out at times, in one form of another, for no apparent reason, even among the seemingly peaceful and polite, not only in speakeasies but at private parties, college proms, or sports matches. The people liked it. I suspected it was an element essential to their well-being. A good fight was more to them than just a fight. Maybe it was spiritual relief they craved, a more satisfying and immediate remedy for their ennui, obscure torments, overwhelming moral burdens, crushing duties, humiliating impotence, doubts, or whatever ailed each of them, than booze, sex, politics, gambling, or religion. Maybe it was something without which they did not really feel alive.

Violence was everywhere. It was almost part of everyday life. You could never forget it. It took many forms. Once I saw two gangsters' automobiles, black open touring cars, go down the main boulevard of the proper little town, between the decorous houses and the well-mown lawns, side by side, at great speed, disregarding traffic lights, shooting at each other like warships in a naval battle, frightening elderly ladies with blue wavy hair in hairnets out of their wits, and almost killing Mike the cop at the intersection. I never found out who these gangsters were, where they ended up, how many died, and why.

One morning Ernest, the city editor, sent me to see one of the bullet-ridden corpses that were occasionally found on lonely roads. It had been conveniently dumped by the cemetery gate during the night. "Find out who he is and why they bumped him off. Follow the story. He's a Wop like you, Mr. Smith-a," he said. I rushed to the spot. A policeman I knew was standing guard by a body sprawled on the ground. Its face was covered by a newspaper. It was the first dead man I had ever seen. "A Wop like you," Harry the cop said, touching the body lightly and kindly with the tip of one boot. I followed the corpse to the place where the autopsy was performed and waited until I was allowed inside to interview the medical examiner. My dead countryman, a Sicilian immigrant, lay naked on a marble slab. The skin from his chest was draped on both sides like thick curtains, his rib cage had been lifted like the lid of a box. I felt sick. The medical examiner was washing his hands, and his helper, holding a towel ready for him, said in a flattering officious voice: "You certainly know how to split 'em open, doc."

A few days later I went to the dead man's house, deep in Brooklyn, for the funeral, hoping to discover some underworld secrets. The thick bony corpse had been put together again, combed with brilliantine, made up with strangely non-Sicilian pink cheeks, dressed in a stiff shirt, wing collar, and dinner jacket like a headwaiter. He was lying on the dining-room table surrounded by flowers and lit candles. His wife, children, relatives, a few nuns, a priest, and silent menacing men dressed in black, standing with their backs to the wall, were all around. The priest, the nuns, and some women were kneeling in prayer; a few disheveled women were crying loudly and shouting invocations to saints or praise of the dead man's virtues and merits, paid to do so according to the old Southern custom. His fat widow, in a new black dress, tears streaming from red eyes, held my hands, looked into my eyes, and asked me: "Why did he have to die? He was such a good family man, loved his children and his parents and his wife. . . . He never missed

208

Mass. He had applied for citizenship. He loved America."
I discovered no secrets.

And all this violence, squalid and dangerous business, these ruthless criminals, these violations of every law, these shady joints which one would have noticed with a knowing smile in the Suburras near the ports of Marseilles, Naples, or Constantinople, somehow became more terrifying under the majestic trees, against the tidy landscape and the trim gardens of the dignified and proper and virtuous little American town. The dichotomy between the two realities, the righteous and impeccable and the violent and criminal, both (I realized) deeply rooted in the American past, was disturbing and frightening, just as a well-born, blonde, and beautiful American whore somehow would seem more of a whore than a slatternly, hairy, deformed girl from Alexandria or Beirut.

Chapter 11

A FEW DAYS after I began work in the summer of 1929 I fell desperately in love. Her name was Ann. There was not another like her in the world. I do not know whether it was her unique beauty which had fired my love and made me feel at times as empty and fragile as a sucked egg or whether it was my love which made her seem to me like a goddess. I know perfectly well, at my age, that a diligent retrospective inventory of a girl's graces is a sadly futile way to prove her fascination to the incredulous. I imagine that a zoologist who has spent months alone in the jungle deludes himself that he can easily explain to anyone his infatuation with a young female gorilla merely by describing the willowy long arms reaching her ankles, the tiny bloodshot eyes like precious rubies, the large contagious grin, the jolly red bare buttocks, the soft fur all over her body, and the reckless agility with which she swung from tree to tree.

Nevertheless, I will try to describe my old love, if only for my sake.

Ann was a blonde, ash-blonde to be exact, her hair straight and light, close to her head and collected in a flat bun at the back. She had steady aquamarine eyes, a slender straight body, and wore no perceptible makeup. She was a serious and tranquil girl, somewhat distant; did not speak much, listened attentively, frowned occasionally, and often smiled beautifully. What particularly pleased me was her skull. Her forehead was gracefully convex; the arched bones under her eyebrows deliciously stretched the skin; her cheekbones were faintly high and prominent, her jaws well designed and strong, a little too strong perhaps. All this, I admit, would in time have given her a somewhat horsy face, full of character, to be sure, more suited perhaps to a handsome man than to a fragile lady, but Ann was nineteen that year and her spare beauty was not yet austere. It still had the indeterminate blurred vagueness of childhood, the glowing fuzziness of a perfect peach. What she would look like twenty years later was the last of my preoccupations. Only the here and now counted for me.

What I liked about her (besides her skull) was the fact that she did not conform to current models. She did not look like the popular girl at a college prom, the boast of raccoon-coated boys, the reckless flapper with unruly curls sticking out from under her bell-shaped felt hat, the shaved nape, the gummed eyelashes like spokes of a wheel, the thickly rouged lips, and the round red discs painted on her cheeks as on a Russian wooden doll. Ann did not roll her stockings under her knees, wear her snowboots undone, never got tight, did not have a barker's raucous voice and his feverish, puppet-like gesturing. What I mean is, she did not look like one of the pretty dolls who were ready to jump into the dark back seat of a parked sedan with the first boy, a boy whose name they had not quite caught, to burn his candle at one end. Not that I spurned the timesaving advantages, blessings, generosity, and ineffable delights of such girls. They were wonderful and indispensable. I was addicted to them. But I could never fall in love with one of them. I never did.

In fact, Ann's beauty was not the kind that could be appreciated at a distance or across footlights. She would never have been considered by Florenz Ziegfeld; would not have been welcomed unclasping her bra on a burlesque stage, with the customers' elephant trumpet calls and stamping of feet. The ivory *bibelot* perfection of her face and body could be savored best a few feet or, better, a few inches away. I enjoyed it (as one enjoys, say, "The Reading Girl" by Fragonard) at close quarters, sitting by her on a sofa (when I admired her profile and the cut of her nostrils), across a dinner table (front view), or on a beach. By the sea, in the incandescent light of a summer morning, she let her hair down like a golden veil over her shoulders, and wore a modest one-piece black cotton bathing suit, which, when wet, clung to her like varnish. Her wrists were as fragile as *grissini;* her hands, tiny, soft, with tapering fingers, demanded fondling as kittens do; her legs were slender, long, and the color of bread crust; her feet, narrow and slightly bony, often disappeared under her when she sat down on a sofa.

She looked earnest, clean, morally and physically clean, honorable, straight, and wise. Above all, she looked chaste, as serenely and proudly chaste as a vestal virgin, but by no means forbidding or austere. She could be as friendly,

open, and gay as a hunting dog, as defenselessly affection-
ate as a cousin. I suppose it was also her quintessential
American look that made me a zombie in her presence. She
was as unmistakably American as the pink two-cent Washington postage stamp, as the Stars and Stripes, definitely
more American in my eyes than the frizzy-haired big-bos-
omed dolls who won the title of Miss America each year at
Atlantic City. She seemed to me, in fact, the very incarna-
tion of that particular America I preferred, the ideal America I longed for, to which I attributed all kinds of perfections. What I wanted to clasp in my arms was not only a
beautiful and desirable girl but probably also her elusive
and partly imaginary country. She was the opposite of an
insidious, voluptuous, deceitful, lazy, fleshy, and weak
Mediterranean odalisque.

I imagine I also fell in love with her because she was the
anti-Circe. She did not turn men into pigs or monsters by
her magic arts, not intentionally anyway. It was clearly my
own obscene nature and not her fault, if, in her proximity,
my trousers often bulged. It was particularly embarrassing
when I danced with her or when I had to stand up suddenly.
I then had to plunge my left hand into my trouser pocket
as if to shift an electric torch that had got there inadvert-
ently. Whether she really was the anti-Circe I imagined or
had been made by the forces of evil a more dangerous and
infallible Circe, one who did not look like a sorceress at all,
whether she would have been pained or secretly proud to
discover what ignominious effects she could provoke, I do
not know. She probably did not worry about the matter.

Ann lived with her widowed father (a small, energetic,
bushy-eyebrowed naval officer, retired), a younger sister,

Betty (who was merely a pretty girl without magic), and her white-haired grandmother in a modest old wooden house not far from us. I had often noticed her in the street, at the movies, on trains, or in shops. It was impossible not to notice her. Every time I spied her head in a crowd or her slim silhouette walking toward me in the distance, my breathing became difficult. Trying to look indifferent and to hide my abject condition, I glanced at her casually as if she were a tree. We never exchanged a nod or a smile. We had not been properly introduced. We met purely by chance late one night, in the early summer of 1929, just after I got my newspaper job.

We met at a party. It was the gayest, noisiest, rowdiest, and surely the most expensive party I had seen outside the movies. It was given at a new estate, several miles east, where the houses grew larger and wider apart, the small plots became gardens, and some of the driveways graceful winding avenues. It looked vaguely English, with trimmed hedges, newly planted young trees with their temporary supports, wide lawns, movie-set rosebushes, and a small pool at the back. I never found out who owned all that. Like many people there I had not been properly invited. I had simply been told by a friend, James Armstrong, a few days before, to be ready in dinner clothes, on my doorstep, at a certain time that evening, to be picked up by him, and to ask no questions. He told me, while driving there, that it was all right, not to worry, this kind of thing was done in America. The party, he said, was being given in honor of a young brother and sister by their parents, for some reason or other, and, within a radius of many miles, presentable young men, who did not know these people's name either, wearing freshly pressed dinner clothes, their hair neatly parted and plastered down with water and gum, were picking up their perfumed, rouged, and curled girls in their chiffon dresses, to take them to the same place. He also assured me we could consider ourselves not plain vulgar gatecrashers but virtually old family friends of our hosts, because he knew somebody who knew somebody who believed he had met them once. James and I were escorting no girls. He said that was a good thing because stags often had, after a certain hour, a much better time, a much larger freedom of action, wider choice, better luck, and surely fewer worries and responsibilities. That was his theory anyway. "Forget your Old World scruples," he said. "This is a free country."

Moreover, he pointed out, there would almost surely be no parents, to whom one had to ask to be formally introduced and explain one's presence, as in stuffy, old, and backward countries. If there were (which was almost unheard of), they would try hard not to be conspicuous, but lurk in a distant little room, and, if necessary, encourage the young guests to eat, drink, be merry, and raise hell, as if the old people were not there. They would even smile benignly and shrug their shoulders, James said, if an occasional old piece of furniture or a Chinese vase was smashed, somebody got a black eye, peed in a spirit of fun in the umbrella stand, or threw some other guest from a first-floor window. But, he added, the parents had almost certainly gone away, fled, as they always did, possibly to a similar party somewhere else, where exactly the same sort of things would be enacted as in their own house but strictly among the middle-aged.

This was not new to me, of course. I had learned that, when young Americans received their contemporaries, they usually seemed particularly anxious to conceal their parents as if they were for some reason ashamed of them. Was the parents' heinous sin that of having generated off-spring? The young severely scolded fathers, mothers, and aunts if they allowed themselves to be seen creeping through the front door or timidly tiptoeing down the dark hall and up the stairs. The parents themselves seemed to find this natural, not to resent it at all, in fact to welcome it with relief. Usually they abandoned the premises long before the first guest arrived or (for all I know) shut themselves up in the cellar or the attic (their bedroom being almost always employed as a cloakroom).

The fact that the generations could not mix as if they were hostile tribes always puzzled me. *Chez nous,* of course, at that time, we still had to meet our parents' friends, sit down to dinner with them, eat with our best table manners, and listen politely to the grownups' conversation. This, of course, was sometimes irksome but seldom uninteresting. Even dull elderly people were worth watching attentively. Sometimes we joined the conversation, asked the guests some respectful question or tried to satisfy their avid curiosity about the customs of the young. The mingling of generations was accepted, in fact, as a matter of course. We thought (if we thought about it at all) that it allowed us young Barzinis occasionally to observe at close quarters some of the well-known men father knew, meet unusual people, well-read and well-traveled Americans, recently landed Europeans studying the American scene with incredulous and stupefied eyes, or wise old foreign residents who had a treasure of funny American reminiscences and had developed a few useful rules to survive in such a bizarre environment.

Meeting older people, furthermore, gave us the feeling of not having been catapulted onto the earth, anonymously and singly, from nowhere; of not being, so to speak, our own first progenitors, obliged to invent civilization from scratch, as many of the American young seemed proud to do. We, the young, felt, of course, and with confidence, that we were wiser and knew more answers than decrepit men in their forties or fifties, but we were also pleased to be the last links of an endless chain stretching back into the remote past. In fact, we thought the purpose of the chain was to produce us. But even the old seemed not to dislike meeting the young. We probably made them feel useful, allowed them to imagine they were handing down the quintessence of their experiences, and delude themselves they would learn at firsthand what the young were really thinking and doing. Dinner parties followed by long *conversazioni* were all that were held in our house. We never gave dances, not even a small one animated by the Victrola or the radio.

James and I were among the first to arrive at the great party. The house looked almost empty. It had evidently been cleared for action. Precious carpets, *bibelots,* vases, and furniture had presumably been stored away. Only priceless tapestries and old masters were left on the walls. They were so beautifully clean and impeccably restored they looked brand-new, as if made the day before. Were they fakes? They could not be, I thought, because fakes are always made to look old, as old and ruined as possible. But then one never knew. Most Americans were so fond of the spick-and-span in all things that they would probably be more readily attracted by the newest-looking and brightest-colored fakes than by the drab and worm-eaten.

One buffet loaded with food stood in what must have

been the dining room, with a few eager black waiters in attendance like artillerymen at their guns; another small buffet was set up in the garden by the swimming pool. One bar, with a red-faced barman behind it, was stocked with bottles which looked infinitely more authentic than the tapestries and the old masters. Ice buckets, from which the gold necks of champagne bottles stuck out at an angle, various bottles, glasses, and ice stood on other tables here and there. A small band played polite music in what must have been the living room. Another small band played out-doors, near a wooden dance floor, smooth and waxed, set up on the lawn, surrounded by Venetian lanterns. The French windows were open and their white curtains bil-lowed gently in the soft breeze.

"Holy tit," said James, looking around, "this must have set these people back a million dollars." The exact signifi-cance of a religious invocation which recalled primitive Florentine paintings of the Madonna and Child against a gold background escaped me. But he was right. It was an expensive party.

When we arrived, a few young people on their best be-havior were nibbling food, sipping drinks, and making em-barrassed conversation in the dim light. Some couples were dancing elegantly and sedately, the boys keeping the girls at least one foot away. James and I knew (or recognized) some of the guests, but could not guess (and nobody could tell us) who, among the young people, were the girl and boy for whom the party was being given. "Never mind," said James. "You might want to introduce yourself to them like a goddamn European. It would only embarrass them." After a while more and more cars arrived. As they were being parked, their headlights slashed circularly, like turning lighthouse beams, through the French windows.

More young people entered, laughing, finishing in loud voices jokes they had started in the garden on their way in. They welcomed friends with shouts of surprise, jostled each other, rushed to the bar, boys grabbed girls and dragged them to the dance floor. The noise increased. The bands played louder and with more enthusiasm, their two musics mingling in a confusion of melodies. One danced to the throb of the drums. As time passed, the voices rose higher, the guests became more boisterous. A boy I had met once took me by the arm, cried, "What the hell are you doing here?" and pushed me to the bar. "What will you have?" he asked me. "Everything is on the house, ha-ha." He obviously had had a few drinks already. I took a glass of not very good champagne. I never drank hard liquor at parties. The taste of the bootleg stuff was usually nauseating anyway, and I was always afraid the poisons would make me sick. "Champagne is for ladies," the boy said. "Drink some he-man stuff. This will grow hair on any man's chest." I explained I already had sufficient hair on my chest, and repeated what I always said when American friends tried to make me drink some of their counterfeit booze: "I don't need it, you know. Being Italian I can easily do, sober, all the things you can do only when drunk." He laughed uproariously and slapped me on the back. "You're a funny one," he said.

By and by, the house and garden were swarming with young people who, as the hours passed, became rowdier and noisier. They danced more energetically. The girls' shoulder straps slipped down, their hair came undone and fell in disorder over their faces. Unsteady young men cut in on dancing couples with commanding authority. Guests ran after each other, wrestled good-naturedly, laughed uproariously at some joke. At one point, a beautiful dark girl did a wild solo dance, surrounded by applauding boys with shining eyes. A boy slipped ice cream down a giggling girl's décolletage and, plunging a hand under her dress, tried to retrieve it, while she squirmed, screamed, asked for help, and, weak with laughter, could not really defend herself. A boy wrapped himself up in a tablecloth, grabbed a guitar, tried to set fire to a chair, and said he was Nero. Another boy diligently poured whisky into flower vases, saying: "It's good for them." Everybody was having a wonderful time.

A little later embracing couples filled each step of the carpeted stairway. Girls sat lovingly on boys' knees, here and there. More couples disappeared behind the well-clipped hedges in the garden, filled the parked automobiles or invaded the upstairs bedrooms. I found a couple in a bathroom, oblivious to their surroundings, he proudly sitting on the throne with a hurt expression on his face and she, humbly on her knees in front of him, pleading: "You know, Jimmy, I didn't mean it. . . . I'll never do it again." I apologized hurriedly, shut the door, and went into the open air looking for necessary solitude. At one point a happy riot started by the swimming pool. Boys were pushing each other into it fully clothed, or jumped in spontaneously to show they were not afraid to spoil their clothes and turn their starched shirts into wet rags. By and by, the dancing couples in the living room and the garden dwindled to the resigned few who had found nothing better to do. The music became desultory and limp, most of the servants disappeared. Here and there a few drunks had already passed out on sofas or on the floor. A pale boy on the verge of collapse was held up like a puppet by a charitable friend who was trying to make him walk up and down a garden path.

A few cars were still arriving. In one of them was Ann. She came with a group of gay young people who had heard about our party at another party, smaller and less expensive, no doubt, and had decided to look in on ours. Most of them were tight. When Ann saw me, she deliberately thrust her arm in mine, and said urgently: "Luigi, you aren't drunk, are you? You must help me. You must get me home. Please. I can't stand it one more minute." How did she know my name was Luigi, how did she know I did not drink, how did she know I would do anything for her? Feminine intuition, no doubt. I reassured her, went looking for James to get the key to his car, and found him tightly enlaced with an unknown red-haired Clara Bow on a sofa in the library. He gave me the key, winking broadly, and said: "What are you up to, eh? I told you stags had more choice and better luck. . . . Don't worry about me. I'll get home somehow, or I won't go home at all." And went back to kissing the very low creamy décolletage of his Clara Bow, who lay back on the sofa, limp, moaning a little, with her eyes closed and her arms abandoned.

Ann clung in silence to my right arm as we drove away, which made shifting gears a little difficult. I said nothing either. I did not ask her what or whom she was running away from or where she lived. I clutched the steering wheel hard so as not to let her see my hands trembled a little, and drove slowly, carefully, steadily, as if I were transporting a Murano glass statue. Whenever I could, I glanced at her sideways. Sometimes her profile appeared and vanished rhythmically in the light of street lamps. She looked tired, relieved, and a little *décoiffée,* but more beautiful than I had ever thought. She smelled of good soap, of well-washed hair, of healthy skin. I dismissed several times the diabolical temptation to stop the car on a dark and lonely side road, as I would have done with any other girl. Maybe I was afraid she might have resented it. Maybe I was more afraid she might have liked it. And why take one cheap chance, why try for a few improbable minutes of bliss, when what I really wanted was the rest of our lives?

When I reached her house, she let go of my arm, relaxed, and sighed gratefully. I got out, opened the car door on her side, bowed slightly like a uniformed chauffeur, and said: "Here you are, Ann." She did not ask how I knew her name was Ann and where she lived. She merely said: "You were wonderful. I'll always remember this." We walked together up the few steps to her front door. I watched her turn the key in the lock and could only stupidly say: "Good night, Ann, sweet dreams." She turned around and smiled. She was smaller than I thought. Her head only reached my nose. She put a finger to her lips, kissed it, and stamped it gently on my mouth, a very American gesture. Then she asked me, "Please call me up tomorrow," and vanished.

Chapter 12

Of COURSE, the really big background story of that summer, as it had been for several years past, possibly the biggest since the fall of Adam, the event future historians would describe and analyze at length, I never had to write about. It was the profound and vaguely sacrilegious transformation of man's life on earth. This revolution rumbled on like distant thunder and lightning behind the landscape. It changed the meaning of words, gave new significance to old gestures, insensibly modified everybody's life. Everybody—well, almost everybody—around me seemed not only to have been freed from want, exactly in accordance with original American expectations and the Founding Fathers' promises, but actually to be getting richer and richer every successive day, and to be looking forward with tranquillity to an ever-multiplying income down the coming years and decades, forever and ever. What was bizarre was that nobody appeared particularly surprised or shocked by the phenomenon. Simple people I knew, even the Lithuanian tobacconist, the Italian cobbler and shoeshiner, the Irish real estate agent, the high school French teacher, talked as a matter of course about buying soon more luxurious houses, more powerful cars, rare fur coats, and complicated household appliances, mostly on the installment plan so as to enjoy them in a hurry and pay for them at leisure; planned to give more automobiles to wives and children; meditated on new magical investments; studied grand-ducal tours of Europe, and discussed ambitious and expensive futures for themselves and all their descendants.

None of those I knew, of course, questioned the fact that he was not getting rich because he had worked harder, come out on top, beaten competitors, or created, founded, discovered, or invented something new, bigger, and better. Most of them had simply put what money they had saved into the Stock Exchange and had plunged into debt up to their chins in order to gamble for higher stakes, all or nothing. "Gamble" was surely not the exact word. It was a fabulous lottery in which every ticket seemed to win. Every afternoon these people whipped open the paper at the financial page, eagerly but not anxiously, as casually as one looks at the thermometer on a fine day, in order to reassure themselves, absolutely unnecessarily, that everything was still all right, that in conformity with the new inexorable course of things they had become measurably wealthier during the last twenty-four hours.

I was obliged to admit that the Americans had finally found, for the first time in millennia, the secret of abolishing poverty. To be sure, they had not yet completed their task. There still were pockets of destitution, hunger, and misery, which I as a reporter often had to look at with my own eyes. The President himself had warned his country-men with statesman-like prudence: "We have not yet reached the goal, but we shall soon, with the help of God, be in sight of the day when poverty will be banished from this Nation." The phenomenon was exhilarating, to be sure, but somewhat unsettling. For one thing, it threatened to make most of the Americans' own ancestral wisdom and traditional virtues grotesque and meaningless, the dodder-ing prattling of old folk, as for instance Thoreau's famous advice to "cultivate poverty like a garden herb, sage." It also threatened to make venerable, God-dictated lines in the Holy Book sound foolishly obsolete, lines like "The poor always ye have with you"; "He that giveth unto the poor shall not lack"; "A good name is rather to be chosen than great riches"; "The poor shall never cease out of the land." To whom would the poor's share of the Kingdom of God belong when they were definitely no longer with us? Who would be left to go through the needle's eye when everybody was turned into a millionaire fat camel?

These were by no means idle speculations. The Bible had notoriously been, together with the search for plenty and the hope of a new innocent society, one of the greatest motive forces in the Rise of the American Civilization, as powerful as the Koran in the Arabs' triumphal sweep from Mecca to Roncesvalles. Its words echoed in famous pro-nouncements of American history, its rhythms breathed in the writing of great American essayists, orators, and poets when they tried to rise to solemn and inspired heights. Maybe Lincoln's "fourscore and seven years ago" is a memory of the Psalms' "threescore years and ten." But I was astonished, in those proudly pragmatic, incredulous, and scientific years, to see how the ghost of the Book still haunted the United States. It was to be found in the night table of almost all hotel rooms for the consolation, reassurance, and possible redemption of sinful travelers. It had been so much read in the past that it survived even among the impious in the form of proverbial wisdom and familiar idioms.

This I noticed particularly, because in Italy the Old Testament was practically unknown, few families had a copy, and it was usually quoted by priests in hurried incomprehensible Latin and by them only. Americans quoted (and still quote) the Book without stopping to think where the words came from, words which are broken-up refuse on the beach of history: "holier than thou," "eye to eye," "beat swords into plowshares," "grind the faces of the poor," "man does not live by bread alone," "the skin of one's teeth," "the root of the matter," "out of the mouths of babes and sucklings," "the apple of the eye," "lick the dust," "eat, drink, and be merry." "We hanged our harps upon the willows" had possibly generated a cowboy's song. Even some titles of contemporary books or plays, surely written by ungodly or skeptical authors, were taken from the Bible as stones cut from an old abandoned quarry, such as *The Little Foxes, Green Pastures,* or *Absalom Absalom.*

In fact, America's greatness was almost solely rooted in old Biblical virtues, which had been indispensable for facing dangers, and, above all, poverty: resolution, loyalty, courage, sobriety, a sense of duty, tenacity, prudence, moderation, thrift, love of one's neighbor, and fortitude. Could the fading of the Book as an inspiration for all seasons, could universal wealth and the abolition of risks, fatally weaken, one day, the moral fiber of the Nation? Could an impious and rich America remain for long the stubborn, staunch, brave, and hopeful country it had been when it was poor and pious? If the moral fiber weakened, what could take its place? Avarice, the hunger for power, psychoanalysis, transcendental meditation?

Seemingly forgetful of all this, Americans enjoyed their proliferating prosperity, which made them if not always and thoroughly happy, at least unhappy for new and expensive reasons. They thought they had it made. They saw no menacing clouds in the sky. Judging from the advertisements, one of the few reliable windows through which a young foreigner could spy American life, among the personal problems still worrying them in the year 1929 seemed to be the fear of exhaling miasmatic breath, elegantly called "halitosis" by the ad writers, of which not even one's best friend would warn one, that of not having read enough of Harvard President Charles William Eliot's five-foot shelf of essential books and not being able to scintillate in erudite conversation, or not playing the piano at a party like Sergei Vasilievich Rachmaninoff ("They laughed when I sat down at the piano . . ."). Possibly, also, the United States had no fear of relaxing or weakening because there was the rest of the world to think about. It had thought about it from the beginning, but it was now more and more concentrating its attention on it. The rest of the world was still entangled in old problems, paralyzed by hunger, stupidity, inefficiency, ignorance, bad sanitation, lack of ordinary common sense; tenaciously fighting these vices and shortcomings, the

Americans could make money and still keep their virtues well honed. That was probably one of the reasons why so many of them were considering with commiseration and a sense of responsibility Central and South America, the West Indies, Europe, China, Japan, and the rest of Asia.

❦

The signs were everywhere, particularly noticeable to a practically penniless young foreigner. Immense billboards, lit up at night, visible for miles, and the brilliantly colored advertising pages of slick magazines I thumbed through in the barbershop showed stupendous auburn-haired beauties, dressed for a court ball, with tiaras on their heads, and tall men with long round chins and glossy hair proudly sitting in their new town cars behind uniformed chauffeurs, showing off resplendent new bathrooms, or fingering all kinds of expensive and superfluous goods. Low and shining automobiles, their interiors preciously *capitonnés,* often glided by like gondolas in the summer night, loaded with ladies, bejeweled like miraculous Madonnas in celebrated sanctuaries, escorted by gentlemen with top hats and white plaster-of-Paris shirts, on their way to some legendary party, east or west of the little town. Yachts, all lit up like merry-go-rounds, sailed majestically on the inky waters. Once when I was waiting on a station platform, I saw a private railroad car, one of the supreme marks of wealth at the time, go by at the tail end of a slowly moving train on the other track. The interior was all Louis XV *boiseries,* peach velvet curtains, French prints, and pink lampshades with fringes. In the dim light I could see a young couple convulsively enlaced on a couch like two wrestlers on the mat. They had not had the time to pull down the blind, or thought it unnecessary. Only unknown and unimportant people like me could see them anyway.

How consoling, convincing, and pacifying were the Americans' explanations of how they and their nation were well on their way definitely to solving the fundamental problems of man. I was not spared them, but did not mind the repetitions. I drank them in. These questions were passionately debated by everybody all the time: "Can stocks be priced higher than the capitalization of their dividends and why?" (The answers were respectively "Yes" and "Why not?") Theoretical exegeses had been simplified to the level of a catechism for children. People repeated them to me politely and patiently, with the tranquil arrogance and compassionate superiority of missionaries describing the only true religion and sure way to reach Heaven to a naked savage with a ring through his nose and feathers in his hair. They generously did not think it was my fault, after all, if I had been born in a backward and ignorant country like Italy. What comforted me was not the impeccable logic of their arguments, which I knew by heart, but their unquestioning faith, the faith of teachers demonstrating obvious and incontrovertible theorems. There was absolutely nothing mysterious about the whole thing, they assured me. All I had to do, to take advantage of it, was follow the instructions, ride the wave, and leave the rest to the American people.

I particularly liked to listen to an old man I often met in the speakeasy across the street. He was, he announced proudly, a retired businessman. He had run factories, holding companies, banks, and vast commercial enterprises. He did not look, however, as a retired businessman looked in those days. In fact, he looked seedy, with a wrinkled and dusty suit, was often unshaven and always a little drunk. I imagined he had gone broke right after the war, before the great new American era had dawned. Nevertheless, he did not complain of his ill-fortune (he never mentioned it), but was the most enthusiastic, almost fanatic, champion of the American system I had met. He explained the whole thing to me with tears in his eyes, at great length, again and again, practically in the same words, every time he could get hold of me. (The poor, I had discovered, were for some reason firmer in their faith at the time than the rich, probably because the poor wanted desperately to believe in a miraculous future, and the rich had more abundant reasons to be scared.) The old man was so eloquent I imagined he was dredging up from his uncertain memory old inspirational talks he had delivered years before at luncheon clubs. His strong point (he emphasized it by punching the table at the appropriate passages) was proving that America's prodigious prosperity was here to stay, an enduring self-perpetuating phenomenon, a definitive turning point in history. It had not come from the sky. It was the inevitable and definitive product of a moral, political, and economic mechanism the people had been erecting and perfecting from the beginning.

Prosperity, he pointed out, possibly echoing a famous book, could not vanish because it was first of all solidly founded on Christian teachings, more precisely on Jesus Christ's personal example. Had He not said that what He was about was "his father's business"? "Business" was the word he used, the right word. "Read the Gospel," the old man said. "You'll find many precious tips on how to get ahead in the world, tips to be adopted by each man or, in our case, a whole nation. Take this one: 'Whosoever shall compel thee to go a mile,' Jesus said, 'go with him in twain.' What could be clearer? It means: do more than you're required, don't watch the clock, surprise your boss by delivering twice as much as you're paid to deliver. That's exactly what the United States has done, deliver twice as much as expected. All business is God's business, young man, all work is worship."

But that was not all. Only in America had the Gospel notoriously shaped the people's character and the fundamental laws. The people's character and the Constitution, which was the result of the Founding Fathers' and the people's character anyway, had started an inexorable course of events which, with only occasional setbacks, culminated in the great Hoover prosperity. It was the Americans' impatient search for the new, the better, the different, their capacity to dare and conceive on a colossal scale, that had made their country great and would one day solve all the problems of the world. He broke down the process thus: Democracy, love of neighbor, and self-interest obliged the owners to pay the highest possible wages; high wages begot mass consumption; this made mass production inevitable; and the rest—unrelenting technological progress, efficiency, persuasive advertising, standardization, et cetera— logically followed. Cost of production and prices shrank every year, things became cheaper and cheaper, thus allowing everybody to afford more and more goods. "There is nothing mysterious about all this," he always said. "Nothing will break the chain as long as men love their fellow men, desire more and better things for themselves and others, and are willing to work hard for them. And men are made in such a way that they will always want more and more things and will work harder and harder to get them."

The functioning of the whole system, he liked to repeat, downing glasses of rotgut and belching politely behind the back of his hand, was guaranteed at the moment by the presence of Herbert Hoover in the White House. The President was a typical American hero. He had started life as a devout and penniless Quaker orphan from a frontier farm, studied hard, worked hard, made a pile of money in his profession, beat all competitors, and shown himself a peerless engineer, organizer, financier, and administrator, then turned his time and energy to philanthropy and public service on a world-wide scale. He even refused the President's honorarium, once elected. He knew how the mechanism worked. He knew America's prosperity was based, like his own, on the people's rugged individualism and virtues tempered in the fiery forge of history. Americans had learned greatness on the frontier. Hoover was on the lookout for signs of coming storms, warned his countrymen against corrupting temptations, studied statistics daily, oiled the wheels of the economy, and saw to it they would never slow down. "Every man can be like Mr. Hoover. You, too," the old businessman assured me. "Someday the people of the world will wake up and realize how stupid they were to grovel in poverty. Luigi, you're lucky you're alive, young, and in America this very year."

Of course, cynical and incredulous Europeans, the writers, journalists, diplomats, occasional bankers and rare businessmen who visited Father in his office or dined at our house, had other explanations for the phenomenon. The incredible prosperity was, to be sure, the result of the Americans' conception of life, their virtues, and of their maniacal and suicidal passion for hard work, but also (and perhaps principally) the unmerited product of luck. The people had stumbled on a wealth of incredible and mostly unexpected resources on their land, minerals, forests, navigable rivers, inland waterways, natural ports, vast fertile prairies, such as could be found nowhere else in the world. They had proceeded to depredate most of what could be depredated without a thought for the future, as an army loots a conquered foreign country. They had, furthermore, exploited for more than a century millions of slaves and ill-paid helot immigrants, who still did most of the hard and dirty work.

Now, when Europe was in ruins, had lost the flower of its youth in the trenches, had sacrificed its reserves and plunged into immense unpayable debts to finance the bloody war, was paralyzed by inflation, torn by revolution and civil conflicts, the Americans, behind the safe fortifications of their tariff walls, had ungenerously exploited the favorable historical moment as ruthlessly and heedlessly as they had looted their own resources. They were demanding hungry and ruined Europe to pay its immense debts, which was impossible and unjust. Had not the money been spent to buy weapons and food to win the common war? Had not the Europeans contributed infinitely more corpses? How much was a corpse worth in gold? Certainly, the Americans had fed the starving Europeans, both allies and enemies, but probably more to assuage their conscience, which would have troubled them if millions had died or gone Bolshevik, or to keep alive a debtor who, when dead, could surely no longer pay. The gold of the world was now being stored in underground caves in the United States. One day, doubtless, the Americans would own it all. That day, international commerce would become impossible, as impossible as gambling after one of the players has absconded with all the chips.

Would the Hoover prosperity last? Most foreigners (and, I must add, a few wise and prudent Americans) were afraid the boom would suddenly burst one day, like the tulip craze in Holland, the South Sea Bubble, John Law's miraculous multiplication of paper money, or the Florida real estate market, which had collapsed a year or two before. All booms burst at some point.

I was exalted, awed, perplexed, and sometimes frightened. Feverish exhortations reached me from everywhere, to think big, aim high, hitch my wagon to a star, gamble on America's fabulous future, not sell America short, Be a Bull on America, come out on top, make a pile, bring home the bacon, knock 'em dead, go in and win. I could not escape them. They were part of the air I breathed. "Be king in your dreams," Carnegie had said. "Say to yourself, My place is on the top." Such imperious commands were to be heard particularly at the noisy boosters' club meetings I had to cover every week. Politicians and clergymen talked of practically nothing else. Essays and articles described the rocket rise of successful Americans from miserable farm or tenement to their first million dollars. I heard it said with admiration of a prominent financier: "A good man. He inherited fifty million dollars and ran it into a fortune." All a poor man needed was an idea, tenacity, drive, and, if possible, the right little woman. Essays and articles solemnly insisted that the amassing of great wealth was not only the one worthwhile goal in a man's life but (as the seedy retired businessman in the speakeasy explained) a philanthropic duty. Everybody agreed there was nothing esoteric about the process. Only the fools, the lazy, the inept, the irresponsible, and the egotist refused to face the challenge. They had no excuse. Cheap handbooks, as simple to follow as cookbooks for new brides, taught everybody in simple language how to develop their dormant talents and the tricks necessary to make a packet quickly, possibly in their youth, in order to spend the rest of their life fishing. One could learn for a few dollars how to speak masterfully in public, be irresistible, dominate a meeting, mesmerize superiors or opponents, make friends, sell everything to everybody, and, in the end, with the first million in the bank, spot prodigious investment opportunities, investments that multiplied themselves like amoebas. "You too," said the ads, "can be" one impossible thing or another, not someday but "tomorrow." People hopefully bought these books by the million, as true believers buy sacred relics or bottles of miraculous water at a sanctuary.

The wisdom of the rich was respectfully recorded everywhere. "We have always acted instinctively," Walter Lippmann noted at the time, "on the theory that golden thoughts flow in a continuous stream from the minds of millionaires." A torrent of well-fabricated novels, plays, magazine stories, and films concerned themselves exclusively and lovingly with the millionaires, real or imaginary, old and wise but preferably young and damned, with humble men who had seen their opportunity and grabbed it on the wing. They were the heroes of the contemporary world. "One had to be a knight in the Middle Ages, and an aristocrat at Versailles. One has to be a rich businessman in the

United States today," I read somewhere. The recording of the reckless conquest of power, fortune, and fame, of the lives, hobbies, parties, Homeric squabbles, and erratic passions of the rich, was carried out (faithfully, I presumed) with the worshipful admiration with which monks long before had written about the lives of saints, or Greek poets sung the rivalries and loves of Olympian gods.

Ordinary rules and laws clearly no longer applied to rich Americans. They could do no wrong. Was Zeus immoral when he transformed himself (as many American millionaires were more or less doing for similar purposes, according to the tabloids) into a shower of gold so as to penetrate a pretty girl's bedroom? There was, of course, a great fundamental difference between Olympus and the United States. No ordinary mortal could become a god. Every American could become one. That was the great American achievement. Everybody could seduce Danaë. In fact, it was his fault if he did not. The poor had only themselves to blame for their seedy destitution.

What did I do to conquer power, wealth, and fame? I was doing everything a man could. I followed instructions. I studied the proper books, got up early, improved myself, combed my hair, shined my shoes, brushed my teeth twice a day, acquired a magnetic glance, trained myself to show confidence, studied how successful people had reached the top, wrote short stories in my spare time, read famous authors to capture their secret formulas. I interviewed all the great writers I could reach, those who lived nearby. I once asked Ring Lardner how he had achieved fame. He was not very helpful. "I don't know. By not thinking about it, I guess. By not asking famous writers foolish questions," he said. He was drunk. I had been persistently warned that in every man's life comes a unique moment when the goddess Fortuna taps him on the shoulder almost imperceptibly, a moment known locally as "the break," when the merry-go-round horse comes closest to the golden ring. I always kept my eyes open for "the break," like a bird watcher waiting for the flight of a rare specimen. I silenced within myself the doubts and skepticism of the Old World, which would have dragged me down, if I had paid attention to them, like cannon balls tied to a shrouded body in the sea. I wanted to be bold, adventurous, undaunted like an American. Mr. Clemens seemed satisfied with my work. When I went by his desk, he beamed on me through his pince-nez glasses and said, "Luigi, you know how to read and write all right," rubbed his hands, and chuckled. Jack, the red-haired Irish managing editor, only three years older than I, was putting my name at the top of more stories. "That'll make you famous," he assured me sardonically.

I was drunk with hope but deeply discouraged at the same time. For one thing, I never seemed to get the "break." Sometimes the fear assailed me that maybe I had got it already, perhaps more than once, but had not recognized it. The tide of gold had not reached me yet. The manna which seemed to rain indiscriminately on everybody was for some reason not raining on me. I had to get along with my miserable fifteen dollars a week. I missed most of the fun. I had to borrow a rusty old car from a friend whenever I needed one, never had that extra five-dollar bill to buy orchids, pay for a sumptuous dinner for a stupendous girl, lobsters, partridges, and champagne, or light a cigar with, as young men did in the movies. I was haunted

237

by the suspicion that the party next door to the one I had been invited to, the party I could see and hear through the open windows and the hedges (young people dancing in the garden under the Venetian lanterns), was always the one I should not have missed. Or, until I met Ann, that the girl who flashed by in another man's car in the dusk was infinitely more desirable than the one in my arms.

What did I expect? I told myself sagely I was only twenty years old and had been working only a few weeks. It was my first job. Surely I did not imagine a scout from the big newspapers or famous magazines across the river would suddenly notice my occasional bylines, ask me for an interview, and urge me to accept a fabulous offer overnight, as scouts picked baseball rookies from provincial clubs in the movies. Life, I told myself, was not a movie. Nevertheless, I hoped it was. Admitting all this, that I could not expect to become rich and famous in just a month, I could not help feeling somehow excluded and neglected. The few powerful short stories I sent to magazines bounced right back, surely unread, by return mail. When I timidly asked Mr. Clemens for a raise, he answered, "So soon?" and laughed. Naturally, young men starting out in life had always been impatient and suspicious. But these, I knew, were not ordinary times, resigned and dreary European times, but the new miraculous American era, the era when the ancient dream of an abundant life and happiness for everybody had come true, or almost. Inevitably, the urgent advice and admonitions to achieve success, the sight of so many people doing it, made me suspect I was not made to live at such a time, that maybe I was a lazy, inept, irresponsible fool.

I tried to console myself, saying (without really believing it) that money and fame were not everything, and I looked for other excuses. Maybe I was excluded from the universal blessings because I was a foreigner, an Italian, surrounded by an invisible wall of prejudice and hostility. Evidently, Italian young men really had only a few careers open to them in the United States. They could become gangsters, priests, singers, or sports champions. Outside of these, there was only mediocrity, and none of these careers fitted me. I had not discovered the passwords that opened all doors, I had not penetrated the secrets so many Americans around me seemed to know as a matter of course, the secrets the guidebooks to success could not disclose, because, clearly, if their authors had known them, they would have been doing more profitable things than writing cheap instructions for the incapable and the defeated.

"Italy," Ernest, the city editor, told me once affectionately, "you always talk about Italy. Forget it. What has Italy got that the United States does not have, more and better? Do you realize that one big New York bank, not the biggest, mind you, you name it, could buy your goddamn country tomorrow morning if it wanted to, museums, masterpieces, ruins, Pompeii, Venice, St. Peter's, the Pope, the King, Mussolini, the Army, the Navy, everything, without feeling the strain?" In his eyes I was still a paleolithic fossil, as archaic as the Irpinian peasants whose Eden on the stinking garbage dumps I had repeatedly described. He wanted to convert me and help me. He did not have to convert me. I was already converted.

Chapter 13

"ONE OF YOUR COUNTRYMEN, Mr. Smith-a," Judy said over the phone with a bored voice. "Must absolutely see you. Says it's urgent and personal."

It was a little after half-past two of a warm afternoon late in June or early in July. I was alone in the darkened office, under the slowly moving fan, in the muffled thunder of the rolling press. I had just returned from a hurried lunch, Manhattan clam chowder and crackers ten cents, apple pie ten cents, coffee five cents, and, feet on my desk, like a veteran American newspaperman, like a police reporter from *The Front Page*, a cigarette in my mouth (two packs for a quarter), was examining one of the first copies of the day's paper, one of those faint copies which look as if printed by ghosts for ghosts. I was preparing to savor slowly, with admiration, but also, as usual, with some apprehension, a big story of mine spread on the front page. I feared that, as usual, it would turn out to be not as good in cold print as I had thought it was a couple of hours before when I had written it. I was also wondering how Ann would like it.

Local Italians came to see me once in a while. They all said their business was urgent and personal. They usually wanted some advice, occasionally gave me tips for what they hoped would be a good story that would destroy one of their enemies, wanted an announcement or a classified ad published, which they called an *articolo*. Some of them occasionally asked me to write a letter for them in English or Italian. They were usually people I knew vaguely, the cobbler, the iceman, the vegetable dealer, a waiter, the grocer, the shoeshine man. When this countryman of mine walked in, I could not quite place him. He was a little thin man in his early forties, with black shining hair as curly as lamb's wool, a dapper suit, yellow shoes the color of geese feet, a phosphorescent necktie adorned with a fake diamond pin, rings on his fingers, and a cheap straw hat in his hands. He advanced ceremoniously, a little too ceremoniously, smiling and bowing to me.

He told me his name was Mike something and we shook hands. Sicilian accent, I thought. I had a vague feeling his face was not new. I had seen him somewhere before. *"Buongiorno,"* I said. "Sit down. *Che cosa posso fare per lei?* [What can I do for you?]" The question, I knew, was too brutally brusque for a Sicilian. With Sicilians one must always go through long preliminaries, exchange flattery, talk about the weather, the deterioration of morals, the beauty of the old country, the execrable taste of watery American coffee, life in general, and then, as slowly and guardedly as Indian scouts in the woods, approach the point. The real subject, however, must never be explicitly mentioned. Each concept must be carefully hidden behind elegant circumlocutions and euphemisms. But then I was Milanese, matter-of-fact, businesslike, in a hurry, a *Front Page* journalist, possibly a future American. I could not afford to waste time with archaic provincial subtleties.

Naturally, I did not expect him to blurt out and tell me clearly, at once, in so many words, what request he had in mind. I sat back in my chair and waited. He spoke the curious pidgin of the Sicilian immigrants of those years, the native dialect mixed at random with Italian and American expressions, as well as Italianized American words. Many of these were incomprehensible. They often had an entirely different meaning in Italian. *"Cotto,"* for instance, Italian for "cooked," meant "coat"; *"olivetta,"* "little olive," meant "elevated railroad"; *"gli sciabolatori del re Erode"* did not mean, as one would think, "King Herod's swordsmen," but "the shovelmen of the railroad," et cetera.

He inevitably started by praising me, my extreme youth, the eminent position I had achieved on the paper, which I owed to my capacity and my merits and not to somebody's protection. He praised my English prose. I concluded the little town was part of his territory, he was a local, tried to read the paper, had heard of my work, and knew vaguely who I was. Then he started praising my father, one of the glories of Italy, a great man, *molto rispettato,* a friend of Kings and Presidents. Finally, he approached very prudently and circuitously what could be an answer to my question. He wanted to know whether, by any chance, my father needed a handyman, a *domestico* in the house, a very loyal, faithful, devoted, and reliable henchman, a sort of bodyguard. He could do everything, cook, wash, shine floors, shoot straight. "You?" I asked. He nodded and said

"Yes," reluctantly. My question had once again been too abrupt. Obviously, he had expected me to fence lightly around the problem of the *domestico*'s identity for a minute or so.

At that point I was struck by lightning and suddenly remembered who he was. I had seen him a few times around some of the speakeasies and roadhouses. He was presumably an inspector of sorts, sent by his organization to make sure that none of the beer and whisky was purchased from the competition. Evidently, what he was looking for that afternoon was a good hiding place. He needed it in a hurry, one that was far from Sicilian eyes. There was no better place than the house of a distinguished *Settentrionale* above suspicion. Nobody would look for him there. Unfortunately, my mother had sworn that her house was not a station in the Sicilian underground, that if one more of those dubious and dangerous fugitives had to be sheltered, after our experience with the little cook, she would go back to Italy forever by the first boat. Besides, none of us particularly liked bizarre Sicilian food, pasta with sardines and wild fennel. And father needed no bodyguard.

I shook my head sadly but firmly, and said, no, we did not need a *domestico,* not even a very faithful one, I was sorry, I could do nothing for him, and turned back to my pale newspaper and my front-page story. Ernest, the city editor, had just come back from lunch, his straw hat on his head and a toothpick in his mouth, and was also looking at the new paper. He was not listening to our conversation. He would have understood nothing if he had, and, if he had understood, he would not have been interested. Nevertheless, Mike kept glancing nervously at him. He realized time was short, as more people would arrive within minutes.

This made him break down, as much, anyway, as a Sicilian can. He became almost explicit. He conveyed to me the information that he needed work badly, that very day, did not have a bed to sleep in, was hungry, unemployed, anguished, at the end of his tether, and had I do not remember how many children to feed. He was, of course, too well dressed and too well fed to be at the end of anything. The brilliantine in his curly hair, the rings, and the pin were not signs of ultimate destitution. I knew enough, however, not to contradict him. I nodded without smiling, full of sympathy, as if I believed him.

He was obviously scared and, as the minutes passed, getting more and more nervous. So was I. He almost jumped when Mr. Clemens showed his pale face at the door and said hello. Mike repeatedly dried his forehead and his hat band with his handkerchief. His ears twitched. He looked at me. I knew (I also knew he knew I knew) he must have been in a desperate fix, possibly a matter of life and death, if he had turned to a complete stranger for help, and to a boy at that, and not, as a Sicilian must do, to one of his relatives. Evidently, he could not do that, did not want to endanger them, condemn some of his parents, grandparents, uncles, brothers, cousins, *compari,* or sons, blood of his blood, to death. It could also be that, for some reason, his family was after him, too. And why, if he had betrayed his own, did not he turn to his enemies for protection, as all traitors do? I imagined he must have committed one of those unforgivable Sicilian crimes, an *infamità* so serious that everybody must condemn him, his family, his allies as well as his enemies; one of those mysterious violations of the unwritten code to punish which rivalries, feuds, and gang wars were temporarily suspended; one of those abom-

244

inable sins for which Sicilian fathers strangle their own sons with their own hands. Probably squealed to the police. I studied his face but asked no questions. One never does. It is always useless or dangerous. If you ever got a straight answer (which is almost impossible), you would suddenly be in the embarrassing possession of unwanted knowledge that might endanger your very life. You would be turned into a *tiro-a-segno* target.

What could I do with him? "Let me see," I said thoughtfully, to gain time. My duty as an honest man, a future American citizen, was, of course, to turn him in immediately. How? Ernest had by then gone out to the printing shop, I could not use my phone in front of Mike, but I could casually stroll over to Judy and whisper to her to call my friend the sergeant at the police station. Would Mike give me time to do that? Would he shoot me or make a dash for the street door? And what would I turn him in for? I knew nothing about him. He had admitted nothing. Maybe (as is often the case) he had no police record, there was no warrant out for him, nobody knew he existed or wanted him. Suppose he was a police informer and was freed after a few hours. What would happen to me? But then again he might like to be turned in. Jails are safe. I could not ask him, of course. The question "How would you like to be locked up?" would have been once again too abrupt. To formulate it with the proper gradual *convenances* and to get some sort of an answer would have taken us at least the rest of the day and part of the night.

At this point I began to think reluctantly, with some shame, of my duty to myself. What could I get from him if I found him a safe refuge? I allowed myself to dream. Maybe I could gain fabulous contacts with the underworld, meet some of its legendary leaders, discover some of their secrets. The idea was absurd, of course. He did not look important enough. Nevertheless, I saw myself, as in a movie, writing a devastating exposé in several installments for one of the large and wealthy magazines. This would make me instantly famous, pay me enough money and allow me to leave the country for a while. I could buy a diamond ring, propose to Ann, buy a car to take her around, a splendid car with outside exhaust pipes. Maybe this was the "break" I had to recognize, the open door to success. Why hesitate? Were not fame and money what I should have wanted?

He was talking to me. He was imperceptibly pleading: "Help me, *per l'amor di Dio.* I will recommend you to Santa Rosalia. . . . If you help me, you'll have my gratitude forever, that of my brothers, my sons, my friends. . . ." Yes, I thought, Santa Rosalia was a good reliable saint to have on your side, but what about the enmity of Mike's enemies? Did anybody know he was coming to see me? Did anybody see him come in? Was he followed? What would his enemies eventually do to discover where I had hidden him? Kidnap me? Torture me? He went on in a solemn, reassuring low whisper: "If you have an enemy, just let me know. You'll not have that enemy for long." I had heard of this promise before. I knew it did not really mean much. It was rhetorical, part of the Sicilian grandiloquent humbug. Besides, I had no enemy. Twenty-year-old boys from Milan, aspiring Americans, working hard, had no enemies, and, even if they had, would fight them honorably and would not have them traitorously mown down by machine guns from a passing car. I was irritated to discover that I was nevertheless stupidly thrilled by the momentary feeling of sham omnipotence. For a second I imagined the surprised expression on the face of Mr. Clemens, or the particularly arrogant rival I had at that time for Ann's heart, or one of my nastier professors, if suddenly faced with an avenging gun.

All these confused ideas and the slowly moving hands on the clock made me jittery, almost as jittery as Mike. "Thank you," I answered politely, as if I were refusing a drink. "I'll think about it, if I ever have an enemy." Evidently I had no alternative. It was absolutely necessary to hide the man. It was the only thing to do. But where? I quickly thought of and discarded two or three places, the old prizefighter's houseboat, the painter's livery stable. . . .

Suddenly, the perfect refuge came to my mind. Nobody would find him there. "Can you work as a *contadino?*" I asked. He admitted, as enthusiastically as a stone-faced Sicilian can, without raising his voice, that yes, he had been a *contadino*—a peasant—in his youth, at Marineo, his birthplace, not far from Palermo, where his father had run a small farm. As a boy, he had taken care of sheep, pigs, vineyards, olive trees . . . . "Vegetables?" I asked. Of course, he assured me with shining eyes, cabbages, beans, onions, garlic, eggplants, zucchini, peas, broccoli, lettuce, peppers, tomatoes . . .

I interrupted the nostalgic inventory. I explained that out on the garbage dumps, far from anywhere and anything, a few Italian families lived in shacks and grew vegetables. I told him I would take him there. They were good people, friends of mine. They might take him in. He could help them in their work, help defend them from intruders, and, since he was such a good shot, kill rats on the run.

"What part of Italy do these people come from?" he

asked suspiciously. "Irpinia? Where is that? Far from Sicily?" He had never heard of Irpinia nor of Avellino, its capital. I gave him the geographical assurances he needed. Yes, far from Sicily, maybe three hundred miles, and without Sicilian relatives or connections that I knew of. He finally allowed himself to smile. "Good," he said. "When do we go?"

I instructed him to leave the office through the printing shop entrance, where there was great confusion at that moment (a lot of boys were there with their bikes to get the freshly printed copies to distribute). Nobody would notice him. These, of course, were strange instructions for a simple unemployed innocent man looking only for work and a room, which is what I should have pretended to believe him to be, but I had no time to waste. I told him to meet me after sundown at a spot not far from the only gasoline station on the road nearest the garbage dumps. He said, *"Bacio le mani"* ("I kiss your hands"), and vanished, which was another form of Sicilian humbug, of course, as he could not kiss my hands in a small American newspaper office without provoking incredulous and ribald reactions.

When he had gone, Ernest asked me idly: "What the hell did this countryman of yours want?" "Nothing," I answered. "You Italians sure talk a lot and make a lot of gestures to say nothing," he said. This, of course, was not true. Sicilians rarely wave their hands when they speak.

Later that evening I found Mike where I had told him to be, waiting in the shadow under the railroad tracks, which, at that point, passed overhead on steel trestles. He nodded imperceptibly when I appeared and followed me, some distance behind. We walked for a few minutes (nobody was following us) in the stinking summer night. I introduced him to the Irpinians, who were happy to get one more man to help them, a poor *paesano* far from home, the father of many children, who had no job and no place to sleep. We all dined happily in the miasma of the rotting garbage, the good odor that meant American wealth to the poor truck gardeners. Mike showed them what a good shot he was by striking a rat or two dead on the run. The Irpinians laughed. When I left, he shook my hand and repeated: "Remember, if you have anyone annoying you . . ." He took me aside and gave me the number of a public telephone booth somewhere (Bensonhurst, I think) where I could get news of him if I mentioned my name.

Days later I learned he was gone. I found out from the Irpinians he had worked very hard, enjoyed their food and wine, played with their children, killed a large number of rats, cooked pasta with wild fennel and sardines, and sung lamenting Sicilian dirges. They said he walked once in a while, at night, to the nearest telephone. Then, one evening, he had said goodbye, thanked them all, shaken hands, kissed the children, and left. A voice, answering the telephone number he had given me, told me days later: "Mike is all right. He thanks you. He is in your debt." Obviously, if he was still alive, his crime could not have been a very serious one. Maybe girl trouble.

Chapter 14

My daydreaming was delirious and obsessive, but I firmly kept it vague about the actual details of the future vicissitudes, possible dénouements, and triumphal consummation of our love. My desire for Ann was as painful and persistent as St. Anthony's fire, known as shingles. It never left me. Something had to happen. What? Where? This I knew, that I did not want it to be sordid. One memory haunted me in particular. One night, a friend of mine and I had taken two girls to his house (his parents were away). I was in one bedroom with my girl, a charming, laughing, inexpert but eager little brunette. We were happy and carefree. From the other room came the sounds of wrestling and muted cursing, for hours. At one point we heard what my friend must have considered the ultimate argument that would have convinced the most chaste and stubborn virgin to give up the struggle, a magic formula the possession of which would transform the gauchest man into an irresistible Casanova. He screamed: "What do you think it's for? Only pissing?"

I did not want it to take place in what was then the most common way, in the back of somebody else's parked car, littered with old papers, cigarette butts, chewing-gum wrappers, and empty bottles, while another couple was embracing in the front seat, and all this among heavy alcoholic panting, desperate entreaties, curses stifled by kisses, moans, contortions, acrid smells, and, at the end, viscous handkerchiefs thrown out the window. We had to be alone. I could not even imagine the scene in a borrowed bedroom, the room of a slovenly friend, with its dubious sheets, or the cheap hotel room which had seen the sweating love of unnumbered, ill-washed, and halfhearted couples. No. My Ann was Atalanta, the sacred virgin who ran faster than all her suitors and was so pure that her nakedness defended her like an opaque chiton. It was difficult to imagine a setting that would not have been degrading and sacrilegious.

It had, as the song said, to be love, love in its noblest, most sublime form. It had to be beautiful, honest, trusting love, an immense tenderness flooding us both while an irresistible unknown puppeteer gently moved our naked bodies, taught us untried caresses, and made us one. It had to have an unpremeditated inevitable quality. There should be the ineluctability of a slow landslide, the power of mounting volcanic passion, mine perhaps as evident, prominent, and overbearing as Vesuvius, her own half-concealed under incandescent sands like the *zolfatare* at Pozzuoli, which reveal themselves by almost imperceptible tremors, rare puffs of steam, and sometimes a sudden all-obliterating eruption, followed by deathlike peace.

Sometimes I mentally staged the ecstatic moment outdoors. I wanted heavenly music, Brahms perhaps, a whole symphonic orchestra in the background which only we two could hear, possibly also the roar of a waterfall, and beautifully colored, sweet-smelling, exotic flowers all around us. I placed our embrace on soft grass, against a sunset as beautifully colored as those on American railroad calendars, or under the cold light of the moon, occasionally in pitiless summer sunshine which would reveal the ivory statuette perfections of her body's smallest details. The moral setting gave me more difficulties. How could I prevent shame, regrets, and remorse from tarnishing the sublime moment? (Such emotions still prevailed at the time.) How could we abandon ourselves to our love if I was tormented by the fear of consequences, the suspicion of having defiled the girl I worshiped, and if she imagined for one moment that I was just another Wop smoothly lying his way to Paradise? Evidently, everything would be easy and relaxed if I could imagine our embrace placidly taking place the night after a wedding, in that invisible part of the films which followed the words "The End" and which one privately staged as one walked slowly home. Sacred vows surely exorcised all sordid shadows. But I could not bring myself to imagine such a preposterous thing as our marriage, even a make-believe one, for the time being anyway. What would we eat the next day?

How could I persuade her? Unlike as with Atalanta, who, as everybody knows, was finally brought down when she stupidly stopped to pick up the solid-gold apples Venus had artfully dropped on her course, gold apples would not budge Ann. She was not particularly interested in money. Besides, I had no money. "Wealth, I think," she once said quietly, and I loved her for it, "is important for people without much imagination, particularly the very rich, don't you think? They are right, of course. It fills the ghastly emptiness of their lives. But there are many more precious things. . . . The rich probably neglect them because they are inexpensive. Nothing inexpensive seems worthwhile to them." Not being interested in money did not necessarily mean she could be attracted by a mad adventure of starvation and drudgery with a penniless twenty-year-old boy. She was no ascetic saint. She might have endured a brief period of poverty, but only as a temporary test, I imagined, if she loved a man as Anna Karenina loved Vronsky, or as Virginia loved Paul.

And was I loved by her at all? In her Anglo-Saxon eyes I probably looked interesting and exotic, a curiosity, a young foreigner with whom it was pleasant enough to while away a few hours, even many hours, entertain an *amitié amoureuse,* a more pleasant boy than many loud-voiced jovial college men, a boy with whom one could, at the most, by giving him some hope, maybe experience one day the delicious thrill of going as close as prudently possible to the red flag which signals the thin ice without falling in. And, for my part, was I really determined to seduce her? Was I not also frightened by a reckless irremediable gesture which, however improbably, might have forced rash decisions on us, and swept her and me into years of complications and dismal unhappiness?

Therefore I obliged myself to avoid realistic, concrete, and pedestrian hypotheses in my daydreaming and to content myself with locating our imaginary idyl in dreamland, on an improbable island at times, where we would land after an improbable shipwreck. The island had to be warm, of course, provided with clean running water and soft grass. There would be the waterfall, wonderful flowers, exotic fruits hanging from the trees, and singing birds. Love-making in such a place and in our situation was inevitable, almost obligatory, there being practically nothing else to do. The inevitability of it all would happily exonerate us (me, at least) from all worries, scruples, doubts, and remorse, and her of all will to resist. However, I never allowed myself to go deeply even into this. Evidently, the whole thing was too absurd. Under what circumstances could the two of us have embarked unaccompanied on a ship, preferably a Conrad sailing ship, in the South Pacific? How was it possible to imagine a shipwreck, conveniently close to a suitable uninhabited and paradisiac island, from which we two alone would survive while the weathered sea dogs of the crew succumbed? In fact, when I dreamed of it, I skipped all details, kept the whole thing very nebulous, and allowed myself to contemplate and enjoy only the final scene, the divine embrace.

I played occasionally with another, more sober and plausible alternative dream. If I had become somebody overnight, the journalistic or, better, the literary revelation of the year, I could have faced Ann with sufficient arguments to reassure her. I would have acquired a name. I would have a future. This was by no means as foolish as it might have sounded. It was almost realistic. Had not Scott Fitzgerald managed it only a few years before? Had he not made his own youthful and impossible hopes come true? Other boys were doing it. Alberto Moravia had done it that very year. He had become famous with his first book at the age of twenty-one. If an editor, publisher, or producer had advanced me an adequate sum on the basis of a brilliant idea, I could have bought myself some elegant clothes and the snappy car I dreamed of, say the Stutz Bearcat or the racing white Mercedes or the open black Packard roadster with green leather upholstery which I saw every day in the dealer's window. I could then have entertained Ann in a subtly tasteful way, a Continental European way, and could have kept off richer, taller, better-connected, more enterprising rivals. Having a clear prospective ahead of us, we could have tranquilly anticipated our future happiness without being tortured by worries and remorse. I had discovered that the only real way open for an Italian in the United States to stop being considered exotic was not, as many were trying to do, to speak and dress like an American or Anglicize one's name (Rossi easily became "Ross," Bartolomei "Bartholomew"), but become, if not famous, at least notorious, and possibly also rich. (This I knew the year Frank Sinatra was only eleven years old, the son of an immigrant fireman, and still living in Hoboken.) Therefore, my daydreaming about the supreme ecstatic moment, when I would hold my chaste naked love in my arms, gradually became inextricably enmeshed with another one, older, more persistent and American, that of the sudden revelation of my genius, the conquest of fame, money, and success.

I do not know whether this fixed idea, that only a proper marriage or, in an emergency, a cheap make-believe imitation, in front of some sleepy village judge in the middle of the night, could really liberate two young people in love, who wanted to go to bed together, from anguish and remorse, and make them free to enjoy themselves fully, was, half a century ago, strictly American and Protestant or was a widespread provincial and middle-class prejudice, a remnant of the nineteenth-century petit bourgeois code, as common in Europe as in the United States. It was not always a forbidding impediment by any means. In real life, many couples on both continents overcame it with ease. In fact, it was often no more than the shadow of a passing cloud. I do not know, that is, whether I was contaminated by this prejudice at an early age in America (possibly at the movies, which staunchly defended the sanctity of marriage at the time), a country where the minister's permission seemed to be an essential prerequisite for copulation; or had imbibed it in my strictly moral and hard-working native city, Milan, which was (and still is) definitely bourgeois, more Mitteleuropa than Italian; or possibly acquired it from my fussy mother, who despised, above all, not sin but the degrading messiness and complications of a life of perennial deceit and surreptitious assignations. This prejudice was sporadically important in my early life, and then only when I fell deeply in love with a chaste and angelic girl. Most of the time (and in later years) it left me absolutely free, in the tranquil knowledge that codes of behavior and reality did not always necessarily coincide.

I tend, however, to hazard the thought that the prejudice was more widespread and commanding in the United States than anywhere else in the Western world, possibly because American society was predominantly and suffocatingly middle-class, and because many American girls in those years instinctively used their beauty as bait. They allowed a boy to enjoy it only after the proper ceremonies had been gone through, possibly with everything that went with them, engraved invitations, lots of guests and friends, a church bedecked with flowers, wedding march on the organ, morning clothes, top hats, rings, champagne, rice and old shoes; or, if all this was not possible, at least a dash in the night to Elkton, Maryland, where a yawning official or clergyman in his pajamas and dressing gown, assisted by his wife in peignoir and curlers, would perform a short improvised ceremony at any hour of the night for a few dollars and produce a valid certificate.

I also thought that the precipitate divorces and quick new marriages prevailing in the United States, which shocked Europeans, were not, as many believed, ominous signs of ineluctable moral decay but proof of the Americans' stubborn attachment not only to *bienséances* and rituals but also to their own rigorous morality. In other countries couples would have thoughtlessly plunged into each other's beds without worrying overmuch about documents and legal status. In America many actually could find no peace and happiness without the consent of the authorities and the right certificates. One gentleman I once met on a boat to Japan, a pineapple millionaire from Hawaii, confessed to me sadly that he, though an unbeliever, being the descendant of generations of missionaries, was irremediably incapable of demonstrating his manly vigor unless the girl in his arms had become his legal wife, and that the many expensive divorces and new marriages he had to go through as a result had cost him a large part of his fortune. This, of course, was exactly the opposite of what happened to many husbands I had heard about in Europe, to whom their legally wedded wives were definitely unappetizing precisely because they were their wives, and had to find consolation and relief elsewhere, often at great expense, in the arms of girls who were not always as attractive or skillful as their own wives.

I remember one particularly disturbing illustration of this curious American fixation. A friend of mine and I had been invited to Vassar for the weekend by two charming girls. The year must have been 1928 or 1929. We dined by candlelight, danced, drank a little, and generally enjoyed ourselves. A terrifying snowstorm was raging outside. It was pleasant to lie cozily on soft carpets (or was it a bearskin?) in front of the open fire, toast marshmallows or roast chestnuts, with a warm, soft, and delicately perfumed, erudite girl in one's arms. Suddenly my friend and his girl startled me by shouting they could bear it no longer. They could not wait. They had to get married immediately, at any cost, anywhere. The nearest place where this urge of theirs could be placated was, I was told, Greenwich, Connecticut. I had the only car (borrowed from a friend). It was my moral duty, they imperiously pointed out, to drive them there without wasting one minute. The night being what it was, I tried to discourage them. I preached the virtue and the moral advantages of continence, told them that, also from a strictly hedonistic and pagan point of view, postponement would add infinitely to their ultimate pleasure, as desire was notoriously the best part of love. Finally, if they really could not wait, why did they not do things the way Italians had been doing them for centuries? Why did they not, for instance, rent a well-heated hotel room with a bath in Poughkeepsie and get the whole thing over with, without bothering me?
They did not listen to reason. They pleaded, appealed to my good heart and to my sense of honor. They were des-

perately in love, they said, their love was holy, unique, and they were sure it would last their whole lifetimes. She took both my hands in hers, pleaded with me, and sobbed, her eyes full of tears. I answered that, if their love was going to last that long, a few hours more or less would make little difference, but I could not convince them. They paid no attention. In the end I yielded. The three of us (my girl was left behind) started on the shortest route to Greenwich, across country, on twisting country roads. We constantly lost our way. The headlights merely illuminated a vortex of white snowflakes against the black curtain of the night. We had to get out every so often to clean and read road signs blanketed by the snow. We also had to get out all the time to scrape the windshield free of the snow that froze solid on it. The only tool we had was the lid of a flat fifty-cigarette tin. The cold was Siberian, and the car, of course, like all cars at the time, was not heated. For warmth we had one girl, one blanket, and one bottle of booze. We took turns at driving, with one hand on the wheel and the other under an armpit to keep it warm. The driver had the feeble heat of the engine to keep his feet from going numb, and the bottle of whisky. The boy in the back had the girl in his arms and the blanket.

I remember the voyage as a nightmare that would never end. We finally arrived in Greenwich, with the help of God and the luck of young people in love, at the first ash-gray light of dawn. It was still snowing heavily. We stopped at the first hotel, where we took three rooms, to recuperate, warm up, wash, shave, and eat some breakfast. As soon as I had recovered, I went down the corridor to look for my friend. We still had to go and find a willing judge or minister or whatever they needed. When I entered his room, I found him and his girl naked in bed, laughing, as happy as little children, eating a good breakfast with relish. "The hell with marriage," they said. "It's an old-fashioned institution, passé, contemptible. We're surprised that you of all people, a sophisticated Latin, should worry about such trifles. . . ." They told me they would think about it. They might get married later in the day or, even better, go home to their families and go through a regular ceremony at a later date. I was speechless with rage. I slammed the door, got in my car, and went straight home, more hours of driving in the whirling snow.

Such are the disadvantages of living in epochs of fluid and changing moral values, when the old has not yet lost all its strength but the new is already beckoning.

I saw Ann, the first few weeks, more and more often and at shorter intervals. In the very beginning I took her out a couple of times on formal dates, to some of the less sinister roadhouses I knew, black tie, flowers, a borrowed car, an advance from Mr. Clemens, the works. Soon the formal dates became rarer. More often we walked, dressed as we were, the two of us alone or with a couple of friends, to the nearby cinema, twenty-five cents, and afterward to the drugstore for a soda or to the beanery for a sandwich. After a week or so it did not really matter where we went as long as we were there together, because what made the evening for me was the glow of her presence, and for her, I presume, basking in the warmth of my admiration. Our conversation gradually absorbed us to the point that we felt alone anywhere, in a bus, on a park bench, in a noisy subway car, at a party, in a nightclub or a railroad station.

What precisely we talked about I do not exactly remember. I know we talked endlessly. She told me about her mother, who had died when she, Ann, was a little child. We explored the problems of Man, life, destiny, God, afterlife, love, sex, the sexes, the future of the world, America and Europe, recklessly, irresponsibly, by hearsay, without adequate preparation and experience, as young people did then and probably still do. We also talked about us, our hopes, our dreams, our future, and more frivolous things too, movie stars, scandals, our neighbors, new tunes, new dances, and childhood memories.

That summer she was between her junior and senior years at college. She was majoring in pedagogy, of all things, but her real passion was literature, French literature in particular. She spoke charming French with a gentle American accent and mostly the wrong genders, as all Anglo-Saxons do. She would ask me, for instance: *"Es-tu contente?"* I had to explain I was *content,* as Nature had placed me in the *genre masculin.* She confessed she wrote poetry, which she refused to show me for a long time. She explained why she found a deep intimate satisfaction in teaching, trying to help children to become good and useful adults. Literature, the books she loved to read and the poetry she wrote, gave her joy, of course, but also a hollow feeling of futility. I read her favorite American novels, she read the French books I lent her. Once I improvised a translation of some Leopardi and some Dante, possibly trying to prove Italy was not all tomato sauce and garlic. It took us longer every night to part on her doorstep. We bid each other the last good night a hundred times. Then we sat on the dewy steps, getting our bottoms wet, Ann embracing her knees, and talked more. Occasionally, she would say: "Go home this minute, Luigi. I'm dead tired and you have to be at the police station at half-past seven." And we went on talking.

We walked the woods at sunset. I took her riding with my painter friend. She sat gracefully in the saddle, gracefully and easily, with a straight back and a high head. Like most young women, she looked incredibly more beautiful on horseback than on foot, which was, in her case, almost unbearable. We sometimes went dancing at the country club and swimming on Sunday morning on lonely beaches (sand dunes, moaning gulls, and strange clumps of tall grass looking like a giant's green hair swept by the wind). We usually went swimming with her sister, Betty, and another cheerful boy called Harry, who knew everything about baseball, wore white linen plus-fours, spoke only in wisecracks, and played the ukulele. The first time we went, carrying sandwiches and pop bottles in paper bags, we found their favorite beach had been surrounded by a fence. Harry helped Betty over the brand-new padlocked gate and ran ahead with her. It was my turn then to get to the other side, where I stood poised to catch Ann. She slid into my arms naturally, as if she belonged there. Her cheeks were cool against mine. I kissed her or she kissed me, I do not know which. Then she turned up her face to look into my eyes. The smile that appeared on her lips was like the first sun at dawn. She said nothing, merely made a tiny, almost inaudible noise, like a child who has eaten a very good piece of cake.

After that, I saw her every night, as a matter of course, without either mentioning the fact that each of us would no longer go out with another date. I also telephoned her once or twice during the day, if I knew where she was, to tell her about the great story I was writing or to make plans for the evening. I was accepted by her family and, in the end, welcomed and practically adopted as a distant foreign relative. Her house was old and small, not at all chic in the style of the day. It had the good smell of tidy American houses at that time, floor wax, lemon oil, the ghosts of vanished roast beef and mutton, potpourri, good soap, and a soupçon of disinfectant. The furniture was handsome and old. There was too much of it, obviously inherited from various branches of the family. I supposed it had been reduced as the family had become smaller, or poorer, or life had become more expensive, but with reluctance, the best pieces preserved and crowded together like poems in each shrinking edition of an anthology. Here and there were a few good pieces of Georgian silver, some old American pottery, a Chinese vase or two, and one handsome Chinese lacquered screen. There was a Civil War drum and a framed American flag with fewer stars than customary at the time. Her father had been stationed in Shanghai at one point in his naval career.

I liked Ann's family, grandmother, father, and sister. I probably did not see them clearly. They were enveloped by the rosy mist of my love for Ann as Homeric heroes were by the clouds the gods disposed around them to protect them. They were (or seemed to me) vastly different from all the people I met ordinarily. Whether they were fossil survivals of a vanished America or forerunners of the future, a sample of what Americans would be when they stopped running, if they could stop running and still be Americans, I did not know. They had some money, the captain's pension, his salary (he had a job in the city with a shipping agent), possibly also the grandmother's *rentes,* but not much, yet they did not feel guilty about their inadequacy, and did not seem at all anxious to go out of their way to become rich. They owned only one old car. They talked about the Stock Exchange boom, of course, about money, other people's strokes of luck, everybody did then, but they did so lightly and somewhat irreverently, as if money was not something sacred, and did so without envy. Strange.

They did not seem to worry either about their rank in society and were amused by other people's scrambling to emerge. I often suspected this pose of theirs might have been a sign of conceit rather than humility. They probably believed their own position, due to eminent ancestors I had never heard of, did not need to be proclaimed or proved, and that absolutely nothing could be done to improve it. Their manners were, technically speaking, no manners at all, but a gentle and benevolent disposition of the spirit. This confirmed something I had heard from European connoisseurs of American mores, that not many Americans had what were known in Europe as good manners but those who did had infinitely more sincere, *raffinés,* and easier manners than courtly, stiff, and arrogant Europeans.

They wanted me to feel at home with them, but above all in their country. They told me old family stories, explained their national habits, vices, and virtues, taught me slang words, sang ancient songs for my benefit (Betty played the piano), described parts of the United States I had never visited, and sometimes talked about the spirit which blew through their country's history and moved the people. The captain told me once: "This is a great country, Luigi, not because it is rich. Don't let Americans fool you. It's rich because it's a great country. Here we believe in man, try to encourage his capacity to improve himself and his lot, try to free him from his shackles. This is all there is, the American idea in a nutshell. We're no better than other people. We only try to be. Sometimes we seem worse, more stupid and irresponsible or demented, because foreigners do not know what imaginary impossible goals we're striving to reach. We're not always successful, I must admit. We know man makes ghastly mistakes, does not always see the right path, has a deplorable attachment to his vices, and has a hard time fighting his lower instincts. Mistakes are costly, inevitable, but necessary. They allow people to change course, to avoid pitfalls and delusions in the future." The captain called things by their names and, when he and I were alone, used some polite curses and four-letter words. I was flattered by this. It was a touching proof of acceptance and intimacy.

Ann's grandmother, a white-haired lady dressed like a proper grandmother, with a black-velvet ribbon around the neck and lace collars on dark dresses, had been to Italy in her youth. Her eyes shone and her voice became vaguely lyrical and tremulous when she mentioned names like Siena, Pisa, Lucca, Gubbio, or Giotto, Cimabue, and Bellini. She was enchanted to hear my father had been born in Orvieto. "Oh, Orvieto," she almost neighed, "the good wine, the great cathedral, the frescoes by Signorelli . . . Have you read what Edith Wharton wrote about Orvieto?" She spoke a few Italian sentences, mostly old-fashioned ceremonious formulas, obviously learned from a handbook for nineteenth-century tourists.

One Sunday they invited me to dinner at one o'clock. It was to be an introduction to American home cuisine, part of my education. The two sisters cheerfully cooked, the grandmother rained gentle advice on them, we three men

(Harry was also there) set the table. Then everything was placed on it, *all'americana*—the turkey, the baked potatoes, the salad, the gravies, the pies—and we sat down. The captain uncorked a bottle of good Burgundy and pointed out he was not violating the law, which forbade only the manufacture, transportation, and sale of alcoholic beverages but said nothing about owning and drinking. He had legally filled his cellar in time, years before, with enough bottles for festive occasions to last his lifetime. "Foresight defeats fate," he said. "That's what I learned in the Navy." He then carved the turkey. I watched his easy conjurer's skill with awe. In Italy, and in our house, birds were cut up in the kitchen and father was not required to perform such a delicate surgical operation in front of impatient guests.

We had a wonderful time. I ate ravenously everything put on my plate without asking questions. An exact knowledge of the ingredients might have discouraged me. There were delicious and unfamiliar tastes. I had never eaten such good American food before. I did not know it existed. "Why can't you eat like this in restaurants?" I asked. The captain explained that, in his youth, one ate like that—well, almost like that—in restaurants and on trains, some of which had the best American food in the country, but later the restaurants had been captured by gangs of foreigners, French, Italian, Greek, Chinese, German, and what have you. Few Americans became cooks. They thought it demeaning or dishonorable, for some reason. And now the people seldom had the time and patience to cook their own national dishes at home. We told stories, laughed, teased each other, passed the cranberry sauce, the potatoes, the gravy, the butter, the bread, and the sliced turkey all around. The captain had to uncork another bottle of wine.

266

The grandmother started reminiscing with dreamy eyes about Florence, where she had met an Italian cavalry officer who wore a sky-blue cape, a helmet like a Medieval knight, and carried a beautiful sword. His name was Count Asinari di San Marzano. No, I was sorry, I had never run across him. He must be a doddering retired general, if he was still alive in 1929, I said. They talked about Rudolph Valentino. Harry cried I looked like him, which of course was not true at all, but all the others said I did and cheered, just to embarrass me. The captain, who had traveled and seen the world, explained Italians had no great respect for women, flattered them and treated them as if they were immature, weak, inept, and muddleheaded angels. This women found irresistible. They all fell for it. It gave them a chance to relax, to be taken care of.

Betty wanted her grandmother's opinion: "Tell us exactly what happened between you and that Italian officer in Florence. We want the truth. Did he treat you as if you were an irresponsible idiot? Did you find him irresistible?" The grandmother was shocked and flattered. "No," she said. "He was a proper gentleman. He treated me with great patience. I'm afraid I was an independent and capricious American girl. We took a few walks. We danced. He waltzed beautifully." "And you still remember him after thirty years," cried Betty. "Your eyes are full of tears." The grandmother blushed. The captain pointed out that if his mother had only stayed a few more days in Florence he might now be a countryman of mine, a *capitano di fregata*, raised his glass to me and started singing "O Sole Mio."

At this point Ann, who had said nothing, lifted her face, looked into my eyes, smiled sweetly, and said in a quiet voice, as if she and I were alone: "What do you do to girls that they fall in love with you, forget family, home, friends, their own country, everything?" My throat choked. My breathing stopped. I swallowed some mince pie with difficulty. I could not answer. What did she mean, and did she mean anything at all? "Stop teasing Luigi," said the grandmother protectively, and patted my sleeve. "He's our guest."

At this moment a car stopped in front of the house and a horn blew joyously three or four times. Through the windows we saw a young man rushing up the steps three at a time. "Stewart!" they all screamed, and ran to the door. The captain said: "How the hell did he get here? He must be a deserter. The MPs must be after him. He is supposed to be in the Caribees with the fleet. Call the police." They all surrounded Stewart as he came in, and cried: "When did you get here, how long are you staying, have you eaten, are you hungry, what a surprise, sit down, there's plenty of food, have a glass of wine, how healthy you look!"

Stewart was tall, thin, sunburned, manly, about twenty-five, smartly dressed in a seersucker suit. He threw his straw hat on a chair, kissed the grandmother and Betty lightly, kissed Ann more seriously and squeezed her to his breast, shook hands with the captain, Harry, and me, said, "So you're Luigi," and sat down at the table on an added chair. "Just in time," he said. His glass was filled, a plate was put in front of him, piled high with food. Between mouthfuls he explained that his ship had been damaged and had to be rushed to the Brooklyn Navy Yard for repairs. He had not telegraphed nor telephoned, so as to surprise them. He had borrowed a car and here he was. Ann sat by him, filled his glass, and said: "It is a lovely surprise. I got your last letter yesterday. You said you hoped to be here for Christmas, at

268

the earliest." He kissed the tips of her fingers and said: "I didn't damage the ship myself, on purpose, as you may think. It was just luck. How pretty you look." And went on eating.

After dinner the captain took pictures of his two daughters, Harry, and Stewart on the front steps. Nobody asked me to join the group. I talked quietly with the grandmother, who said: "Don't let them pull your leg, Luigi. They don't know anything. They are barbarians." The old lady looked at me as if I were a cavalry officer of the 1890s.

Chapter 15

EUROPEANS DID NOT KNOW that the infernal, relentless, free-for-all, demented scramble for wealth and rank offended many sensitive Americans, too. I knew. They were shocked by its inevitable cruelties, gross injustices, and shrill vulgarity, by its gladiatorial lack of mercy for the old, the weak, the timid, and the inept. Nevertheless, I had to admit that, in spite of all its iniquitous faults, which I saw clearly, it was preferable in the end to the resignation, the swampy immobility, interrupted by an occasional bloody revolt, of life in Europe at the time. Admittedly, life in Europe appeared to travelers and expatriates as more dignified, decorative, cultured, and decorous, but under the surface, I knew, it was even more unjust, cruel, and vulgar than American life. It was cursed by poverty, ignorance, hunger, despair, hatred, fear, as well as the resigned and cowardly acceptance of all ills as irremediable. In fact, most people in Europe bitterly believed that all change was for the worse because old ills could be exchanged only for new and more unbearable ones.

On the other hand, the undignified climbing up the greasy pole to gain more money and a higher status, the insane desire to provoke one's neighbor's envy at whatever price, gave Americans an aim of sorts in life, spread affluence, clothed the naked, fed the hungry, provided jobs for millions, cured the sick, put roofs over the destitute, inextricably mixed the social classes, allowed some of the best men to emerge, and, above all, furnished the public treasury and private philanthropic organizations with ample funds to improve the world, face and foresee problems, build schools and libraries which might eventually transform the nature of man, as well as construct hospitals, stadiums, bridges, roads, and model jails on an unprecedented scale. It was a Good Thing, I assured myself, one of the Great Achievements of Man, a Stage on the Road to Progress, which, as Victor Hugo wrote, was notoriously *le pas de Dieu dans l'Histoire.* In short, it was something to be accepted, almost always admired, and póssibly imitated.

Granted all these beneficial advantages, I was still haunted by doubts. To begin with, the current scramble seemed misnamed. Only a few really became rich and famous in the end. Most of the others led mediocre lives. And were they happy? To be sure, almost everybody was better off than people in other centuries or in other countries, but, driven by impossible hopes, Americans knew no peace. They still slaved like peasants of old from morning till night, weighed down by debts, worries, and moral imperatives, from youth to old age and death. It was saddening to watch good Americans, these New Men, free and self-reliant rugged individualists, each of them his own master, docilely crowding like cattle onto the morning trains on their way to work and returning, at the end of the day, in droves, dazed by fatigue. Work, of course, was all right. What was life without work? I myself was happy working hard and would have been wretched without work to do. But I could not bring myself to believe this unrelenting struggle without pause was what life was all about, the principal goal of man on earth, the main reason for the establishment of a thoroughly new nation across the Atlantic, the world's best hope, created to remedy the intolerable flaws of Europe. I could not believe that that was all and that there was not something else, something better.

These thoughts often haunted me, but I tried hard to exorcise them. I dared to discuss them with only a few friends. I suspected I was attached to such vaguely sacrilegious doubts only because they helped preserve the dignity of the defeated and decadent continent in which I had been born and to which I was still stupidly attached; or because they could be useful in justifying and ennobling my eventual, almost certain, future failure in America's pitiless competition. I was not alone, of course. Many people around me, behind their cheerful and optimistic countenances, were not quite convinced that to scramble breathlessly and work themselves to exhaustion was man's principal mission in life. I discovered nobody was really happy; in fact, when you got to know them well, many more were thoroughly unhappy than happy, as unhappy as the Europeans but for different reasons. Of course, those who, in the American game of snakes and ladders, got stranded at one point in the wrong box or never even started were unhappy; but those who, halfway through, discovered that they, in spite of their struggling, would never reach the final box in the end were even more unhappy. Most unhappy of all, however, were many successful people, who should theoretically have been the happiest, because every one of them thought he had not really gone as far as he deserved, and felt cheated, or because, with success, his new problems had multiplied and become unendurable. Wise and thoughtful people were more than unhappy. They were terrified.

Many of those who praised the pleasures and the compassion of the Old World and deplored the contemporary American madness, perhaps partly to console themselves for their inadequacy, were, of course, European immigrants, like the old Irish priest I knew who lamented the deterioration of his flock, their loss of the simple faith, their new shameless devotion to expensive automobiles, luxurious living, jazz, and lust; or the old Sicilian gardener who sadly deplored the decline of his autocratic life-or-death authority over his children and his wife; or the retired Latin scholar from Bavaria. He was a small old man with a white goatee and gold-rimmed eyeglasses, who had come to America at the end of the previous century but had never really adapted himself to the rules of the new life. He kept on comparing the United States to an idyllic Bavaria which existed only in his memory and, had it ever existed, would have vanished long before anyway. He secretly wanted to civilize the United States. He sometimes stopped me on Main Street, took the old pipe out of his mouth, and talked to me as to one of the few who could understand him. Confidentially, in a low voice, with a strong German accent, he would quote familiar lines like Horace's *"Virtute me involvo probamque pauperiem sine dote quero"* ("I wrap myself up in my virtue and court poverty without a dowry") or Juvenal's *"Cantabit vacuus coram latrone viator"* ("The poor man sings gaily when confronted by the hold-up man"). He then winked and looked around, as if the dead language and the memory of the dead poets were subversive secrets between us in a country which despised Latin, poverty, and ancient wisdom.

One afternoon I was dispatched to cover a grass fire on the salt meadows by the water's edge. Four fire trucks had been called and they had easily put it out before I arrived. "Why so much fuss for such a small fire?" I asked a fireman I knew, who was neatly rolling a hose. He told me it might have been dangerous if it had spread, because there were large gasoline tanks, buried not too deep and not too far from where the grass had burned, which might have exploded. Even so, I said, nobody would have got hurt because there were no houses anywhere around. The nearest thing to a house in the flat open landscape was one distant dilapidated houseboat in the creek. It appeared to be moored by the shore but more probably had been sitting a long time on the muddy bottom. It looked deserted. I strolled over. Maybe I could write a good story if people lived on it and had miraculously survived the danger.

I approached it at the same time as a tiny old man walking from another direction. He was evidently the owner, had fled with his most precious belongings, and was now coming back. A bird cage dangled from one crooked finger and an old violin case from his right hand; a bundle of clothes and some books were clutched under one arm. "Hello," I said with professional cheerfulness, and told him who I was and what I wanted. "Hello," he said, wiped his feet carefully on a worn-out doormat, and politely asked me in.

He was a very small and light man, as light as a jockey, probably in his seventies, pink-faced, with wisps of white hair, patient blue eyes, and a squelched nose twisted to one side. He unlocked the door, let me in, hung up the bird cage, and put down his burdens. "We both want coffee," he said, and started making it. As he busied himself, we talked about the fire and the danger of the gasoline tanks exploding. He wore old ill-fitting clothes, probably picked up in the garbage dumps not far away, but spotlessly washed. The cabin was clean and tidy, as rooms of solitary old men who become manic housekeepers often are. Everything was scrubbed, shining, and in its right place. A few ancient prints from the *Police Gazette* were nailed to the walls.

Sipping the hot coffee, I asked him to show me what belongings he had thought worth saving. Maybe I could whip up an elegant and moving feature story listing the few things an old man considered as precious as his own life. He waved to the canary bird, his old clothes, his fiddle, the few books, and said: "I don't own much." Among the books were a well-thumbed Bible, Walt Whitman's *Leaves of Grass,* Emerson's essays, Thoreau's *Walden,* and Henry George's *Progress and Poverty.* "They can be read time and again," he explained. "In the long run they are the cheapest. I thought the other books were not worth saving." He dismissed a small shelf with a gesture of the hand.

Among the treasures he had brought back was a large scrapbook. It contained yellowed clippings from old sports pages and a few chocolate-tinted photographs on cardboard of a young prizefighter posing stiffly, his shining hair carefully parted and combed, and his eyes glassy. "That's me," he explained, "or I should say that was me." He told me he had been featherweight champion of the United States in the eighties, exactly what years I cannot remember. "I was goddamn good," he boasted. And he taught me right there and then his secret punch, the punch that had brought him to the top. He called it "the corkscrew." You kept your right (or left) fist low, close to the side of the body, and shot it out as if to hit your opponent from below, but then your elbow suddenly turned upward in mid-air, your arm twisted in a spiral or corkscrew motion, and the blow fell unexpectedly from above on the side of the other man's chin. The old champion showed it to me in slow motion, then made me try it on his own chin. He laughed as he jumped lightly up and down and cried: "Don't be scared. You won't hurt me. Go ahead. Use the weight of your body. Shoot." He explained the corkscrew punch would be useful for defending myself from malefactors. "It might save your life one day, you never can tell."

I asked him how he lived. Was he alone in the world? No. He had a grown-up and married grandson, a small-businessman, who came a couple of times a year to see if he was still alive. The grandson was probably ashamed of a grandfather who lived like a hobo, and often tried to convince him to enter some charitable institution. "A nice boy but a bore," said the old man. He had saved a little money (nothing much in 1929), had few needs, and could still take care of himself. In fact, he liked his solitary life. He had his chores to do, fetching clean fresh water, gathering driftwood, tidying up, cooking, washing, and sometimes walking to the nearest store, a couple of miles away, for his few necessities. He had his memories, his canary bird, and his books. "I sometimes sit watching the boats go by and the gulls," he told me. "You call them all gulls and think they are all the same. They are of different breeds, different colors, and have different habits. They are very interesting to watch. A few come to eat out of my hand like tame pigeons." He quoted some of their Latin names.

Then he had his violin. He took it out of his case and showed it to me. I looked inside and, on a worn-out label, made out the dim words "Guarnerio, Cremona." I was stupefied. What a story this was going to be in the end even without embellishments. "Old Boxer Saves Million-Dollar Fiddle In Fire. 'It's My Dearest Treasure,' Says Ex-World Champ." "Do you know it's a Guarnerius?" I asked. He nodded, lowering his eyelids. Of course he knew. It had been his father's, his grandfather's, and possibly his great-grandfather's, he did not know for sure. "Do you realize," I told him, "that if you sold it you could live in a suite at the Ritz the rest of your life and wear diamonds?" "I know," he said, "but I don't want to live in a suite at the Ritz and I don't like diamonds. I like it here with the gulls." He put the Guarnerius under his little chin, and drew plaintive and gay music from it, ghosts of popular tunes of the eighties.

I do not remember his name, after so many years, but I am sure it is possible to discover it from old records. I could probably find somewhere the article I wrote about him in the summer of 1929. He, surely, was among the Americans who did not believe the world had changed just because more and more people were getting richer and richer every day.

Suicides fascinated me. They particularly fascinated me because they should have been as incongruous in the contemporary American scene as prostitution in a Marxist country. Why should men do away with themselves on the very threshold of the most prodigious era humanity had ever seen? Evidently for the same unknowable reasons why so many of them drank themselves into trembling stupor, isolated themselves, like stylites on top of their columns, in all kinds of absorbing pursuits, dedicated themselves to fanatical cults and crusades, joined the wandering hobos, or exiled themselves to effete Europe. Suicides were not frequent in the little town and most of them were uninteresting. Nevertheless, I tried to investigate them, even the obvious ones, in the scant time I could spare for them. I would snoop around the suicide's house, open drawers, read old letters, talk to relatives, with an afflicted expression on my face, and gather neighbors' gossip, in the hope of discovering some revealing clue.

Once (to cite a single case), a man, a stranger, was found poisoned in his little room at the YMCA. Only his name was known, not his profession nor where he had come from. He left no message of farewell. I asked to see the form he had filled in before being accepted as a guest. In answer to the question, who should be warned in case of accident, sickness, or death, he had written the name of a woman and a local address. I went there and rang the bell. There was no answer. It was late in the afternoon, that day's paper was out, and I had the time to wait. I sat down on a large whitewashed stone marking the path to the back door and lit a cigarette. Children were playing and shouting all around me. The house was small and unpainted in what must have been, even in the old days, a shabby section for modest people.

When the woman appeared, a bony, pale, worried-look-

278

ing middle-aged spinster with a shopping bag, I was embarrassed and ashamed but forced myself to tell her the man was dead and ask her a few questions. She did not cry out and did not weep. She merely stared at me incredulously, turned paler, clenched her jaws and the fist clutching her bag. I followed her into the house. She was (I discovered tactfully) a spinster, in wretched health, a schoolteacher out of a job. The man had been her fiancé. He was also very lonely and poor, a poet, who, of late, had tried to make a living selling lots in new developments. The real estate firm had gone bankrupt, owing him some money, all the money he had, with which he hoped to marry her, pay for her cure, and finish the great poem he had been writing for years, the poem that would have given him fame or, at least, some notoriety. After she had told me all this, she suddenly wept, silently, without sobbing, a grimace distorting her mouth, tears filling her eyes. "He has not even written me a farewell letter," she said disconsolately. Maybe he had, I tried to assure her, it would surely come in the mail the following morning. You wait and see. Then I apologized for my brutal intrusion and left, my story already writing itself in my head.

The love of the lonely, wretched, and destitute couple, the end of their last dream, and his death could, of course, have taken place anywhere. A nineteenth-century Russian, Chekhov or Turgeniev, could have described all this with a wealth of humble, tender, and apparently incongruous details, in a low voice, beautifully. He would have placed the couple in St. Petersburg, streets filled with snow, made them members of the liberal intelligentsia rejected by the arrogant establishment, despised by neighbors, harassed by the police. He would have described the miraculous blossoming of young love between the two middle-aged people, the man's ardent laboring at his poem, her health slowly improving. Chekhov or Turgeniev would have written a splendid farewell letter, the end of the story, which would have arrived by mail the next day, a letter she would not have been able to read because she had killed herself, too. Matilde Serao would have placed more or less the same plot in Naples at the end of the century, amid street vendors' cries, the strumming of guitars, laundry hanging across the narrow streets, the hunger and desperation of the people, and the incredible beauty of the *golfo*. She would also have pitilessly suggested the poem he was writing was irremediably bad.

But this was America, not St. Petersburg or Naples; the year was 1929; the sovereign was Herbert Hoover, not Nicholas I, Alexander III, or Umberto I. The elderly couple were free, in a free country. They were not revolutionaries. The police did not harass them. In fact, every opportunity was open to them. All they had to do in this rich and generous country was stretch a hand in the right direction, answer an ad or two, get a job, improve themselves, follow the instructions, study at night, do all the proper things, and they would have been happy, healthy, and prosperous. Moreover, there was any number of private philanthropic, lay, or religious institutions all around them, to which they could have turned for help. The point of the story, of course, was just this: that it was still possible then in the United States for a man to do away with himself as he would have done in wretched times and miserable countries; that what had driven him to death and oblivion even more irresistibly than in old Russia or Italy had been not poverty but probably the very universal prosperity around him. It was an American tragedy, after all, a tragedy which could only have taken place in the United States in 1929, the tragedy of betrayed expectations.

Other suicides I investigated were similarly lonely, poor, sick, and unfortunate people, but some were not. I supposed most of them lacked the agonistic spirit, the will to go in there and win, or were cursed with a sensitive soul which made the gross vulgarity of much of life around them unbearable, possibly for the same reason that two of my Columbia schoolmates, good friends of mine, killed themselves in the following months. They were both young, healthy, and brilliant, among the best writers in the class. They surely would have quickly reached the top. One of them had a friend, his best friend, who always jokingly told him, "Take gas!"—almost meaningless and not very funny advice. This young man turned on the kitchen jet one night, lay down, and died. He left a simple note: "I took gas."

I could understand why the poor sometimes preferred death to misery. But some suicides were not poor at all. Some may possibly have been *anciens riches,* too well-bred and inept, who, I imagined, had been tormented by one of the forms of American discontent, the discovery that wealth is satisfying and life-filling only when there is not much of it to go round and the rich can commiserate with and do good to the many poor. More puzzling were certain *nouveaux riches* who also killed themselves. A few were enviable people, who had made a pile and even a name for themselves in their own fields, whatever they were. Their affairs were prospering. Invariably, they had smart wives, children in the right schools, amusing friends, lovely houses, and flocks of automobiles for all seasons. Why did they want to die?

Other failures, living ones, fascinated me. Larry, for instance, a colleague of mine, a reporter like me, to my eyes a decrepit old man, surely old enough to be my father. When he was sober, he got his facts right and wrote a tidy story. He was usually drunk. At times his dewy eyes rose beseechingly toward me over his typewriter. He said nothing, but I understood the signal, nodded, and, as soon as I was through with my work, took his place and completed his. He always said: "You're a good boy, Mr. Smith-a, to help a poor sick man. God will reward you." The time Ernest, the city editor, was in a clinic, I had to give orders to Larry. I was embarrassed and timidly worded my orders as requests for advice. "What do you think should be done?" I would say. "We should have a man, a good man, cover this, don't you agree? You're the only reporter experienced enough to go and get the facts, don't you think?" I tried to send him not too far, on foot (the walk would sober him up), and possibly away from tempting speakeasies.

Sometimes, after work, he dragged me to his favorite spot across the street. "You can't let a poor man drink alone," he would say. I went in the naïve hope of keeping him from downing too much booze. I barely tasted the little glass of amber liquid placed in front of me, which smelled of nauseating chemicals. His drinks disappeared inside him one after the other as if he were made of sponge. After a few he became reminiscent and protective. He told me again about his brilliant youth, the stupendous jobs he had

had, his successes, the women he had made love to, and what Arthur Brisbane had told him. He warned me to avoid mistakes: "Discipline yourself like an athlete, try fiction, that's where the money is, and don't get married."

In his wallet he kept a picture of a girl dressed in the fashion of 1910 holding a baby in her arms, the wife and daughter he had lost somewhere. "My girl must be about your age now. . . ." he said. "I'll get them back, by God, as soon as I free myself from this run of bad luck." He also preserved a precious clipping, the story he had sold to the *Saturday Evening Post* years before. I had to read it several times. To my cruel eyes it was sweetly sentimental but elegantly written, grade B stuff, professional but not very good. Larry was evidently a dismal failure, more pathetic than others, since he had at one time almost got to the top of the greasy pole. I wondered whether he was a failure because he drank or drank because he was a failure. In other words, had he been born in some other country or at some other time, when a man was not expected to surpass his rivals and win the *gros lot* in order to be considered merely alive, where a man was just allowed pleasantly to be what he was and not what luck, his native talents, tenacity, and his capacity to cut corners made him, would Larry have been sober?

This desperate craving for drink, like the many suicides, I never really understood. It was baffling. It went with failure, of course, but also with success. Writers and artists drank because they were sensitive, dejected, and easily hurt, dull people drank because they were dull and bored with their own company. Booze consoled the inept and unlucky and sustained the conquerors. It warmed the heart of the downtrodden working class but also stifled the millionaire's remorse or filled the emptiness of his life. The Puritans drank to forget their moral strait jackets, the hedonists drank because what are the pleasures of the flesh without drink?

Take Ernest, the city editor, whose place I filled for a while. He was a brilliant young man who could go far. He taught me all I know about reducing a vast gaseous piece of prose to spare solid matter. He wore a stiff straw hat at work, like a butcher, never sat down, nervously tapped his lighted cigarette on the edge of his desk to let the ash fall, and compulsively kept unraveling the paper spirals of which the pencils were made, until they were reduced to stumps. He drank all the time.

Once I went to see him in the clinic where he was being treated for delirium tremens. I found him in bed with a bandaged head, looking like a turbaned Indian. He explained what had happened to him, a stupid little incident. I was terrified by his tale. I had never heard anything like it. Nothing like that ever happened in Italy. It seemed that a band of musicians in uniform, "red uniform with gold trimmings," he specified, as small as cockroaches, visited him all the time, playing pleasant tunes. They came marching in under the closed door, climbed on his bed, gave their concert on his stomach, and marched away in formation, always playing. He was always sorry to see them disappear and one day decided he must capture one to keep him company and later to take home as an animated *bibelot*. The drummer was the easiest to catch, as he marched alone at the end of the group.

That day, at the right moment, when they had all gone under the door and only the drummer was left behind, Ernest plunged from his bed. That was how he had split his head, hitting the door. All this he told me laughing, as a matter of course, as if it were something that could happen to anybody, any day. I said nothing. I could not speak.

Sometimes I ended the day in a rundown livery stable. It had probably sheltered the spanking horses of a proud family at the time of Rutherford B. Hayes. Where I presumed the opulent mansion had been was now a row of cheap two-story stucco commercial buildings facing the street—a quick lunch, Saverio's shoeshine and repair parlor, a cigar store, a florist plus notary public. Hidden behind them, like dear memories that had to be protected, surrounded by weedy and refuse-strewn vacant land which surely had been the old garden, were the old box stalls and the carriage house slowly disintegrating in the heat. I liked the smell of the stable and the talk of the man who ran it with the help of one black handyman. He was a lean middle-aged bachelor, always in ancient riding clothes. His real profession was not riding but painting. He had studied in Paris and Munich, had lived a few years between Rome, Florence, and Venice, spending the little money he had inherited. His work showed all those foreign influences, and his admiration for Whistler, but also something more definitely American, a non-European clarity, boldness, and enthusiasm.

He said he liked me to visit him because he wanted to paint my head, and did a few desultory sketches. In reality, he like to drop a few Italian or French phrases and names like Fantin-Latour, Terborch, Bernardino Luini, Ensor, Simone Martini, or Karl Schmidt-Rottluff, without having to explain who they were. To be sure, I did not know who most of them were, but nodded wisely and was flattered to

285

be a member of an exclusive club of two, besieged by demented and ignorant Philistines. In his stable, the anxiety about being left behind in the frenetic American race and the embarrassment of being Italian were forgotten. In fact, being an Italian became a privilege. My painter friend looked upon the rest of his countrymen with loving pity and condescension. *"Poveretti,"* he would say of them. "One day perhaps they will understand."

Some evenings, at sunset, to exercise the horses that needed it, we took long-reined quiet rides where the countryside was still what it had always been, gray grassland with clumps of black trees against the distant pink sea under the red sky. We talked. "Most American Presidents," he explained once, "have been great horsemen (Washington, Jefferson, and Jackson were particularly good), down to McKinley and Teddy Roosevelt. Our troubles started when Presidents no longer knew how to sit a horse. Because the art of statesmanship is the art of managing something alive that has a will of its own. Now all these politicians know is machinery. They hope to change all kinds of things overnight by merely pushing one pedal, turning a crank, or passing one law." He was thinking of Prohibition, of course. He would also complain of what was happening to Nature. "It's majestically beautiful, infinitely more beautiful in America than in Europe," he said another time. I agreed. "But once men's activities reach a spot, there you see shoddy tanks, ugly factories, broken-down shacks, and festoons of wires dangling from drunken poles, everything cluttered up with rusty tin cans, rags, bottles, refuse of all kind, junk, and stinking garbage." We were riding and he contemptuously swung his whip in a circle pointing to such things around us.

I was curious to know why he was content to run a shabby livery stable and did not take advantage of such a historic moment. He should have become famous and made a lot of money, I told him. He should have painted portraits of the rich and their bejeweled wives (there were enough new millionaires around anxious to arrange instant heirlooms and ancestors' portraits for their descendants). At worst he could have illustrated stories in magazines or painted the more distinguished advertisements, ladies and gentlemen with their Pierce-Arrows in front of Palladian mansions. He looked at me with disgust when I suggested these possibilities. "I'm a millionaire of sorts already," he would say. "I don't have to catch a train in the morning, I serve no boss, and am doing exactly what pleases me. How much is that worth?" Another time he explained: "Not everybody came from Europe to this country in search of gold, Luigi. Many also wanted freedom, which is the tranquillity to live your life, think your thoughts, worship whatever you want, write, paint, or loaf. Real Americans don't like to be pushed around, Luigi. This is really what this country is all about."

I was also puzzled by another friend who refused to follow the herd. Bob was a very rich young man who worked with his father, an opulent downtown broker. He was engaged to a sweet girl, Elaine. She was slim and beautiful, moved languorously with a certain hesitation, and, as if lost in thought, did not always seem to hear what was being said. Bob had a theory, that in order to love the house in which he was shortly to live with her, in order to feel it was really their own, they had to build it with their own hands as their ancestors had done. He bought a piece of wild land not far from the ocean. He knew something about carpentering, bought handbooks, drew plans, and dedicated most of his summer evenings and weekends to measuring, digging, sawing, hammering, planing, and carrying heavy things. Elaine looked at her sweating fiancé in overalls with adoring eyes, thought the whole project just wonderful, and honestly tried to help, but Nature had not made her a construction worker. She handed him the wrong tools, and precariously held the ladder for him with long ivory hands.

I spent a few Sundays with Bob and Elaine, my mouth full of nails, hammering away. To be sure, Bob, too, was an oddball, like the painter or the old prizefighter, a stubborn man who did not allow the contemporary American imperatives to influence him. At the time, anybody in his position was expected to commission some renowned architect to build him a very expensive marble residence in imitation Regency style, with swimming pool, stables, fountains, and carefully landscaped gardens. His ideas, however, while not contemporary, 1929 American, were by no means European. I had never heard of an Italian or French or Austrian millionaire who took off his coat and built himself a château with the help of his wife in order to love it more. Maybe an English nut, a Ruskin and William Morris addict, might hypothetically have constructed a thatched cottage, but then the English, from my point of view, were not entirely European, nor sane either.

On the other hand, if one considered the matter carefully, one had to conclude that in reality Bob was more American than most of his money-chasing compatriots. He just followed alternative traditions. For one thing, he showed an almost religious respect for work, real hard work, done with one's callused hands outdoors and not at one's desk with telephones, files, secretaries, and dictating machines. He followed Jefferson's example at Monticello (he had turned himself into an architect and lent a hand in the construction). He also showed a Jeffersonian contempt for his own Hamiltonian wealth, besides a Calvinist desire to prove his own self-reliance. He had a hunger for responsibility (it will be nobody else's fault if, in the end, the plumbing does not function and the roof leaks); yearned for durable spiritual values which he believed could be secured not through meditation and prayer but only through pragmatic activities. Finally, the whole project smacked vaguely of an American utopia. Whether he knew it or not, it was surely inspired by Fourierist or Transcendentalist dreamers of the past who also had built their own dwellings and had sought happiness in this world, salvation in the next, and the miraculous solution of all problems in brotherhood, the honest sweat of their brow, and contact with Nature. In all agrarian colonies, fatally doomed to dismal failure, people loved each other and lived a long time in the open while building houses and barns with their own hands. The early immigrants to America, ever since the first English refugees settled on the Virginia or New England coasts, and the pioneers in the West, had done it.

An elderly lady, American from way back, the tall, gray-haired, and portly mother of a friend, was busy in her kitchen one day, wearing pince-nez glasses, dressed majestically in spotless white like a head nurse. She was storing jars of fruit and vegetables for the winter. She gave us coffee and told me, rhythmically waving a wooden spoon to emphasize each word: "This won't last, Luigi. It has never lasted before. All this talk about a new era, of why it will go on forever, is a lot of bunk. We Americans often get drunk on words. The flood will come, sooner than you think, to punish us for our sins and our pride. It came in 1893. Luigi, listen to me, build yourself an ark." Her rows of glass jars looked ominously ready for a siege or a famine.

Chapter 16

THE SPLENDID SUMMER was slowly on its way out. Rain had washed and cooled the air. The real heat was over. The lawns were turning emerald-green again. Here and there the leaves of the big Huguenot trees were already trying to turn red, yellow, orange, bronze. I duly warned Mr. Clemens I was going to leave shortly, as soon as the School opened. He said: "I'm sorry to see you go, Mr. Smith-a. Where will I ever find another reporter like you?" What he probably meant was, where could he find one as eager to work as hard at that price?

Our house had been empty for a few weeks. I lived alone in it. Emma was getting married in Milan in September. Father and Mother had gone to Europe with little Ugo for the ceremony and the festivities. Ettore, who was studying tropical agriculture at Cornell, had got himself a summer job as assistant manager of a banana plantation in Jamaica.

He had grown into a silent, shy, sensitive boy, a dreamer who read a lot and wrote secretly. He wrote both languages, English and Italian, very well. Curiously enough, he disliked the way Nature had made him. He always seemed to be doing things suited to quite another man, an adventurous swashbuckling extrovert. It had probably been this other man who had taken up tropical agriculture, for which Ettore had no particular vocation, so as to contribute one day to the development of an Italian colony in East Africa. I think he was influenced first of all by Father's Kiplingesque, unreal, and romantic concept of the future of Italy, as well as by the movies. Personally, he might have been attracted also by the opportunity a job in the tropics offered him to flee, with a lot of books and writing paper, from the perennial torture of life among crowds in the cities of Europe or America, the ice and snow of New York or Milan winters, to warmth, solitude, and Nature among native workers, far from exasperating bosses. I believe he was also trying to escape from the Barzini delusion and curse, the idea that the easiest and surest way to make a living was to write. Besides, it had somehow been tacitly agreed that I was the one who would write, and one in the family, he possibly thought, was enough.

He never considered becoming an officer in the colonial army, which, of course, was the easiest way at that time of finding a refuge in the tropics. He disliked soldiering, harsh manners, coarse language, idleness, the inevitable native mistresses, discipline, superiors, and weapons. He chose to pursue the scientific production of tropical fruit surely not in order to become rich himself, which was improbable anyway, but to turn one of Italy's showy and financially bankrupt possessions as far as possible into a money-making investment. This last idea was surely due to American influence. He did not find peace in Jamaica that summer. His was a troublesome plantation. One night the workers mutinied, tried to drag him out of bed, and probably wanted to lynch him. He saved himself by talking to them eloquently while brandishing a gun. It was difficult for me (when I received his letter describing his hair-raising adventures) to imagine my gentle eighteen-year-old bookish brother impersonating the hero of an adventure movie, Douglas Fairbanks or Tom Mix. But then one can never fathom how far a shy man will go to prove to himself he is not the man he is. In 1943 Ettore was among the first to organize Italian underground resistance in Milan. When the SS looked for him (he had been betrayed by a traitor who had infiltrated his group) and, not finding him, arrested Father as a hostage (Father, of course, was too eminent and popular to be kept in prison for long), Ettore refused to run away to Switzerland, a few hours away by mountain paths, and gave himself up. We never saw him alive again.

My helpless love obsessed me more and more as the summer died. Stewart was away, cruising the Caribees with the fleet, and I saw Ann practically every day. We both knew we had come to a point at which something had to happen. She often came to dinner in my house and, on the night the servants were out, she would cook supper for the two of us. We ate in the kitchen like Americans. We played at being married. We talked about an imaginary future, the names of our children, their characters, their careers. We laughed a lot. Sometimes we wept in each other's arms, and kissed each other's salty tears. The whole thing was unbearably delicious torture. We often surveyed our quandary and came up with no answer. That I loved and wanted her more than anything in the world, she knew. I had told her so often enough, and written it to her in prose and poetry. I also knew that she loved me, although she never allowed herself to pronounce the words. But I could sometimes read her love in her expression, the feel of her hands, the sudden smiles that lit up her face, the touch of her lips, the tears that filled her eyes, the way she often clung to me, and the excessive care with which she occasionally did the simple cooking for both of us. I discovered then that cooking, too, can be a tender act of love. That there was no visible future for us was evident. We both agreed the only and wisest thing for us to do was to stop meeting, not gradually spacing our dates but from one day to the next, cold turkey, so to speak, that very evening, and forget each other. We decided this many times, almost every day, but we never had the courage to do it. We always found a compelling reason to meet the following day, surely for the last time. The next best thing, I always timidly suggested, was to forget everything and sleep together. But this was a fateful step, the passage of the Rubicon. I did not want to push her. I did not want to beg either, or put her up against an ultimatum. The decision could be only her own, a spontaneous one, I told her. I thought then I was being a gentleman, an Anglo-Saxon gentleman. I now realize I was wrong and cowardly. I was putting an unbearable burden on her shoulders. It was my duty to decide for both of us.

Ann knew (she explained it often) her future could be only what she had believed it was going to be before she met me. She should marry Stewart, or somebody else more or less like Stewart, but more probably Stewart because he was there. He had the same background as hers, came from a good Protestant family, American from way back, had gone to Annapolis and into the Navy like her father. He would be an admiral one day. He was honorable, bright, and energetic. They had known each other for years. They understood each other almost without speaking, like brother and sister. There would be few surprises in their lives. They would produce a number of blond and well-behaved children, who played baseball in vacant lots and always washed their hands before dinner. They would own rumbustious dogs. They would subscribe to the right magazines, vote for the right President, visit the dentist once a year, go to church on Sunday, play tennis, have nice friends, move from one naval base to another but without ever realizing they had moved, because life would be more or less the same and their friends would be interchangeable in every one of the bases, and every new house would look and smell like the preceding one and like the house she lived in now. They would retire in the end to some warm spot in the United States, where Stewart would play golf and she would dedicate herself to gardening and some worthy cause.

She said these things without joy, with resignation, but without bitterness either. That Stewart loved her there was no doubt. That something in her loved him, too, was also clear. Stewart had officially proposed, the last time he was in New York, and was now waiting for an answer. "I don't want to rush you," he had said. "But you know you're made for me, I'm made for you, our life together will be what you were born for. Anything else would be a mistake." And, in a way, he was right.

Our love was only an accident, an unfortunate accident,

like her grandmother's flirtation with the Italian cavalry officer in Florence or my meeting with Natalie on the *Duilio*. I was, of course, attractive, entertaining, and tempting, a mysterious animal; I could probably make love more tenderly, sensitively, inventively, and artfully than Stewart, and go on for many more years. But I was a foreigner, as Natalie's father would have pointed out, an entirely different and unpredictable sort of human being, a Catholic and an Italian. And were the arts of brilliant conversation and inspired copulation the main things in life? Were they not a way Nature had to tempt us away from the path of common sense? I was too young, too, much younger than Stewart, had not yet finished college, had no money and no certain prospect for the future. What kind of a career was that of a journalist, a writer, a *letterato,* if you please? Who could tell whether I would make it in the end, was strong enough one day to make the bell ring with a sledgehammer blow, wear a literary admiral's stripes within a few years, or, more modestly, pay the bills and save money for my old age? When she diligently explained these things, which she did often, too often, more or less in identical words, she caressed my hand, never looked squarely at me, and had tears in her eyes. It was as if she were trying to convince herself rather than me. I said nothing. She was absolutely right, of course.

She was absolutely right, of course. Some of the most delicate and poignant short stories written in those years kept coming back to me with rejection slips. I tried in vain to get a spare-time job on a big newspaper for the winter. Once (to mention one attempt), sent by a mutual friend, I want to see the New York *Herald Tribune* city editor. He was a legendary figure at the time, the best in the city. His name was Stanley Walker, a nervous little man. I was paralyzed with fear. So much depended on our meeting. I could barely speak to him. I carried scrapbooks of my stupendous stories under my arm. He received me courteously in the editorial room and showed me around the place. He pointed to several old men working hard at the copyreaders' and headline writers' U-shaped table, patient and tame white-haired old men, their heads bent over their work like students at examination time. "They are all former editors-in-chief of this paper," he said with slightly excessive pride, pride in a country, his own, in which only efficiency counted, a man was worth strictly what his work could produce at the moment, where old age and past honors did not entitle him to any privilege. The sight filled me with fear and compassion. Mr. Walker did not even open my scrapbooks. He gave me no hope. "We don't need anybody," he firmly explained, "but if we did, we have a long waiting list of experienced young men, all Americans, all bright, older than you, raring to go, all ready to drop good jobs in the boondocks to join us....Let me know how you make out," he also said. "Come and see me from time to time," and: "Let's go and have a drink."

We rode downstairs to one of the most famous speakeasies of the day, called Bleeck's, where some of the most famous men in New York met. He introduced me to all his friends. "Meet Luigi, Mulberry Street's answer to an editor's prayer. The only Italian in captivity who can use a typewriter as well as a stiletto." I shook hands with all of them, surely the most celebrated writers, columnists, playwrights, actors, men about town, whose names escaped me, putting down my glass to do it. I had only one arm free, as the other kept my precious unopened scrapbook close to my ribs.

I also tried to follow up my idea of exploring the secrets of the Sicilian underworld with Mike's help. I had saved his life, hadn't I, and he owed me a great favor. It was now his duty to save my life. After much mysterious negotiating (in the end, I had to promise I would not write a word without the approval of the parties concerned), he finally solemnly announced that his *capo*, Don Turi, would grant me an audience.

Don Turi lived in a decayed section of Brooklyn in a house surrounded by an iron fence. The house was old, but the fence was new. Don Turi was a kindly old gentleman, fat but still fast on his feet like an old house cat. He had watchful and alert black eyes, younger than his face; wore a woollen peaked cap indoors and a travel rug over his shoulders to protect himself from colds. He received me in a room whose walls were practically papered with framed photographs from the old country. There were peasant brides and grooms galore, some of the girls in their ancient costumes; young men in the last war's military uniforms, and some in *carabinieri* dress uniform holding the regulation Napoleonic hat with plume (known technically as *la lucerna,* or oil lamp) under an arched arm. *Carabinieri* and bandits have always been recruited among the same people in Italy. There were also many priests, nuns, monks, and one bishop smiling benignly at me.

Don Turi sat on an American straight-backed armchair, with a silent and attentive young man sitting behind him, his oldest son. Oldest sons are always present at their Sicilian fathers' more important interviews and never speak, because their job is more or less that of what is now known as a tape recorder. They must listen and remember, in case something happens to the old man, but they cannot be played back by third parties. Don Turi spoke his obscure dialect, slowly and with royal dignity. He seemed to use the *pluralis majestatis* like the Pope, but, in fact, when he said "we," he literally meant many men, the *amici* and *gli amici degli amici*. This is, more or less, what I think he said:

"Mike told me what you have done for him. It shows you have generous sentiments and are a gallant young man one can rely on. This is very rare among North Italians, Americans, and other foreigners. We thank you. We're in your debt. We never forget our debts. You know that. We never forget wrongs done to us, either. Someday you may need our help, Don Luigi, even when I am no longer here." (Mike and his son murmured, "As late as possible, with the help of God," as automatically as the faithful answered " . . . *qui tollit peccata mundi*" when the priest said *"Agnus Dei. . . ."*) "That day," Don Turi continued, "you can count on us, provided, of course, your request agrees with the laws of honor. Not today, however, the way you suggest. Mike says you want to defend the Sicilians' name from defamation, explain to the American public what laws we obey, and how we help each other like brothers in this strange, difficult, and hostile country." (That, of course, was the explanation I had given Mike.) "It is a noble wish. We commend you. But I'm afraid the moment is not opportune. We're at war. We Sicilians in America must think of ourselves like the Jews in Egypt before the Exodus. Everybody around us is our enemy and our oppressor. We have to be very prudent. Prudence, the Church teaches us, is one of the cardinal virtues. We showed our trust in you when we agreed to receive you in our house. But we cannot go further. Whatever you might write will be either accurate or wrong. If accurate, you will not be able to produce proof when it is denied and you will be accused by some of betraying us. Something unpleasant might happen to you. If it was wrong or exaggerated, it certainly would not have been worth your while to come and see me. Whether accurate or inaccurate, what you might write will be misunderstood anyway. Nobody understands (or wants to understand) us. You'll be bothered by the police, who are dull, ignorant, corrupt, and brutal people, mostly Irish. They will never leave you alone in order to get my name and my address, which they already have anyway. Yours is a dangerous errand, believe me, you yourself do not realize how dangerous. For your own sake it is my duty to discourage you, as I would discourage a grandson of mine. Some other time, perhaps, but not now." He gave me a glass of sweet wine with a biscuit, then shook my hand, and dismissed me, walking me ceremoniously to the iron garden gate. That was the end of that.

The question which vaguely obsessed me in those months was: Which way is America going? We now know the question should have obsessed Herbert Hoover, the American people, and the rest of the world more than me. (We now also know that it can be answered only if one answers another question first, to which there has unfortunately never been a single answer, but a number of tentative hypotheses, some of them enticing, some ludicrous, *tot capita tot sententiae.* This question is: What exactly is the United States?) Like everybody else, or almost everybody else, I dismissed the larger implications of the first question —let the Great Engineer and the wise men of the world worry about those—and narrowly concentrated on its possible repercussions on my immediate private life. A definitely reassuring answer could obviously sweep away doubts or indecisions, permit me to plan my future with some confidence, and incidentally also, if I had clear and brilliant prospects ahead of me in the American future, finally allow me to sleep with Ann, with a clear conscience.

Everybody, of course, was aware of the fact that everything was changing around us under our very eyes. Evidently, the country was not, could not, be what it had been for generations until a few months or even weeks before. "This is a revolutionary country, Luigi," Ann's father told me. "But we are not afraid of revolutions here. Jefferson said a little revolution is good for political health. It is a sign of life." (He meant, of course, an American glacier-slow, relentless transformation of society, with occasional demonstrations of popular discontent, and not the insane, bloody, and disorderly revolts, led by demented demagogues, which were then tearing some European countries apart.) We all knew we were passengers on history's roller coaster, and that our car was climbing higher and higher. We were also thrilled and proud of the privilege. There were pessimists too, of course. Some of them, wise and dyspeptic, reminded us that what had gone up in the past had, sooner or later, to come down. But, curiously enough, nobody foresaw the catastrophic collapse of everything which would follow within a few weeks, the following October, and the real revolution that would sweep and transform the country, more subversive than the whisky distillers' occasional riots against revenue men which Jefferson had praised.

So I was not worrying especially whether the great prosperity would turn into an economic cataclysm, which seemed then an impossible nightmare, but about something else. The signs of the times (I was a great newspaper reader, which is probably the reason I had such confused ideas) pointed, as they always do in historical phases of transition when the old sun sets and the new rises at the same time, in two opposite and contradictory directions. The American future was, according to what you read and the people you met, ultimate Byzantine degeneration and corruption, *or* a brave new world never seen before, a world without poverty, disease, insecurity, and injustice. It was impossible to choose, as both views were corroborated and supported (like everything in America) by indisputable and abundant documentation.

Would the country become, as some persuasively demonstrated, more and more a raw, pitiless, anonymous, unprincipled, money-mad mass society, flooded with shoddy goods, tortured by unsolvable problems and frightening injustices never before seen on earth, a place in which living pleasantly would soon be almost impossible? A country in which it would be hopeless for an ordinary, obscure individual without powerful friends, or *amici,* to defend his dignity and personal liberty, and live free from anguish? A country which, dominated by an egalitarian frenzy, would trample upon and steam-roll all differences in taste, culture, and racial backgrounds, and pulverize everybody down to a humiliating lowest possible denominator? Or would the people utilize their proliferating wealth finally to transform their country into what they hoped it would be someday, what many tried to believe it already was, the greatest nation on earth, and endow it with all the conveniences and improvements it needed? Would the people soon manage to approach the utopia the Fathers had dreamed of?

It was, as I say, possible to believe both. The more intelligent and articulate Americans, professors, writers, and journalists, or the well-read, well-traveled, and more discriminating, saw mainly the revolting vulgarity, the gross hedonism, the corruption rampant everywhere, and the stupid materialism. Many of them fled, as they had always done, abroad, to the Left Bank, or (the rich) to sumptuous palazzi, *hôtels particuliers,* and Medicean villas, where they could read the Paris *Herald,* and surround themselves with obsequious servants and fastidious friends. The expatriates were not real pessimists. They were proud to be Americans. They were merely impatient and disappointed but still hopeful Americans. I considered the two contrary views with some perplexity. At the time, in my ignorance, I had not learned the fact that the contradiction was built in, as old as the Republic. Nobody had told me the United States was not a nation, as European nations are nations, but a nation *sui generis,* in reality a cosmic dust of people, all different, mainly held together, as iron filings are held together in a fixed pattern by a magnet, by one single hope, that of building a new perfect society tomorrow. This is why they can only occasionally be united to fight a war or bring about a fundamental devastating reform, and then only when they are convinced that they are engaged in a crusade to improve not their life alone but the whole world.

This wonderful hope, which is always also a stern moral

imperative inside each American, is held to as tenaciously and unreasonably as a religion. If it were to fade away, I think, the iron filings would scatter, the coach and horses would turn into a pumpkin and a brace of mice, and the United States would vanish. What would be left would be a lot, of course: millions and millions of people, all dissimilar and unrelated, Wasps, Jews, Italians, Blacks, businessmen, gamblers, cowboys, Red Indians, millionaires, rednecks, evangelists, intellectuals, brush salesmen, farmers, inhabiting the same immense continent, all energetic, hard-working people, making money, but each pursuing his own private goal, without a common national purpose, without a feeling of unity or a sense of common mission. They would lose the faith in themselves and their destiny which had previously supported them, lose their wonderful American self-assurance, the arrogance of people who know they are right, and they would also lose their power.

In my abysmal ignorance I was also not aware of the fact that Americans, men engaged in their unending Sisyphean labor without rest (the name should perhaps be SisyphUS), which they are condemned never to finish, had always been tormented by the perennial discovery that their achievements were always late and inferior to the dream, that every gain had to be paid for with heartbreaking and irremediable losses. From the beginning their expectations had always been so high that the results, no matter how spectacular, were bound to be disappointing. Impatience and a feeling of frustration were the two faces of America. The impatient had always rushed furiously forward, sometimes blindly, at greater and greater speed; the frustrated had always wept over the mistakes, the delays, the spoiled opportunities, the corruption, the betrayal of the old ideals, and the despicable frailty of man.

Personally, for many reasons, I preferred not to believe in an imminent or even distant *Götterdämmerung.* I was young. I did not deny there were evident and sometimes shocking signs of decadence, injustice, and corruption all around me, but paid more attention to the opposite signs. Could not the corruption be a remnant of the past rather than an introduction to the future? I saw the people boldly fighting (as they did not fight in other countries, my own in particular) against decadence, injustice, and corruption. I saw the vigor, the stubborn optimism *à tout prix,* the resolution, and the political health of the Americans. They might not always have been conscious of what they were doing, they sometimes seemed to act by instinct like ants, or to be swept away by mass emotions. Nor did they always know where they were really going, but were fiercely at work getting there, wherever that was, beyond the setting sun.

Nothing could stop them. They never relaxed. They tried and tried so tenaciously every possible way that they could only succeed in the end. They had always triumphed in the past, had they not? They could not fail. These signs, proudly exalted by politicians, journalists, Rotary Club speakers, best-selling writers, and the ordinary people, were as conspicuous as the contrary signs of decadence, but few of the writers or intellectuals I admired bothered to describe them. When they did, they derided them. Why I did not know. Probably because evidences of the Americans' stubborn, enthusiastic, and relentless tenacity, having always been part of the landscape, were practically invisible; because they were the heritage of ordinary, dull, and unsophisticated people; or because such signs were so common they were boring.

The day the dam burst, Thursday, October 24, 1929, I was the make-believe editor-in-chief of our imaginary School paper. It was a frantic day. There were two very big stories to worry about. An Anarchist had tried to kill the Italian Crown Prince Umberto in Brussels, and the price of shares had reached bottom on Wall Street; the ticker took all day to transmit the new quotations, and thousands of people were presumably ruined. Which story was to occupy the last column on the right of the front page? I consulted my editors and debated the matter within myself. The attempted murder of the Prince was enticing not so much for the bare fact itself (many princes had been and were being shot at all the time like clay pigeons) as for the circumstances: In the light of Dr. Pitkin's theories, there was little doubt the Brussels story was to take precedence.

Umberto was young, almost as handsome as John Gilbert. (He had inherited his *allure* from his uncle, Danilo of Montenegro, the real-life prototype of the *Merry Widow*'s Prince Danilo. I ordered one of my men to check that and prepare a brilliant little box.) He was in Brussels on a romantic errand, an errand that would presumably make the hearts of millions of women throb. He was there to celebrate his engagement to a young and blonde princess, Maria José of Belgium. She was (still is, for that matter) the daughter of King Albert, one of the legendary popular heroes of the First World War, known as the heroic leader of the little martyr country. The young Prince and Princess were going to crown their love dream that day. In reality, their wedding had, as usual, been decided long before by grubby politicians in the two countries' chancellories, mostly for devious or secret reasons, but journalists did not tell the public that and, for sordid reasons of their own, preferred to exaggerate and illustrate profusely the ladies' magazine novelettish angle. As Umberto, all dressed up in his gorgeous uniform with golden epaulets, his chest covered with decorations, and Medieval orders of chivalry around his neck, was riding to the Royal Palace, a small obscure man surged from the cheering crowd and either threw a bomb or shot a rusty gun, I forget which. As so often happens, the excessive eagerness and inexperience of the Anarchist made his hand tremble. He missed his target and was immediately arrested.

The story was, as I say, very tempting. There were many attractive elements. While, in the light of its national history, the American public should definitely have been on the side of the obscure revolutionary, who was, after all, only trying to destroy another George III, I knew Americans were in reality abnormally and unnecessarily fascinated by royalty. They were also easily moved by youthful love in a splendid Graustarkian setting. They were as a rule attracted by any dramatic story, by the contrast between the resplendent and handsome hero and his shady and malevolent enemy, and by the happy ending. I imagined the Prince had intervened with the police, asking them to treat the unfortunate man gently, and possibly also forgave him his mad gesture. Princes (and Presidents) always do. It is part of the job, like being occasionally shot at. I was sure the agencies would eventually send us his generous words. A noble and magnanimous quote would have made the story even more irresistible.

On the other hand, the Wall Street story did not look half as attractive. The Exchange had had occasional slumps in the past, some of them almost like landslides during the summer, a few serious ones during the previous days. It had been suffering from hiccups. But it had always punctually recovered. As the afternoon wore on, in fact, prices rose again. Some of the most august financial and political leaders entrusted the agencies with their own amused tsk-tsks, deplored the ill-informed people's panic, invited them not to sell America short, to trust their country's future. The biggest men in Wall Street, we were informed, had met at Morgan's at noon and they surely would know how to fill the breach. They had always done it. Richard Whitney, the Morgan broker, bought United States Steel in a loud voice for more than the stock was worth at the time. Personally, I had never been particularly interested in speculation, the money game, and the Stock Exchange, as I had never been attracted by gambling. In fact, the whole thing bored me. I knew little of economics and always skipped the financial pages, their intricate and incomprehensible or frenetically optimistic stories. To tell the truth, I looked upon the Street and all it represented with snobbish contempt.

The reason why I finally decided to give the Stock Exchange collapse the most eminent position on the front page had therefore nothing to do with intuition or foresightedness. I admit I did not realize the day would be remembered for decades to come. As so often happens, an event destined to shake the world from its foundations and change the life of every man, including that of multitudes as yet unborn, appeared to many contemporary observers as one more damned thing which followed other damned things of more or less the same importance. A famous

American journalist who was in Petrograd the day Vladimir Ilyich Ulyanov, *dit* Lenin, had the newly elected Constituent Assembly brutally disbanded by soldiers and sailors, and assumed absolute power, told me, many years later, that he (the journalist) had not realized the event would determine the fate of the world forever. He told me:

"I wrote a dramatic but prudent story, remembering how often subsequent events make fools of eager eyewitnesses, brought it to the telegraph office, and went to dinner in my usual restaurant with other journalists. It was the best in Petrograd. Everything was reassuringly the same: the tzigane band played brilliantly, the obsequious headwaiter in his tail coat tactfully suggested some delicate and dainty *spécialité* or the *plat du jour,* the waiters pushed around nickel-plated *wagons* full of steaming meats, the food was exquisite, and the wines just right. . . . All around us were chic ladies, well-born and well-tailored languid gentlemen, as well as officers from great regiments. It was absolutely impossible to deduce, in the restaurant or in the tranquil streets on the way back to our hotel, that something momentous and irrevocable had taken place."

One of the two reasons why I finally decided the crash was to occupy the most eminent position was my ignorance and diffidence in financial matters. I was afraid of not attributing to the event the importance everybody else obviously would attribute to it. The other reason was my nationality. I was afraid I was interested in the attempted murder of the Italian Crown Prince because I was Italian, and that possibly made me see in the event many more attractive qualities than ordinary readers would perceive. I wrote "Wall Street" at the proper place on the layout in bold letters with a greasy pencil and a tranquil conscience.

I was sure that was where my nonexistent, purely hypothetical readers would have wanted it.

Stewart returned on leave at the end of October. I did not see him. I did not see Ann either. In fact, I found unlikely excuses not to see them. Sometimes I fancied myself as a noble self-sacrificing philosopher or a chivalrous old-fashioned gentleman, who made himself scarce in order to leave his love absolutely free to follow, if she wished, the dictates of her tedious Anglo-Saxon common sense. More rarely I saw myself as a contemptible coward, incapable of fighting for his (and possibly also her) happiness, who tried to prolong at all cost a blissful state of ignorance, afraid to read radiant and inane happiness on Ann's and Stewart's faces, the happiness of definitive decisions taken, all doubts finally dispelled. To be sure, Ann rang me up several times. Her calls disturbed me. American girls almost never called young men at the time. They could do so only in emergencies, or, at normal times, could call relatives, very old friends for a specific reason, and elderly men. There being no emergency, how exactly was she classifying me? I also resented the consoling and vaguely propitiatory tone of her voice. I told her I was terribly busy in town and practically all my evenings were taken.

I was not lying. I worked very hard at the School, on some project or other for Dr. Pitkin, surely harder than was necessary, spent days in the library and at the typewriter, consumed empty hours angrily debating futile problems with my schoolmates. I kept on looking for a spare-time job. I also impatiently pursued all the girls I could lay my hands on. I went dancing in the evening, drank a little for the first time, smoked one pack of cigarettes after another, ended the night in some girl's flat, returning home later and later, sometimes at dawn, on the first train, and, more and more often, not at all. I treated the poor kind girls with brutal contempt. Curiously enough, most of them seemed to like it. To be sure, those who did not dropped me, or I dropped them. Others who, as good athletic American women, would have knocked a boy's teeth out or smashed his head in with a broomstick if he tried to be less than abjectly respectful, accepted it from me because I was Italian. They were fascinated by the new exotic experience, one that, of course, would not last long. In fact, I never again had such success in my life.

Naturally, at the end of a few weeks, worrying madly, working frenziedly, sleeping only a few hours at night, making love as indiscriminately, frequently, and senselessly as a streetwalker on the waterfront, I was exhausted. One morning I felt really sick, so sick that anybody else would have gone to bed and called a doctor. I got up. On the train to town I met Ann's grandmother. With a queenly gesture and a gracious smile she invited me to sit in the empty place next to her. She looked at me, then put a gloved hand lightly on my knee, frowned, and told me I looked awful. "What is the matter, Luigi?" she asked solicitously. "Have you a fever? Did you take your temperature?" I answered gruffly that I was all right, never felt better, there was nothing wrong with me, a little overworked perhaps, nothing to worry about. Then I courteously inquired about her own health and that of the captain and the girls. I could not get myself to include Stewart. I could not pronounce his name. She assured me everybody was very well and we talked about the weather and the Stock Exchange slump. When the train pulled into the catacombs under Pennsylvania

Station, the old lady got up, and, standing in line on her way out, with me behind her, turned her head a little and said casually: "Stewart has left. He's gone back to his ship. Goodbye, Luigi." Not one word more. She did not say whether Ann was engaged or not. I did not dare ask.

That afternoon I felt fagged out, anxious, shaky, and a little sick. I broke my date for the evening and went home early. The house was empty. Ettore, of course, was in Ithaca. Mother and Ugo were still in Italy. Father was in town, had left word he would dine out and would be back very late, after the last train, probably by taxi. The maid, who was on her way out, told me he had taken his dinner clothes with him. I relaxed in a deep armchair, with an open book on my lap, and very slowly felt a little better. Stewart, I thought, had left. That was something anyway. But what had been decided? The afternoon wore on, the light gradually turned peach, then cardinal's red, then bishop's purple. I did not bother to switch on the light. Maybe I dozed. It was almost night when the phone rang brutally. It was Ann.

She said briskly: "Grandmother told me you're sick but refuse to admit it. What's the matter with you? I'm worried."

I reassured her. I was perfectly all right, nothing wrong, a little tired perhaps, not having slept well the night before. She went on resolutely: "Don't be silly. Is there anybody with you? Have you taken your temperature?"

I said, in the wan voice of a wounded man on the battlefield, that there was absolutely nothing to worry about, I was alone but I could easily take care of myself, I could warm some bouillon when I felt like it and there were apples and crackers in the house somewhere.

"I'll be right over," she said in a very efficient and determined tone, the voice of an American philanthropist rushing to the scene of famines, epidemics, floods, or earthquakes to take charge of relief operations. I did not have the courage and the strength to dissuade her. After all, to have Ann near me, even if she was tied to a man who would never understand her and know how lucky he was, was surely better than solitude. Besides, it was not absolutely certain she was engaged. I was fool enough to hope she had postponed her decision once more, to gain time, or even rejected him.

Within a few minutes she was there. She was more beautiful than I remembered, slightly *décoiffée* (she had obviously rushed from her house without tidying herself), her eyes shining with medical missionary zeal. She took charge. She dragged me from my armchair, pushed me into my bedroom, turned back the bedcovers, ordered me to undress, pulled my trousers off, handed me my pajamas and indicated the bathroom where I was to put them on. All this, of course, no Italian girl at the time would have had the courage to do, with the exception perhaps of hospital nuns. No decent, well-brought-up young lady pulled a man's pants off him, no matter what the circumstances.

A ce propos, we Barzinis always quoted what happened once, in the 1860s, to my maternal great-grandfather, Leone Bassano, as a luminous example of the American girl's bravery in face of an emergency and her lack of false prudery. He was a Venetian who manufactured and sold Murano beads. His specialty was *avventurina* (the family liked to believe he had invented it, but this was surely untrue. I saw *avventurina* from classical Roman times in museums. Maybe he had just reinvented it). *Avventurina* is chocolate-brown opaque glass with gold flecks. It was usually cut in the shape of a semiprecious stone and made into brooches. It was particularly fashionable in Great Britain and the United States. You can see it on the breasts of many Anglo-Saxon ladies in daguerreotypes. Leone Bassano went frequently to London on business. Once, on his way back, crossing France on a fast train, he found himself alone in a compartment with a young American lady. At the time, each compartment was separate from all the others, there was no communicating corridor, and the only way to get out was to wait for the next stop. Express trains, like the one he was on, stopped very rarely. My great-grandfather had bought a French novel along the way and found nothing better to cut the pages with than his sharp and well-honed Solingen straight razor. At one point he had to get up, to open or close a window, or to fiddle with his baggage on the rack. The train lurched and he sat down heavily on the open razor. He cut himself very badly high on the thigh, almost where it begins to be called a buttock. The blood streamed out in a flood. He had probably severed a vein. The American young lady, a well-born, well-brought-up, proper, and demure girl, who had kept strictly to herself until then, realizing that the poor man would bleed to death before the next station, resolutely took off his trousers and underwear, and quickly made a very tight tourniquet at the appropriate place with a handkerchief. She saved his life, unperturbed by the sight of an unknown mustachioed foreigner's private parts. Grandmother, Leone's daughter, when telling this story for the nth time, always commented: "If the lady had been Italian, she would have howled, wept, prayed to an appropriate saint or two, or fainted, and my father would have died."

Once I was comfortably in bed, Ann made me swallow a handful of aspirins with a bit of water, stuck a thermometer in my mouth, looked at her wristwatch with a professional frown, ordered me to stay absolutely still, and scurried downstairs to make tea. I relaxed. An immense feeling of beatitude slowly invaded me. It was evident that, whatever had been decided between her and Stewart, she still loved me enough not to want me to die. This was not much, to be sure, in a country where philanthropy, the care of suffering animals, the feeding of starving populations, and the nursing of the sick were national imperatives, but pleasant enough, surely better than the contrary.

When she came back with the tray, she looked at the thermometer with almost imperceptible disappointment. Obviously, I had no fever to speak of, not enough to justify the rush to my house, the fuss she was making, the Florence Nightingale efficiency. She sat down in the gloom and watched me sip the hot tea. Then she approached, sat on the edge of the bed, and looked at me as if she were on the verge of telling me something important. I thought: "Here it comes. Now she will say she loves me but not that way and that she will be like a sister to me." She said nothing. Maybe a sister was too intimate, I thought. Maybe she could go only as far as first cousin. I held her hands, thanked her, kissed them, kissed her wrists, and told her how much better I felt thanks to her. "Maybe my sickness was only in my head," I said, laughing weakly. "Your very presence cured me. You must be a healer." She laughed noiselessly and caressed my cheek as a nurse does a child's.

At that point I slowly pulled one hairpin from her coiffure, then another, a third, a fourth, almost innocently, as if pretending to play a simple joke on a school friend in

315

class. She did not try to stop me. She only smiled. In those years, and with particular girls, the slightly old-fashioned ones careful of their dignity and self-respect, to undo their hair was still a symbolic and intimate gesture. It was allowed to a few very dear friends, and then only rarely. It was, in a very minor way, a daring and exciting gesture too, the very first step to love-making, what the bridegroom did to his bride once they were finally alone in the bedroom.

When only a few hairpins were left in Ann's practically undone coiffure, she shook her amber-colored hair completely free, until it streamed down over her shoulders. She then leaned down and kissed me, holding my head between two hands as if it were a vase. I knew then, kissing her, she could not be engaged to Stewart. It was not a friendly, cousinly, or sisterly kiss. It was not an adulterous or stolen kiss either. It was more explicit and eloquent than a long and poetic declaration. That was probably what she wanted to tell me but didn't. My happiness knew no bounds. I felt as if I could have floated in air, levitated like a Counter-reformation saint, lifting her in my arms, until we rested on a pink Tiepolo cloud in a lapis-lazuli sky. I invoked her name, "Ann, Ann," and said nothing more.

Keeping my lips glued to hers, I started, almost in spite of myself, to unbutton her dress (there was a row of tiny buttons down the front) with trembling hands. The gesture was a little shabby, an almost automatic routine, something my hands had done on their own many times before with other pretty but indifferent girls. The kiss was a warm and sincere one, full of passionate love and tenderness, certainly, but also functional. It kept her still. It kept her mind off what I was doing. It could allow her to pretend she did not know I was undressing her. But she was not fooled. She did not like it at all. She brusquely pushed me away, wrenched herself free, and got up. "Luigi, that's not for us, is it?" she said with reproach in her voice and ordered me: "Turn your face to the wall." I turned my face to the wall, heard the swish of her dress falling around her feet, heard her pick it up to put it tidily on a chair. I heard her undo, unstrap, unclasp what else she had underneath. Finally, I felt her body against my back. I turned round and furiously tore the pajamas from my body. She murmured, "I love you, Luigi," in my ear. It was the first time she had allowed herself to say the words.

Making love to Ann was surprisingly like the first time for me, too. (It was clear it was the first time for her.) We were swept away by an irresistible senseless hurricane, we did not know what we were doing, and yet, in our frenzied rage to destroy each other, to reduce the loved one to a gasping comatose state begging for mercy (and to do it again as soon as the loved one revived), there was a curious feeling which I had never sensed before, a feeling of peace, of innocence, of intimacy, and of familiarity, as if we were children at play, had known each other always, had always held each other naked in our arms, and an immense feeling of liberation too, the feeling of passengers in a balloon when the moorings are cut, the feeling of having been freed from the constrictions of one's solitary private body.

We then lay side by side in the darkness, holding hands, without speaking.

Epilogue

IN THE AUTUMN OF 1929 and the winter and spring of 1930, life was becoming more and more difficult for practically everyone as each week passed, millions of people were being fired, industrial plants were closing, solid, ancient, and glorious firms went bankrupt, brokers jumped to their deaths from the tops of skyscrapers. The price of stocks sank ever lower after brief and short-breathed rallies. All this I read in the newspapers. But even had I not read it in the newspapers, I would have been aware of the disaster. People I knew were down-and-out, some put up their houses for sale (a useless gesture, as nobody was buying anything), or boarded them up and left, because they could no longer afford to live there. Shops sold their stock at clearance sales and closed forever. Some of my student friends abandoned their studies and went back home. An elderly couple, who lived not far from us, were wiped out in the Stock Exchange débâcle. It was too late for them to start life again, so they committed suicide. He shot her with his old Army revolver and shot himself. They were dear people. Unemployed men began selling apples or pencils in the streets, pathetically making believe they were not reduced to begging. Straight beggars were on the increase, still dressed in decent clothes. They asked for a dime for a cup of coffee. No beggar in Italy ever specified the sum he wanted or the exact purpose he would put it to. American administrative punctiliousness, no doubt.

Father, too, was worried. He came home later and later, more and more tired, and said very little. His paper had never made any money, no new newspaper ever does, but its losses had been gradually getting smaller and its circulation had been on the increase. It had been financed by an Italian Croesus from Waco, Texas, a cotton exporter, Pio Crespi, who looked like Tom Mix and wore a cowboy hat. He was a relative and supplier of his Italian Crespi cousins, who made cotton textiles in vast quantities near Milan and owned the *Corriere della Sera*. In bad times, as the need for funds grew, Pio Crespi naturally found it more and more difficult to furnish the money needed in sufficient and punctual quantities. The future looked dim, to be sure, the future of the country, the future of our family, and my own future in particular, which had not looked promising even when times were good. Nevertheless, deep in my heart, I never thought the situation was really hopeless, never thought the lean kine would last more than a few months, a year at the most, and never thought the depression would spread to the whole world.

Why, it is easy to see. To begin with, a man mixed up in a great historical event rarely realizes what is happening,

319

just as the British soldiers rushed back to Brussels too soon from the Waterloo battlefield and broadcast the news that Napoleon had won. As monotonous and persistent as the bad news in the daily papers were the heartening exhortations from eminent gentlemen in the know, the descriptions of vast designs conceived by the President and his Cabinet to turn the economic tide, the prophecies that things would inevitably be better very shortly, the cheerful reminders that American virtues were still intact, that the people would defeat the crisis and save themselves as easily as they had defeated the Germans and saved the world from ruin and slavery only a few years before; that all it took was courage, know-how, energy, hard work, and common sense, things which were in abundant supply. Who was I to doubt the words of great authorities, revered moral and religious leaders, who reassured me practically every day?

I was twenty-one that December (the twenty-first, to be exact), and at that age one tends to be an optimist anyway, and stupidly convinced that only other people will be overwhelmed by ill fortune, defeat, plagues, Spanish flu or other epidemics, just as in war a young man always believes all the others, the men to his right and left, will be killed, while he will be miraculously left intact. I was, furthermore (very often but not always), persuaded for no apparent valid reason that I had a great future ahead of me, and that no silly and temporary slump in Stock Exchange quotations and a world depression would stop me. I had been making very little money when things were prosperous and I did not feel the shock of sudden poverty, accustomed as I was to making ends meet with few dollars. In fact, the sight of rich people suddenly impoverished cheered me. Finally, and this might have been the decisive reason why I was not as obsessed with the crisis as other people seemed to be, I was desperately in love and had little time for silly extraneous preoccupations.

Ann and I were living in a cloud of paradisiacal dementia. We could think of nothing else. We made love wherever and whenever we could, in the woods, the beaches, the gardens, one of our houses on the rare occasions when the rest of our respective families were absent for the evening, in borrowed rooms, once in a little hotel (with great care not to be caught by the house detective), at other times as guests in friends' country houses for the weekend (when she tiptoed to my room). We were transported by an uncontrolled fury, a divine wind like that which drove Paolo and Francesca through the infernal air. The wind was the knowledge that all we had was the present. There was no future for us. We also knew our delirious happiness could not last forever, that the sober and unpleasant problems of life would catch up with us soon enough. Every stolen meeting, caress, and kiss acquired the importance they would have had had we been condemned by medical experts to an early death. We made love like La Traviata and Alfredo—if Alfredo had also been suffering from galloping TB.

One day (it was a peaceful Sunday afternoon around Easter time, we were sitting on the sofa in Ann's living room) she took my hand, looked into my eyes with her own honest and serious American eyes, and said: "Luigi, I will never forget you."

My heart stopped.

"I will always remember these months which will always be a dear part of my life," she went on.

I was frightened by the use of the past tense. What in hell was she trying to tell me?

"There is no future for us," she continued. "Oh, don't say anything." She put a hand on my mouth. I kissed her palm. "You and I know it. We must not deceive ourselves. It would be dishonest and weak. We must face facts. I have come to a decision. It took me a long time. Alone. I didn't want to talk it over with you."

"What decision?" I asked weakly. I knew Ann. I knew her decision, whatever it was, would be unshakable, as solid as a fortress wall. No flood of Latin charm or poetic sentiments, no tender recollections of past delights or bright but improbable prospects of future happiness would make her hesitate. This was the end. I listened to my fate.

"I can't go back to Stewart. You have made me a different girl. You have spoiled me. Poor Stewart. But I cannot go on with you. The longer we cling to each other, the more we will suffer in the end. You know why. I don't have to tell you. And this is my decision. I'm leaving for the Ozarks to teach illiterate children how to read and write. There's a wonderful organization that enrolls college girls to do that. You know I love teaching. You know I will be happy doing it. Don't make it difficult. Don't say anything."

I said nothing. Her decision, of course, was the American equivalent of entering a convent. We made love desperately that evening (after supper everybody had gone to the movies) on the living-room sofa. We both wept.

I finished my second and last year at the School in a zombie-like daze. Ann, a vital part of me without whom I could only partially exist, had not only abandoned me forever but, having done so for a most noble, self-sacrificing, admirable, and chaste reason, had cruelly stolen from me the consoling possibility of despising or hating her. Had she betrayed me with another boy whom I could look down on as mediocre (it was easy at the time for me to look down on other boys as dim-witted and dull), I could have convinced myself she was not the girl I had thought she was and her loss nothing to mourn. I could think of her as a cheap flapper with a *cuisse* a little too *légère,* as the French say, and look for other girls. This was impossible. I read, wrote, and listened interminably to long rows of words, as meaningful as lines of black ants, passed examinations with suicidal indifference, and somehow graduated.

Just before graduation—it must have been at the end of May, 1930—Father solemnly invited me to step into his office. He wanted to speak to me. He asked me to sit down, shot his starched cuffs, offered me a straw-tipped Melachrino, talked about a frivolous thing or two, then asked me what my plans were: "Have you thought about them? What do you want to do after graduation?" I answered firmly I wanted to go back to Italy. I had no doubts. That was the only way open to me. He nodded wisely as if he had known all the time what my decision would be. Within weeks he got me a passage on an Italian liner bound for Genoa and, when I sailed, handed me four thousand lire. This was the last money he ever gave me, the equivalent at the time of two hundred U.S. dollars. I spent it all during the summer with immoral young women. From then on I managed to make what I needed. I left the United States so quickly that I could not even be present at the graduation ceremony of my class. I am sorry I never wore an American cap and gown, like those worn by Harold Lloyd, and do not possess a proper graduation photograph with proud father and mother. Poor Dr. Nicholas Murray Butler had to send me my diploma to Italy by registered mail.

It is easy to enumerate the superficial and obvious reasons which, I was honestly convinced at the time, had made my decision inevitable. In those spring months I had finally reached the conclusion that the damned depression would last a long, long time. Nobody knew when and how it would end. Like all American phenomena, it was the biggest, best, and most intricate of its kind ever generated by man. There was a chance it would go on forever, getting worse and worse. It naturally made getting a job impossible for every new college graduate, even for the well-connected and most brilliant Wasps with pronounceable Anglo-Saxon names and open Anglo-Saxon faces. What chance had a young unknown foreigner who (I must admit) wrote with an accent, and was Italian to boot, at a time when ordinary Italians were looked upon in the United States as barely human? That I had to get a job and to get one soon I knew only too well. Father's paper was sailing in ever shallower waters. His income had shrunk. Mother was watching, if not the pennies, at least the quarters. I hated having to depend on petty occasional handouts.

Then, of course, I had lost Ann. She was, in a way, the symbol of the happy and blessed America I loved, the courageous country the depression had wiped out. If things had gone on as before, hand in hand with her I could have blended with and disappeared in the crowd, an unsuccessful American among many. That door was shut. Evidently, I could only accept defeat, pack up, and go back where I had come from. In Italy poverty and failure were not abominable sins but simple proof of misfortune. Besides, I thought I had better opportunities in Italy than in the

United States, the land of opportunity. In Italy, I would be one of the few journalists who knew English, and could pillage English and American newspapers, magazines, and books with impunity. I would also be one of the few who had already lived in the future and knew the shape of things to come. I had been assured I had mastered the technique of modern journalism and could easily beat all competition. (All this, of course, was a naïve and deleterious American delusion. I soon discovered there is no harder life than that of the returned student. He does not belong to the country where he studied but is considered a foreigner in his native land. Nobody forgives him for what he innocently thinks is his advanced knowledge. He must learn to hide it in order to survive, adapt himself to local customs, ask for advice and protection from older people who know less than he. In my case, the returned student's normal difficulties were multiplied by my name. When I started working in Milan, everybody looked forward with pleasure to seeing me end up soon like Gabriellino d'Annunzio, crushed by the weight of my father's fame.)

The fact that Italy was oppressed and paralyzed by a totalitarian regime could only frighten foreigners. It did not worry me. In a way, it attracted me. I knew (as all Italians knew) the regime was as full of holes as a *colapasta,* the colander in which spaghetti were drained. The majority of good journalists did not believe in it and accepted it as one accepted wars, pestilences, or foreign invasions. Almost all men of culture were disciples of Benedetto Croce, a Hegelian and nineteenth-century liberal who thought Fascism was merely an unpleasant interval alien to the genius of Italy. Most of the men of culture were being employed by Mussolini in the compilation of a monumental encyclopedia, which turned out to be one of the best in the world and one of the few worthwhile achievements of the regime. They were all, or almost all, anti-Fascist. Most intelligent and honest men in every field were anti-Fascist, too. A popular saying was: "If a man is intelligent and Fascist, he is not honest. If he is honest and Fascist, he is not intelligent." I knew I could work in a good Italian newspaper without bothering to pay homage to the official ideology. In fact, one could do better work, because people were bored by the faithful, dreary, predictable repetition of the party line. Then there was the enticing possibility of writing harmless-seeming copy, secretly constructed in a subtle and ingenious way. The clever readers read between the lines and laughed. An old anti-Fascist journalist later told me: "You talk so much about freedom of the press .... Such freedom is necessary only to those who don't know how to write."

﷼

Only the mature gray-haired Barzini knows that the young Barzini's decision to go back to Italy in 1930, write again in Italian, dismiss his American education as practically irrelevant, face the unpredictable vicissitudes of the Italian future and the ordeal of getting ahead in a country where virtue, competence, and hard work were not always automatically rewarded but often derided by the smarter and wiser people, was not, as he sometimes liked to think, a courageous, patriotic, selfless decision, but in reality a demonstration of abject cowardice. The young Barzini was not clearly aware of the fact that American responsibilities frightened him out of his wits. He hid his fears behind complicated, flattering, and noble justifications. What secretly terrorized him was the superhuman burdens an American had to bear. Most Americans, who were saddled with their heavy moral shoulder pack from early youth, did not realize how hard their life was, how much harder than that of other men. A few did. Those who did, fled, dedicated themselves to debauch, got drunk, took dope, wrote beautiful poetry, gave the world great novels, lived tortured lives, or destroyed themselves. The burdens Americans carried were the individual moral duty not to waste one hour of their lives, achieve success and make money, build and produce more and more, and, at the same time, persistently improve the world, untiringly trying to teach all men how to live, work, produce, consume, and rule themselves the American way. And all this *a tappe forzate,* breathlessly, endeavoring to reach within a few years what would have taken more placid and incredulous people two or three generations.

This God-imposed philanthropic mission took, in emergencies, the form of war, sometimes terrible wars in more and more distant countries, in outlandish lands where the people's language, mentality, politics, ideals, and hopes could not be stranger and more incomprehensible to Americans, where they would be misunderstood and grope for solutions in a haze of unhappy uncertainty, stumbling into grievous and irreparable mistakes. Most of the mistakes were inevitably determined by the very ideals of the American people, those, for instance, which made Woodrow Wilson a noble but ineffective and calamitous fool at Versailles. Americans seldom dealt with brute reality and men as they are (as the Americans themselves also are, under their ideological uniform) but as they imagined or hoped men to be, capable of making any sacrifice for freedom, peace, and an ever-larger yearly Gross National Product. In a way, many Americans preferred to live in a consoling world of their own creation, just as many of them preferred the synthetic, the make-believe, the man-made products, to those of God, in other words the imitation chemical vanilla I tasted on my first day in the United States. For years I wondered (I still do) whether living enclosed in their own mental Disneyland would not lead them and the rest of the world to catastrophe, as almost happened in 1929.

Such considerations, however, which occasionally torment my mature days, were not very relevant when as a young man I decided to go back to Italy. I was then preoccupied not so much with the future of the world as with my own. What frightened me most at the time was the concept of life as a bet, either success and money or nothing. Would I make it? Was I strong enough to forgo all the small pleasures of life in order not to be obliterated by failure? I was a deserter, running from the field of battle and seeking refuge in a backward, ancient, pleasant, almost unchanging country, my own, where very few people were then trying to get anywhere and beat their competitors, and those who did employed ancient and nonfatiguing arts. The irony was that, in spite of it all, I could not leave America behind. Something in me was forever American. I worked hard, harder than most, achieved unnecessary but memorable scoops, and tried to reach success alone, unaided, by the excellence of my work, and not by cultivating friends and protectors, joining powerful camarillas and organizations.

The irony is that, in spite of my century-old Mediterranean skepticism, I still believe the world would be a better place if some of the American ideals of my youth had prevailed everywhere and, first of all, in the United States itself.